DESIGNING AND ACHIEVING COMPETENCY

Further titles in the McGraw-Hill Training Series

THE BUSINESS OF TRAINING
Achieving Success in Changing World Markets
Trevor Bentley   ISBN 0-07-707328-2

EVALUATING TRAINING EFFECTIVENESS
Translating Theory into Practice
Peter Bramley   ISBN 0-07-707331-2

MAKING MANAGEMENT DEVELOPMENT WORK
Achieving Success in the Nineties
Charles Margerison   ISBN 0-07-707382-7

MANAGING PERSONAL LEARNING AND CHANGE
A Trainer's Guide
Neil Clark   ISBN 0-07-707344-4

HOW TO DESIGN EFFECTIVE TEXT-BASED OPEN LEARNING:
A Modular Course
Nigel Harrison   ISBN 0-07-707355-X

HOW TO DESIGN EFFECTIVE COMPUTER BASED TRAINING:
A Modular Course
Nigel Harrison   ISBN 0-07-707354-1

HOW TO SUCCEED IN EMPLOYEE DEVELOPMENT
Moving from Vision to Results
Ed Moorby   ISBN 0-07-707459-9

DEVELOPING WOMEN THROUGH TRAINING
A Practical Handbook
Liz Willis and
Jenny Daisley   ISBN 0-07-707566-8

USING VIDEO IN TRAINING AND EDUCATION
Ashly Pinnington   ISBN 0-07-707384-3

TRANSACTIONAL ANALYSIS FOR TRAINERS
Julie Hay   ISBN 0-07-707470-X

Details of these and other titles in the series are available from:

The Product Manager, Professional Books, McGraw-Hill Book Company Europe,
Shoppenhangers Road, Maidenhead, Berkshire, SL6 2QL.
Telephone: 0628 23432 Fax: 0628 770224

Designing and achieving competency

A competency-based approach to developing
people and organizations

Rosemary Boam
Paul Sparrow

McGRAW-HILL BOOK COMPANY

London · New York · St Louis · San Francisco · Auckland
Bogotá · Caracas · Hamburg · Lisbon · Madrid · Mexico · Milan
Montreal · New Delhi · Panama · Paris · San Juan · São Paulo
Singapore · Sydney · Tokyo · Toronto

Published by
McGRAW-HILL Book Company Europe
Shoppenhangers Road, Maidenhead, Berkshire, SL6 2QL, England.
Telephone: 0628 23432
Fax: 0628 770224

British Library Cataloguing in Publication Data
Boam, Rosemary
 Designing and Achieving Competency:
 Competency-based Approach to Developing
 People and Organizations. – (McGraw-Hill
 Training Series)
 I. Title II. Sparrow, Paul III. Series
 658.3

ISBN 0-07-707572-2

Library of Congress Cataloging-in-Publication Data
Boam, Rosemary
 Designing and achieving competency: a
competency-based approach to developing
people and organizations/Rosemary Boam,
Paul Sparrow.
  p.   cm. — (McGraw-Hill training series)
 Includes bibliographical references and index.
 ISBN 0-07-707572-2
 1. Employees—Training of. 2. Executives—Training of.
3. Competency based education. I. Sparrow, Paul. II. Title.
III. Series.
 HF5549.5.T7B576   1992   92-11505
 658.3'124—dc20   CIP

12345 CL 95432

Typeset by Book Ens Limited, Baldock, Herts
Printed and bound in Great Britain by Clays Ltd, St Ives plc

Contents

	Page
Series preface	**xi**
About the series editor	**xiii**
About the authors	**xv**
Acknowledgements	**xix**
Preface	**xxi**
PART ONE: **Theory and knowledge**	**1**
1 The rise and rationale of competency-based approaches	**3**
Rosemary Boam and Paul Sparrow	
Why have organizations started to view their human resources as assets rather than costs?	3
What is meant by human resource management?	5
What is the range of human resource management solutions available?	7
Why have competency-based approaches become so important?	9
What is the context in which competency-based approaches should be implemented?	12
When is it best to adopt a competency-based approach?	13
References	15
2 What is meant by a competency?	**16**
Charles Woodruffe	
Defining a competency	16
The competency–competence debate	17
Competencies and technical skills	19
Competencies and other person variables	19
Listing competencies	20
Generic competencies	21
Clustering competencies	25
Classifying competencies	25
Determinants of competencies	26
Future orientation	27
Rejecting competencies	28
Summary	29
References	29

3   **Identifying competencies**   31
     Rajvinder Kandola and Michael Pearn
     Data gathering   31
     Choosing a method   32
     Competency identification   35
     Competency analysis methods   37
     Conclusion   48
     References   49

4   **Assessing competencies**   50
     Mike Smith and Ivan Robertson
     Analogous approaches   51
     Analytical methods   62
     Miscellaneous approaches   70
     Assessment centres   71
     Development centres   72
     Conclusion   73
     References   73

PART TWO: **Issues and practice**   77

5   **The first step on the ladder—a practical case in identifying
     competencies**   79
     Peter Honey
     Why choose the Repgrid?   79
     The case itself   80
     Conclusion   88

6   **Using competencies in selection and recruitment**   89
     Rob Feltham
     Process   89
     Implementation   91
     Evaluation   101
     Notes   103
     References   103

CASE STUDY ONE   **Safeway plc**   **104**
     Rob Feltham
     Competency classification   105
     Graduate recruitment and development   106
     Note   110

7   **Using competencies in career development**   111
     Stephanie Craig
     Identifying and establishing competencies   113
     Using competencies   117
     Assessment techniques   118
     Managing the output   123
     Implementation   125
     References   127

CASE STUDY TWO   **A competency approach to role and career management restructuring**   **128**
Michael Pearn
The company   128
Objectives   129
Competency model   130
Behavioural indicators   133
Career movements   135

8   **Competence, pay and performance management**   **137**
Derek Torrington and Will Blandamer
Performance-related pay   138
A competency-based approach to performance management   140
Creating a common language   142
Pay/performance link   143
Competency defined as excellence   144
References   145

CASE STUDY THREE   **A competency approach to performance management**   **146**
Clive Mosley and Jane Bryan
The drive towards quality   146
People make equality   147
Developing the HR strategy   149
Competency and personal development   151
Pay and grading   153
Communicating the changes   154
Objective setting and appraisal   155
Evaluating success   155

9   **Using a competency approach in a business change setting**   **157**
Viv Shackleton
Future competencies   158
Background to Finserv   159
Issues   160
Job analysis methodology   164
Design assessment methods   167
Development centre   167
Outcomes and evaluation   171
Application issues   171
Pointers for success   172

PART THREE: **An assessment of the strengths and weaknesses of competency-based approaches**   **173**

10   **Where do we go from here?**   **175**
Paul Sparrow and Rosemary Boam
Existing competency work   175
Forward-looking profiles   177

Good future performance 177
Competency life cycles 180
Updating competency profiles 182
Competency requirement forecasting 183
Pushing competencies deeper into existing personnel systems 192
Linking competencies to strategic issues 194
Conclusion 196
References 196

Glossary 198
Index 200

For my husband, Brian, and our daughter, Alexandra—
without their patience and support this book would
never have been possible

For my wife, Susan, who is the most 'competent' person
I know

Series preface

Training and development are now firmly centre stage in most organizations, if not all. Nothing unusual in that—for some organizations. They have always seen training and development as part of the heart of their businesses. More and more must see it that same way.

The demographic trends through the nineties will inject into the marketplace severe competition for good people who will need good training. Young people without conventional qualifications, skilled workers in redundant crafts, people out of work, women wishing to return to work—all will require excellent training to fit them to meet the job demands of the 1990s and beyond.

But excellent training does not spring from what we have done well in the past. T&D specialists are in a new ball game. 'Maintenance' training—training to keep up skill levels to do what we have always done—will be less in demand. Rather, organization, work and market change training are now much more important and will remain so for some time. Changing organizations and people is no easy task, requiring special skills and expertise which, sadly, many T&D specialists do not possess.

To work as a 'change' specialist requires us to get to centre stage—to the heart of the company's business. This means we have to ask about future goals and strategies and even be involved in their development, at least as far as T&D policies are concerned.

This demands excellent communication skills, political expertise, negotiating ability, diagnostic skills—indeed, all the skills a good internal consultant requires.

The implications for T&D specialists are considerable. It is not enough merely to be skilled in the basics of training, we must also begin to act like business people and to think in business terms and talk the language of business. We must be able to resource training not just from within but by using the vast array of external resources. We must be able to manage our activities as well as any other manager. We must share in the creation and communication of the company's vision. We must never let the goals of the company out of our sight.

In short, we may have to grow and change with the business. It will be hard. We shall not only have to demonstrate relevance but also value for money and achievement of results. We shall be our own boss, as accountable for results as any other line manager, and we shall have to deal with fewer internal resources.

The challenge is on, as many T&D specialists have demonstrated to me over the past few years. We need to be capable of meeting that challenge. This is why McGraw-Hill Book Company Europe have planned and launched this major new training series—to help us meet that challenge.

The series covers all aspects of T&D and provides the knowledge base from which we can develop plans to meet the challenge. They are practical books for the professional person. They are a starting point for planning our journey into the twenty-first century.

Use them well. Don't just read them. Highlight key ideas, thoughts, action pointers or whatever, and have a go at doing something with them. Through experimentation we evolve; through stagnation we die.

I know that all the authors in the McGraw-Hill Training Series would want me to wish you good luck. Have a great journey into the twenty-first century.

ROGER BENNETT
Series Editor

About the series editor

Roger Bennett has over 20 years' experience in training, management education, research and consulting. He has long been involved with trainer training. He has carried out research into trainer effectiveness and conducted workshops, seminars and conferences on the subject around the world. He has written extensively on the subject including the book *Improving Trainer Effectiveness*, Gower. His work has also taken him all over the world and has involved directors of companies as well as managers and trainers.

Roger Bennett has worked in engineering, several business schools (including the International Management Centre, where he launched the UK's first masters degree in T&D) and has been a board director of two companies. He is the editor of the *Journal of European Industrial Training* and was series editor of the ITD's *Get In There* workbook and video package for the managers of training departments. He now runs his own business called The Management Development Consultancy.

About the authors

Editors **Rosemary Boam**

Rosemary Boam has accrued considerable experience in the human resource field since qualifying as a chartered psychologist in 1981. Her expertise lies in the assessment and development of managers. She worked for a number of years at the Henley Management College before joining PA Consulting Group. In her present role as principal consultant, she has specialized in competency profiling and applying competency-based approaches in the selection and career development area.

Paul Sparrow

Dr Paul Sparrow is a lecturer in organizational behaviour and management at Manchester Business School. He is a chartered psychologist. After working as a freelance consultant for a couple of years he took the post of research fellow at Aston University, and then spent three years working as a senior research fellow at Warwick University. During this time he published numerous articles on the future of work and human resource strategy. He spent two and a half years with PA Consulting Group working as a consultant and then principal consultant in the areas of human resource planning, resource development and information technology. He has recently returned to academia.

Contributors **Will Blandamer**

Will Blandamer is a researcher at the Manchester School of Management currently engaged in research, on behalf of the NHS, into pay structures and negotiating arrangements and the role of the personnel function in the wake of the reforms to the Health Service.

Jane Bryan

Jane Bryan studied economics and politics before entering her career in human resources. Before joining PA Consulting Group in 1988 she worked within generalist personnel management roles in both the public and private sectors. At PA she has been involved in a variety of rewards-related assignments for clients including the Department of Social Security, Hunting Engineering, ITN and several local authorities. She is currently a human resources consultant specializing in rewards.

Stephanie Craig

Stephanie Craig is a director of Craig, Gregg & Russell Ltd, a professional consultancy specializing in applying psychology to work. She is a chartered occupational psychologist with many years' experience in the design and implementation of selection and development methods across a wide range of job types and industry sectors. Before the set up of CGR in January 1988, she was with PA Consulting Group, responsible for the development and growth of the Psychometrics Unit and before that she worked for the State Services Commission in New Zealand as an occupational psychologist.

Rob Feltham

Dr Rob Feltham is director of ASE, the business test division of NFER-Nelson. NFER-Nelson is a broad-based publisher of psychometric tests for business, education and the caring professions. Prior to his current appointment, from 1975–1988, he worked as a psychologist specializing in recruitment methods for the Home Office and Cabinet Office. He has previously written a number of articles about methods of psychological assessment, including assessment centres, psychometric testing, validity and cost benefit analysis.

Peter Honey

Dr Peter Honey is a chartered psychologist who works as a management consultant. He worked for Ford Motor Company and British Airways before becoming a freelance in 1969. He specializes in anything to do with people's behaviour and its consequences, and divides his work between designing and running training programmes, consultancy assignments and writing. He has written widely on behavioural topics in over fifty publications. His books include *Developing Interaction Skills, Face to Face Skills, The Manual of Learning Styles, Solving People-Problems, Improve Your People Skills* and *The Manual of Learning Opportunities*. He has advised on the contents of many training films and written the accompanying booklets. He features in the Video Arts production *Talking about Behaviour*.

He is an associate professor with the International Management Centre, a Fellow of the Institute of Management Consultants and the Institute of Training and Development, and a member of the Association for Management Education and Development.

Rajvinder Kandola

Rajvinder Kandola is a partner of Pearn Kandola Downs, a practice of occupational psychologists. He specializes in job analysis, selection and equal opportunities. He is the co-author of *Job Analysis – A Practical Guide for Managers*. Recent projects have included a competency analysis of executive officers within a government agency and the development of a competency framework within a London local authority. He is particularly interested in the use of competency and job analysis techniques for developing fairer selection methods.

Clive Mosley

Clive Mosley came into HR management following a university education in law. He worked initially in the automotive engineering industry in both personnel and employee relations in a range of different roles. He has worked with PA Consulting Group for four years on human resources assignments with clients such as ITN, Glaxo, British Railways

Board, Eastern Electricity and the Department of Social Security. He is currently business manager of PA's Rewards Consultancy practice.

Michael Pearn

Michael Pearn is a partner of Pearn Kandola Downs, specializing in assessment, development, team building and cultural change, and is the co-author of *Job Analysis – A Practical Guide for Managers*. He has carried out competency analysis for a wide range of organizations including pharmaceutical companies, fast-moving retail goods manufacturers and oil companies. He is particularly interested in the use of competencies for development purposes and for assisting in changing corporate culture.

Ivan Robertson

Professor Ivan Robertson is associate editor of the *British Journal of Psychology* and co-editor of the *International Review of Industrial and Organisational Psychology*. His work experience includes several years in industry/national government as an occupational psychologist. His teaching, research and consultancy interests focus on psychological and organizational factors related to work performance, satisfaction and health at work.

He also has an interest in methodological and psychometric issues related to industrial/organizational psychology. Professor Robertson has contributed to several international conferences, in this country and overseas, and has appeared on national TV and radio. Since taking up an academic post in 1979 he has produced 12 books and more than 60 scholarly articles/conference papers. He came to Manchester School of Management, UMIST, in 1981 where he is now professor of occupational psychology.

Viv Shackleton

Dr Viv Shackleton is a chartered occupational psychologist and lectures at Aston Business School on the postgraduate degree in personnel management. He has held university appointments in the US and continental Europe, as well as in Britain. His teaching and research specialisms are in employee recruitment and selection, and managerial assessment.

He is also the managing partner in his own consultancy firm, Shackleton Consultants, advising companies on setting up employee recruitment and selection systems and on the management of people. He is the author of numerous books and articles in the professional and academic press. His most recent book is published by Fontana, entitled *How to Pick People for Jobs.*

Mike Smith

Dr Mike Smith is a senior lecturer at the Manchester School of Management, UMIST, and has wide experience of researching and applying the psychology of selection. As well as writing many books and papers, he teaches one of the UK's most prestigious Masters courses on selection and assessment. His research interests include selection testing, survey methodology, job analysis and job motivation. He has been supported by many research grants including one grant of £250 000 to establish, with BT, the first Teaching Company Scheme in Psychology.

He has served on a number of regional and national bodies, including Manchester University Appointments Board, committees of the Manpower Services Commission and the Council of the British Psychological Society. He is a director of Coutts Career Consultants.

Derek Torrington

Derek Torrington is professor of human resource management at the Manchester School of Management. He is chief examiner for the Institute of Personnel Management, and author of more than 20 books in the field of industrial relations and human resource management. Professor Torrington is currently researching pay structures in the National Health Service, training standards for life assurance sales representatives, and management in schools.

Charles Woodruffe

Dr Charles Woodruffe runs Human Assets Limited. He specializes in the assessment and development of managerial competence, particularly via the assessment centre approach. His clients have been mainly in the financial sector, but have also included parts of the public sector, as well as engineering and high-tech organizations. Before setting up his own business, he worked for PA Consulting Group, which gave him an invaluable grounding and education in the consultancy profession.

Earlier in his career, he was a lecturer in occupational psychology, personality and social psychology and has had many articles published in the main international journals of personality. His most recent book, *Assessment Centres*, is published by the IPM. He is a member of the IPM, and a chartered occupational psychologist.

Acknowledgements

We would like to thank all the individual contributors to this book. The goals we set ourselves as editors were to: move the debate on competencies forward by clarifying definitions; provide detailed and practical guidance on application; demonstrate the range of human resource issues that can be tackled by the approach; and highlight the implementation issues. In this we have been wholly dependent on the considerable skill and experience of our contributors. We thank them for placing the contributions into a coherent framework and for giving us the benefit of their invaluable knowledge.

PA Consulting Group provided the learning base for us, and encouraged us to devote our time to this project. Much of our thinking about competencies has been developed within the stimulating environment of their Human Resource Consultancy.

To Liz Williams and Georgina Cohen, our appreciation for their help in typing chapters, often at short notice. To Mark Parrish our thanks for supporting innovation in the competency field. To Jenny Ertle and her team at McGraw-Hill we owe our thanks for their encouragement of this book and their continued patience with us as editors.

Finally, special thanks are due to Brian Redding and Susan Sparrow for their continued support for our work and quiet acceptance of the many intrusions on family time.

Preface

Throughout the late 1980s many organizations began to focus parts of their human resource management system on the concept of a defined set of 'competencies' or 'competences' for managers. The potential benefits were, and are, attractive indeed. When a managing director or senior manager hears that it is possible to define exactly what is needed in the important jobs in the organization and exactly what people need to bring to those jobs in order to perform effectively, they begin to listen. This 'elixir' of organizational life represents a powerful lever. Pull it in the right direction, and you can:

- choose the right people to join the organization;
- appraise and manage performance according to their competency;
- assess their readiness or potential to take on the challenge;
- identify the gaps to help develop them in the right direction.

Do all these things at the same time, it is argued, and no managing director can fail to appreciate the direct link between money invested in the staff and a financial return based on the resulting excellent performance. Individual managers can also feel that at last the organization is going to tell them 'how' they demonstrate competency in their jobs, instead of listing a series of vague job descriptions that are far removed from what they really do. It is not surprising that the appetite of organizations to find out more about 'competency approaches' has grown.

Unfortunately, these wonderful tools have been largely the preserve of individual academics and consultants. Perhaps as a result, there seems to have been a perfect negative correlation between the increasing interest and published work on 'competency approaches' and the level of confidence that managers have in the writings of the experts. A powerful elixir 'competency approaches' may be, but how do you make the recipe?

This book is intended to address this dilemma. It should be read by managing directors, line managers and personnel managers who want to know how to apply the approach while at the same time avoiding the pitfalls. The book is intended to pick up the academic debate and convert it into practical advice. The chapters have been written by leading academics and practitioners. Each chapter picks on a particular topic and explains exactly what is involved in the approach. The authors also provide advice on implementation issues based on their experience. The chapters themselves are arranged in such a way as to build up the reader's understanding of, and skill in, the approach. It is divided into three parts.

Part One presents the theoretical background and practical knowledge needed to adopt a competency-based approach. This knowledge covers four progressive levels:

- why organizations are adopting competency-based approaches;
- a definition and clarification of 'competency';
- gathering data to identify and analyse competencies;
- measuring the extent to which competencies are held by existing staff.

Part Two considers a wide range of applications and the associated implementation issues, mainly through the use of discussion and case study.

Part Three makes an assessment of the strengths and weaknesses of competency-based approaches. It outlines an appropriate course for future development.

In Chapter 1 we place competency-based approaches within the broad context of recent developments in the field of human resource management. We describe a number of 'triggers' in the business environment which necessitate a more strategic response to the way people are managed. Organizations tend to have responded in six ways: learning by doing; cost reduction and simplification; structural changes; cultural or large-scale change programmes; human resource planning; or resource development strategies based around underlying competencies. We explain the reasons behind the growing popularity of the last approach. We also raise a number of issues that should be considered when adopting a competency-based approach, namely how to create the right environment and understanding for change and when to consider using the approach.

With the scene for the book having been set, Charles Woodruffe addresses the central issue of defining what is really meant by a 'competency' in Chapter 2. He makes an important distinction between the aspects of a job that have to be performed competently—the tasks and functions that define the areas of competence needed—and the sets of behaviour patterns that the individual needs to bring to the job in order to perform with competence—the 'competencies'. Competencies are concerned with the behaviours we must have, or must acquire, to input to a situation in order to achieve high levels of performance. A competency analysis therefore identifies all the behaviours we input into a broad context in order to perform well. It taps a wide range of psychological areas—such as personal traits, motives, attitudes, skills and aptitudes—and summarizes them at a descriptive level. Only when these behaviours have been identified—regardless of the specific tasks—are they grouped together into a named 'competency'. Competencies therefore lie at the heart of effective performance across a wide range of tasks and areas.

In Chapter 3 Rajvinder Kandola and Michael Pearn describe a series of methods that can be used to identify these competencies. The competency profile is the keystone on which every application depends. Practitioners must get the identification of competencies right. Kandola and Pearn highlight two different approaches to gathering data in order to identify competencies. The first involves taking a neutral stance on effective performance (usually in a stable situation) and the second examines values-driven hypotheses (usually associated with a vision that expresses the main corporate values of the future). They outline the main factors to be considered in choosing a data-collection technique and then discuss the relevance of different techniques in relation to the objectives of the reader. Six methods of analysis—observation, diaries, interviews, critical incident techniques, repertory grids, and checklist and inventories—are considered in turn. The pros and cons of each approach are discussed and some example outputs provided to assist the reader. The overview of job analysis techniques demonstrates that there is a wide range of techniques available. In order to build up a balanced picture, the best approach is to combine methods that are quantitative and qualitative, direct and indirect, standardized and flexible.

In Chapter 4 Mike Smith and Ivan Robertson take the reader through the next stage of knowledge—how to measure the extent to which competencies are held by existing managers and personnel. They point out that accurate assessment of competency is central to all the various applications that are discussed later in the book. Assessment of competencies relies on four main approaches. The first approach aims to copy key aspects of the job. Smith and Robertson describe the strengths and weaknesses of group exercises, in-tray exercises, role plays, presentations, written reports, psychomotor tests and trainability tests in assessing competency. A second approach relies on setting up abstract tests (such as tests of ability, temperament, and motivation and interest) which apply to people in general. The assessment of competency may also rely on reputational measures such as supervisor and peer ratings, or a number of miscellaneous techniques such as accomplishment records. In practice, most organizations rely on a combination of more than one method. Smith and Robertson outline the main principles of the two most popular approaches—assessment centres and development centres.

Having read Part One, readers should be armed with all the background knowledge to initiate a competency-based approach within their organization. Part Two is intended to describe the implementation issues that will be faced in applying competency-based approaches to the following areas:

- identification of competencies through a self-administered repertory grid approach;
- selection and recruitment of staff;
- career development;
- performance management;
- cultural change.

The identification of competencies is the first step on the ladder that practitioners have to take. In Chapter 5 Peter Honey provides a practical case study on how to identify competencies. He explains when it is appropriate to use repertory grids (one of the techniques discussed in Chapter 3 by Kandola and Pearn) and takes the reader step-by-step through the use of this powerful technique. The case material he uses to illustrate the technique is based on a manufacturing organization that needed to develop better 'people management' skills at supervisor and foreman level. Honey explains how the technique was administered, the results analysed, and a list of competencies produced.

By Chapter 6 the reader will be skilled in the practical identification of competencies. Rob Feltham draws the strands together and describes the use of competency-based methods in the area of selection and recruitment. He examines how a competency-based approach can benefit recruitment by identifying what it is that the organization needs and ensuring that the recruitment process makes an optimum contribution. This involves linking recruitment needs to the business strategy, taking account of labour market changes and producing a shared understanding of the kinds of people that the organization needs. Feltham then describes a number of ways in which systematic assessment procedures based on agreed competencies can bring a high level of consistency among people responsible for making hiring and promotion decisions. He highlights ways in which organizations can improve the targeting, attraction and evaluation of applicants. Safeway plc is used as a case study to illustrate how they addressed many of the implementation issues.

A second area in which competency-based approaches have been used extensively is career development. In Chapter 7 Stephanie Craig focuses on how organizations can develop staff for the future. She explains how career evidence gathered from an individual's current level is of limited value once people face the major 'career bridges' such as moving from a technical to a professional role, or operational to strategic management. The competency-based approach truly comes into its own by providing guidance on likely performance at the next level. Craig discusses the ways in which career development decisions can be made more meaningful, planned and effective under the headings of: identifying and establishing career development competencies; using competencies to achieve organizational and individual needs; techniques for assessing competencies; managing the outputs for career development; and the implementation issues that need to be resolved throughout the process. She provides a detailed description of a career development workshop—one of the most frequently used techniques in this area.

Chapter 7 addresses the 'structural' aspects of career development, i.e. succession planning, promotion and career development workshops. A career management case study is provided by Michael Pearn. The case describes how the manufacturing arm of a large pharmaceuticals organization used a competency-based approach to analyse three new managerial roles, create a competency model for the three levels of management, design an assessment centre and develop a core group of experts in the organization.

In Chapter 8 Derek Torrington and Will Blandamer take the discussion of competency-based approaches into the area of performance management. They highlight the shift away from collective bargaining towards individual employee relations and the associated emphasis on individual performance. The growth in performance-related pay schemes that has followed has brought with it a number of problems. These revolve around the setting of meaningful objectives for the appraisal system and the appraisee, improving the appraisal process and translating appraisals into pay. Torrington and Blandamer argue the case for competency-based approaches in these areas, raising the need to focus on those competencies associated with 'excellence' as opposed to base-level competence.

As yet there has been little use of competency-based approaches in these areas. However, Mosley and Bryan provide a case study based on a medium-sized distribution organization in which competency-based approaches were applied to the area of performance management.

Viv Shackleton provides the final case study in Chapter 9. The previous cases have developed a detailed understanding of the use of competency-based approaches in specific areas of the personnel system— recruitment, career development and performance management. The last case provides a description of how a medium-sized financial services organization used competency-based approaches—in the form of a career workshop—in a business change setting. This case takes the application of competency-based approaches into a more future-oriented and strategic setting.

The focus of the book changes again in Part Three. In Chapter 10 we assess the strengths and weaknesses of existing competency work on the basis of the preceding chapters. We argue that there is now a sufficiently deep and broad understanding of competencies for the technique to be used in more strategic settings. This brings with it the need to develop more qualitative values-driven techniques to identify and classify competencies. We describe a number of techniques that will enable organizations to conduct 'competency requirement forecasting'. We also outline the 1990s application areas that will feature competency-based approaches—such as structuring careers around competencies, creating strategic skill pools, and using competencies in strategic team-building situations.

Theory and knowledge

1 The rise and rationale of competency-based approaches

Rosemary Boam and Paul Sparrow

The next three chapters in this book will define the nature of competencies, describe the ways in which competencies are identified, and discuss how they are assessed. Subsequent chapters will then describe the issues associated with the implementation of competency-based approaches in a variety of settings through the use of example and case study. In order to appreciate the relevance of the approach, however, it is first necessary to locate a competency-based approach within the range of human resource solutions open to organizations. We must be able to make a case for taking a competency-based approach as opposed to any other approach. This chapter therefore attempts to address the following questions:

- Why have organizations started to view their human resources as assets rather than costs?
- What is meant by human resource management?
- What is the range of human resource management solutions available?
- Why have competency-based approaches become so important?
- What is the context in which competency-based approaches should be implemented?
- When is it best to adopt a competency-based approach?

Why have organizations started to view their human resources as assets rather than costs?

Since the 1960s there has been an evolution in the way we think about the business environment, the management of people, the relationship between the organization and employees, and the nature of management capability (Evans, 1991; Morgan, 1989).

In the 1960s the business environment was relatively stable. Employees were generally seen as an economic resource. Their contribution was tightly controlled by the organization and was expressed in a clear 'contract' between employer and employee. There was little emphasis on individual differences. The talk was all about general motivational theories (characterized by the work of Maslow (1968), Herzberg (1966) and Ouchi (1981)) based on broad human needs. Organizations concentrated on 'the best way of doing things' and therefore competence was seen in terms of mastering specific techniques. Skills and knowledge in a specific field of endeavour were the order of the day for employees.

During the increasingly competitive 1970s and early 1980s the atmosphere became one of change and uncertainty. Suddenly there was no 'best way' of doing things. There was no longer a best way of organizing

people. It all depended on what you wanted to achieve—your strategy—
and your structure was only effective if it 'matched' your strategy. At
the same time our understanding of human motivation became richer
and began to stress individual differences. The focus of attention was on
'matching'—structure to strategy—jobs to structure—and people to jobs.
In this environment organizations wanted a flexible worker, capable of
self-management in certain situations. The employee was still seen as a
'cost of doing business' and in order to reduce that cost it was necessary
to ensure you could harness individual differences and match the right
person to the right job. To do this you had to motivate and 'energize'
employees, who were generally viewed as uncooperative, and this led
to a focus on powerful charismatic leaders with good management
process skills, and a demand for less conciliation.

It was legitimate to respond to the major upheavals of the early 1980s
by 'cutting the deadwood' and attempting to reduce the organization to
a hard core of effective (and marketable) employees.

The mid-1980s saw another change in the way we thought about
human capability. Competitive pressure turned to competitive threat.
Workforces were slimmed down. Individual jobs became more self-
contained, more skilled and varied, and the reduced levels of supervision that resulted created the need to give individuals more control
over their own activities (White and Trevor, 1983). Giving employees
more scope and autonomy meant that organizations had a vested interest
in viewing employees as an asset (no longer just a cost). As an asset,
employees should be invested in in order to add value to them. The
organizations that survived the recession in the early 1980s embarked
on major strategic changes. With the new focus on developing people
there was a growing realization that people were also important in
implementing these new strategies, yet there was increasing uncertainty
over the best way to manage the more flexible (and less organizationally committed) employees.

It was also realized that it was no longer a question of having the right
'fit'. Evans (1991) argues that management has become a balancing act.
Rather than submitting to 'either/or' choices—such as centralize or
decentralize, produce low-cost or value-added products or services—
organizations have to be able to balance opposites. Organizations need
to be opportunistic, but also to plan. They need top-down hierarchy as
well as bottom-up involvement. They have to balance the need for quality with financial imperatives, business generalism with professional
specialization, and good teamwork with the brilliant individual. In this
environment organizations need individuals who can help to define the
situation. Managers need to be encouraged to confront, understand and
deal with a wide range of forces outside the organization and this
implies the need to develop their skills, attitudes, values and mindsets
in a way that will produce a combination of excellence and the ability to
manage the 'tension' within the organization constructively.

What is meant by human resource management?

By the mid-1980s there were a host of 'triggers' that, by themselves, implied the need to manage carefully the skills and competencies of the workforce. In combination, they represented an overwhelming force for change. In order to survive—let alone gain any kind of competitive advantage—organizations had to focus on the quality of their human resources to a degree not seen before. Figure 1.1 summarizes the pressures that a number of authors (Hendry, Pettigrew and Sparrow, 1989; Herriot, 1989; and Toffler, 1970) have identified as shaping the way that organizations manage their people.

The extent and pace of the changes indicated by these 'triggers' served to demonstrate that organizations were only able to implement the planned strategic changes by creating a parallel human resource management strategy. In response to these challenges, a radically different philosophy and approach to the management of people at work, called human resource management (HRM) grew in popularity (Storey, 1989). Human resource management was considered to be the process of analysing an organization's human resource needs under changing conditions and developing the activities necessary to satisfy these needs. The approach was used to integrate human resource policies with strategic business planning, to reinforce 'appropriate cultures' in the organization, and to shift the focus of personnel management towards the contribution of the individual (as opposed to a collective group) (Legge, 1989).

The Harvard Business School (Beer, Walton, Spectre and Lawrence, 1984) defined a number of areas of policy that general managers could mobilize in response to the various strategic triggers in order to bring about four major outcomes within organizations:

- competence of employees
- commitment of employees
- congruence between the goals of employees and the organization
- cost effectiveness of HRM practices

Each policy area represented a major task that general managers must attend to. These tasks were:

- the flow of people at all levels into, through and out of the organization in order to have the right number of people with the right mix of competencies (human resource flow policies);
- the design of reward systems to attract, motivate and retain employees at all levels (reward system policies);
- defining and designing work by rearranging people, information and technology (work systems policies);
- determining the levels of responsibility, authority, power, delegation and decision making (employee influence).

These human resource activities were viewed from a business perspective. As such they were seen in the context of business strategies and operational plans, and addressed with an eye to the bottom line, profits, effectiveness and survival (Schuler, 1990). The philosophy was guided by the following premises:

New technology

- Technical changes in products, processes and information systems
- Redesigned managerial work
- Decision support systems eroding the difference between technical and general managers
- More information, power and knowledge at lower levels
- Market need·for more rapid product development

The drive for quality

- Business pressures for higher quality design of products and delivery of service
- Total quality programmes requiring deeper understanding of internal customer-supplier workings
- Knowing how to deliver what the customer wants

New competitive arrangements

- Changes in regulatory contexts such as privatization, deregulation, conversion to agency status
- Increase in strategic alliances and joint venture arrangements
- Increasing number of acquisitions, mergers, takeovers and diversifications

STRATEGIC TRIGGERS

More flexible and responsive organization

- Decentralization in mature and declining industries
- Short-term performance improvement pressures
- An increased number of people operating at the boundary of the organization
- Moving from bureaucracies to 'adhocracies'
- Reduced rules and formalization
- Overcoming functional, product and national boundaries within the organization
- Accelerated movement of small firms through start up, growth, maturity and decline stages

Internationalization of business

- 'Globalization' of business markets
- Redrawing of new economic groupings, e.g. Single European Market, Pacific Rim

The power of information

- Increase in the availability and quantity of information
- A need for organizations to use information more effectively
- Need to search out and develop experience already in the organization
- Managing relationships with external sources of expertise

Supply of resources

- Demographic pressures reducing the supply of human resources
- Limited mobility of staff (e.g. north/south divide) creating a need to manage with what is available
- Educational provision unable to match organizational demand
- Long-term shift from a buyer's to a seller's labour market in specific regions of the country
- Growth of the 'me' culture with demand for individual development

Figure 1.1   Business pressures creating the need for new competencies in organizations

- HRM has to balance the views of a number of stakeholders such as shareholders, employees, customers and suppliers;
- The policies have simultaneously to serve the interests of the organization, the individual and society;
- There has to be a reasonable degree of consistency or fit between each of the above policy areas;
- This is best achieved by linking the management of human resources to the business strategy;
- HRM is therefore a part of the general management function and cannot be delegated to a functional speciality.

What is the range of human resource management solutions available?

In response to the major strategic changes in the mid-1980s, organizations reacted in a number of ways. The human resource strategies pursued attempted to add value to the organization by identifying, analysing and implementing a set of procedures and activities to solve the various people-related concerns. The people-related concerns can be summarized in terms of six 'strategic' reactions:

- learning by doing
- cost reduction and simplification
- structural changes
- cultural or large-scale change programmes
- human resource planning
- resource development

Each of these 'strategies' brought with it a particular focus of activity. The nature of these activities becomes more apparent when you consider the typical comments managers make about their own organizations in thinking about the various pressures they are under. They tend to jump to a particular conclusion—such as 'we haven't got the right sort of attitudes and culture round here'—and undertake a series of actions to bring about the various solutions described in Figure 1.2. There is nothing wrong in essence with such reactions, but the danger is that organizations tend to focus on one or other of the areas shown in Figure 1.2 at the expense of others. They get on a one-way escalator that takes them down a reorganization route, or into large-scale change programmes, and so forth. The different approaches are not mutually exclusive and in most cases one type of focus will precede another, as organizations 'jump ship' and introduce a new flavour into their human resource management.

Reaction	Route	Main focus of attention
'Crisis—what crisis?'	**Learning by doing**	• Reactive and piecemeal adjustments to the way people are managed • Multiple (but minor) tweaks to HR policies once the wave hits • Politically easy, cosmetic or damage limitation changes
'We're going to have to get a lot leaner and fitter.'	**Cost reduction/ simplification**	• Headcount and budget control or reduction • Emphasis on productivity *measurement* • Prioritization of project workload in line with importance • Focus of reward on performance
'We're not organized in a way that matches our strategy.'	**Structural**	• Top down clarification of levels of control, responsibility and accountability • Changing the information people are exposed to, roles they play, relationships they form • Work redesign based on bottom-up analysis of tasks carried out • Examination of who needs to talk to whom
'We haven't got the right sort of attitudes or culture round here.'	**Cultural/ programmatic change**	• Creation of a 'vision' for the business • Reliance on charismatic leadership • Large scale change programmes • Focus on global themes such as quality, customer satisfaction, market awareness • Attention given to internal management processes • Heavy use of internal communications • Investment in training and education • Emphasis on team building at local level

Figure 1.2 *Human resource management responses and routes to strategic issues*

Reaction	Route	Main focus of attention
'Better see what we've got and decide what we need before we do anything.'	**Strategic/ human resource planning**	• Proactive data collection about what really happens • Attempts to model what might happen • Measuring the cost and benefits of the way people are recruited, retained and developed • Deciding which areas to invest in • Determining a critical path for the changes • Sequencing and managing the implementation against a plan
'We haven't got the right skills and we don't make the best of what we've got.'	**Resource development (competency-based)**	• Deciding what type of work needs to be done • Analysing the way effective people do the work • Communicating the model of effectiveness • Making sure recruitment, development and performance management systems mutually reinforce the same behaviours • Providing line managers with tools to assess and develop individual potential

Figure 1.2 *Cont'd.*

Why have competency-based approaches become so important?

There are two main factors that have led to the ascendency of one of these human resource management strategies—the competency-based approach. These are:

• the failure of large-scale change programmes to deliver the necessary changes in individual behaviour;
• a growing link between business performance and employee skills, such that sustained business performance can only be achieved through improved management capability.

The failure of large-scale change programmes

Once organizations had embarked on some of the major human resource management transformations outlined in Figure 1.2, attention turned towards thinking about the change process itself. Many organiz-ations were tempted to focus on one approach to the exclusion of the others. It was appreciated that managing the process of change was as important as reaching the end goal. Research in the United States (Beer, Eisenstat and Spectre, 1990) focused on the way organizations attempted to change the way they managed people. It showed that the least successful route (but equally the most popular) was the pursuit of large-scale programmes of change—management education, quality circles, mission-philosophy statements and culture programmes. These large-scale programmes took up a lot of time and did not help the organizations become more competitive. Why did they fail? Because, it is argued, they are not in the 'critical path' of business units. The main weakness of the large-scale change programmes are:

- They start with a global and long-term business issue (e.g. quality or customer service) that tends not to be sensitive to, and has little to do with, the short-term critical issues faced and understood by managers;
- They tend to rely heavily on education and training methods that raise expectations and create an unrealistic view of what will be achieved;
- They tend to encourage learning through the use of new words and language (representational learning) rather than changes in what people do (behavioural learning);
- There is therefore a tension set up between what people say and what people do;
- Programmes are often driven by an exclusive project team, with little devolved control to those managers at the sharp end of the business;
- Programmes become vulnerable to a changing business scene and priorities;
- On the basis of experience they are also vulnerable to short-term pragmatists and long-term cynics who say 'this too will pass'.

Beer et al. (1990) argued that large-scale change programmes failed to change organizations because they failed to change behaviour. To sustain a change in behaviour long after the change programmes are dead, you have to create a demand for the new behaviours.

The skills supply imperative

Another factor behind the ascendency of competency-based approaches was that the acquisition of new skills became the underlying imperative of the 1980s. A research programme into human resource management in 20 UK firms (Hendry, Pettigrew and Sparrow, 1988) found that organizations were having to cope not only with numerous external pressures, but also with internal pressures to change the shape and balance of skills within the organization. The early 1980s recession had created 'development gaps' (as a result of downsizing exercises and recruitment bans). In many organizations there were large 'missing cohorts' of people and their loss was experienced for several years afterwards as the cohort worked its way through the management development system. Organizations also had to face the challenge of the 1980s with 'inherited skills bases' that were largely unsuited to the new tasks in hand.

Competitive pressures had presented organizations with a perceived business performance gap and this had largely resulted from skills gaps within the organization. Most of the developments that were made in HRM in the late 1980s were in the areas of recruitment, more flexible pay, flexible employment contracts, training and development and the upgrading or downgrading of skills levels. The vast majority of these developments were part of a deliberate and broad skills supply and retention strategy. The whole concept of skills and abilities had developed towards the need for competencies. Morgan (1989) explained the shift:

. . . whereas in the past managerial competence went hand in hand with the possession of specific skills and abilities, it now seems to involve much more. Increasingly, it rests in the development of attitudes, values and 'mindsets' that allow managers to confront, understand, and deal with a wide range of forces within and outside their organisations.

In May 1991 a Harvard Business School survey of 12 000 managers in 25 countries found that there was an intrinsic correlation between profit growth, job satisfaction and the rating of skills of people within the organization. Managers in every country put quality of education and skills as the most important factor that would effect the success of their company. This is largely because, as Moss-Kanter (1991) neatly summarizes: 'the mean time between surprises is getting shorter than the mean time to make a decision'. Organizations will only survive by reducing the mean time they take to make a decision, and this places great emphasis on the level of management capability.

If we summarize the developments in HRM we can see that organizations are currently looking for an approach to the management of their human resources that will enable them to bring about changes within the 'critical path' of the organization by describing global issues in a way that is sensitive to the local context. It is also necessary to express the desired change by drawing upon the language and understanding of the line managers who are at the sharp end of the business. There is a need for an approach to facilitate and sustain long-term changes in the actual behaviour of individuals while also providing a way of integrating—or 'gluing together'—the approaches taken in the four policy areas (previously outlined) of human resource flows, reward systems, work systems and employee involvement. Performance also needs to be defined in a way that incorporates the view of a wide range of stakeholders (customers, suppliers, shareholders, employees, etc.) and the approach to performance needs to be applicable to all levels within the organization.

An approach whose time has come

A competency-based approach is able to address one of the main weaknesses of large-scale change programmes:

- It is couched in terms of behaviours—what people actually do—not what they say they do;
- It is sensitive to and picks up what managers at the sharp end of the business have to do;
- It also suits the pragmatists because it looks at the underlying nature of effective performance (most managers find it hard to disagree with a well researched competency profile).

What is the context in which competency-based approaches should be implemented?

The scope for using competency-based approaches is enormous. We should not go overboard, however. Putting promising people into punishing environments is not a good strategy. Focusing on competencies should not be marketed as a panacea. Having identified and developed people with the competencies required to perform effectively, organizations still need to create the situations that will harness, and give full potential to, the individuals who have to deploy their competencies. It is also important to create the conditions that promote an understanding of the performance requirements and a demand for the appropriate behaviours.

In this sense, there are a number of changes that should act as precursors to any major competency-based programme. These precursors can be applied to any attempt to manage change. Attention needs to be given to the following issues (Beer et al., 1990) prior to—or at least in parallel with—any competency-based approach:

- increasing performance demands by articulating the new pressures in a clear way and establishing the appropriate performance standards;
- building up an awareness of and learning about the way to cope with the changes by drawing upon internal and external models of best practice;
- changing the structures and roles before defining the necessary skills and behaviours;
- giving line management a stake in providing the necessary leadership, i.e. giving them permission to innovate, replace personnel and/or be instrumental in the changes themselves.
- mobilizing a network of internal and external 'change agents' (such as senior management, personnel, consultants, academics) to help redefine the problems the programme is intended to address;
- starting changes on a pilot basis (often in outlying units) to provide a basis of experience and success before threatening core personnel and their values;
- orchestrating changes from the top, placing the best people as role models, providing realistic time frames and choosing to initiate pilots in a good environment.

Competency-based approaches also provide more than just a slightly more meaningful and relevant person specification. By detailing the behaviours that are associated with effective performance a competency approach shows organizations which 'levers' to pull. It also affords the opportunity to sustain high levels of performance by bringing together and integrating the way individuals are motivated to perform, made more able to perform, and rewarded for that performance.

Competency-based approaches are not the 'poor neighbour' that sits alongside other strategic approaches to human resource management. They lie at the heart of all the other approaches, converting them into a language that can be used for or as:

- improving the selection process;
- improving the assessment of career potential;
- improving the performance review process;
- providing a common language system to convey the nature of effective performance;
- facilitating self-assessment and development;
- providing a basis for coaching and training;
- an essential tool for developing the business culture;
- a tool to help build successful teams;
- a method for identifying the implications for job and organizational design;

When is it best to adopt a competency-based approach?

There is no simple or ideal recipe that can be used to indicate when it is appropriate to consider using competency-based approaches. Should you restructure first, then consider how to recruit, develop and retain people with the right competencies? Is it best to undertake a human resource planning exercise before any other approach is taken? In practice, most organizations introduce new approaches by 'hijacking' an existing initiative and recasting it in the new 'colours'. However, from the analysis in this chapter, there is a logical sequence that organizations should follow where possible (see Figure 1.3).

We feel that a competency-based approach should act as the final integrating approach to change. There is now a sufficient understanding about the nature of competencies—and sufficient application and experience of the approach—for it to have wide potential. The extent to which current practice—in the areas of selection, career development, performance management and cultural change—realizes this potential forms the basis of the rest of this book.

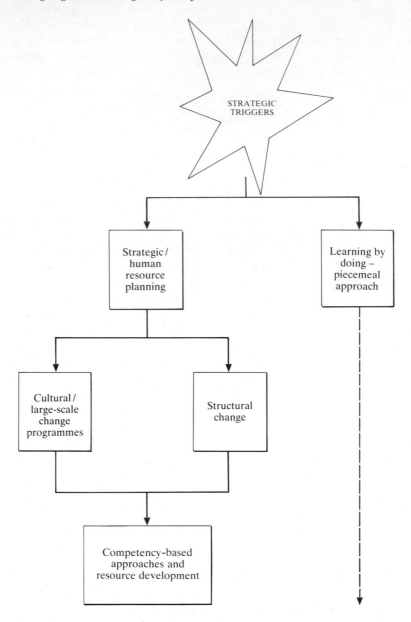

Figure 1.3 *The sequence of human resource management interventions*

References

Beer, M., R. Eisenstat and B. Spectre (1990) *The Critical Path to Corporate Renewal*, Boston: Harvard Business School Press.

Beer, M., B. Spectre, P.R. Lawrence, Q.N. Mills and R.E. Walton (1984) *Managing Human Assets*, New York: Free Press.

Evans, P. (1991) 'Motivation revisited: striking a dynamic balance in the dualistic organisation', *23rd International Human Resource Management Conference*, 3–5 April, Barcelona: Management Centre Europe.

Hendry, C., A. Pettigrew and P. Sparrow (1989) 'Linking strategic change, competitive performance and human resource management: results of a U.K. empirical study', in R. Mansfield (ed.) *Frontiers of Management: Research and Practice*, London: Routledge.

Herriot, P. (1989) *Recruitment in the 1990s*, London: IPM.

Herzberg, F. (1966) *Work and the Nature of Man*, New York: Staples Press.

Legge, K. (1989) 'Human resource management: a critical analysis', in J. Storey (ed.) *New Perspectives on Human Resource Management*, London: Routledge.

Maslow, A.H. (1968) *Toward a Psychology of Being*, New York: Van Nostrand.

Morgan, G. (1989) *Riding the Waves of Change: Developing Managerial Competences for a Turbulent World*, Oxford: Jossey Bass.

Moss-Kanter, R. (1991) 'The new management realities', *23rd International Human Resource Management Conference*, 3–5 April, Barcelona: Management Centre Europe.

Ouchi, W. (1981) *Theory Z*, Reading, Mass: Addison-Wesley.

Schuler, R. (1990) 'Repositioning the human resources function: transformation or demise', *Academy of Management Executive*, 4(3), 49–60.

Storey, J. (1989) (ed.) *New Perspectives on Human Resource Management*, London: Routledge.

Toffler, A. (1970) *Future Shock*, London: Pan.

White, M. and M. Trevor (1983) *Under Japanese Management*, London: Heinemann.

2 What is meant by a competency?

Charles Woodruffe

Defining a competency

The word 'competency' stalked up on the unwary working in the human resources field. The catalyst for its use was Boyatzis's (1982) book *The Competent Manager*. He triggered the popularity of the term which became *de rigueur* for the serious consultant in the late 1980s. Unfortunately, while street credibility demanded use of the word, few were certain in their own minds what it meant. This state of confusion has not really abated with the passage of time.

Definitions abound. Boyatzis defines competency broadly as 'an underlying characteristic of a person'. It could be 'a motive, trait, skill, aspect of one's self-image or social role, or a body of knowledge which he or she uses'. Hornby and Thomas (1989) define competencies as 'the knowledge, skills and qualities of effective managers/leaders' (p. 53).

It often seems to be used as an umbrella term to cover almost anything that might directly or indirectly affect job performance. Given its pivotal role, it is absolutely crucial that there is an adequate and agreed definition of competency. Without precise definition:

- the person wanting to specify an organization's competencies has no clear idea what is being looked for. No technique for identifying competencies can be employed successfully amidst a general confusion over what a competency is;
- there can be no theoretical contribution to what causes individuals to have or to lack a competency and no theoretically based advice on whether they can be developed.

Progress is made by going back to Boyatzis, who distinguished functions, tasks and relevant competencies. In his example, one of the tasks of the planning function is to determine the goals of the organization. The relevant competencies are efficiency orientation, proactivity, diagnostic use of concepts, and concern with impact. Essentially, the distinction is between:

- the aspects of the job that have to be performed competently; and
- what people need to bring to the job in order to perform the aspects to the required level of competence.

It is a distinction that leads to a definition of a competency:

> *A competency is the set of behaviour patterns that the incumbent needs to bring to a position in order to perform its tasks and functions with competence.*

Of particular importance to the definition is the statement that competencies are concerned with people's behaviour. It is a discrete dimension of behaviour. Furthermore it is a dimension of behaviour that is relevant to performance in the job. This job-relevance is true even if for some purposes (e.g. vocational guidance) the competency list might extend notionally to all jobs.

Competencies are behavioural repertoires that some people carry out better than others. From Chapter 3 you will see that it is these behavioural dimensions that should be the focus of the job analysis. What matters to people's performance is the way they behave, and the job analysis must isolate the behaviours that distinguish high performance.

An example of a list of competencies is produced in Figure 2.1. It will be seen that each competency is composed of a cluster of behaviours. These are the behaviours of the high performer.

To summarize, a competency is a dimension of overt, manifest behaviour that allows a person to perform competently. Behind it must be both the ability and desire to behave in that competent way. For example, the person competent at selling will need a competency that includes listening. In turn, that includes knowing how to listen and choosing to listen. Put more generally, people will only produce competent action in a situation if they know how to and if they value the consequences of the expected outcomes of the action (Krampen, 1988).

The competency-competence debate

Having arrived at a definition of a *competency* it is important to differentiate it from *competence*. An essential distinction is between aspects of the job at which the person is competent, and aspects of the person that enable him or her to be competent.

Competencies deal with the behaviours people need to display in order to do the job effectively (e.g. sensitivity) and not with the job itself (e.g. staff management). The job itself consists of a set of deliverables, outputs or roles, each of which requires a number of individual competencies. Some lists of competencies confound these two by putting together what people must be able to do, with what they need to do it effectively. The result is a set of competency dimensions that are not independent. This raises problems when the competency list is put to use. For example, the list might be used as assessment centre dimensions. If the list includes both competencies and job roles, the team of assessors will be unclear about the particular competency to credit with a particular

Breadth of awareness to be well-informed

Develops and maintains networks and formal channels of communication, within the organization and with the outside world; uses information technology to gain information; maintains an awareness of what should be happening and what progress is being made; keeps abreast of relevant local, national and international political and economic developments; monitors competitor activity.

Incisiveness to have a clear understanding

Gets a clear overview of an issue; grasps information accurately; relates pieces of information; identifies causal relationships; gets to the heart of a problem; identifies the most productive lines of enquiry; appreciates all the variables affecting an issue; identifies limitations to information; adapts thinking in light of new information; tolerates and handles conflicting/ ambiguous information and ideas.

Reasoning to find ways forward

Generates options; evaluates options by examining the positive and negative aspects if they were put into effect; anticipates effects of options on others; foresees others' reactions; demonstrates commonsense and initiative.

Organization to work productively

Identifies priorities; thinks back from deadline; identifies elements of tasks; schedules elements; anticipates resource needs; allocates resources to tasks; sets objectives for staff; manages own and others' time.

Drive to achieve results

Prepared to compromise to achieve a result; installs solution within time frame; innovates or adapts existing procedures to ensure a result; takes on problems; suffers personal inconvenience to ensure problems are solved; comes forward with ideas; sets challenging targets; sets out to win new business; sets own objectives; recognizes areas for self-development; acquires new skills and capabilities; accepts new challenges.

Self-confidence to lead the way

Expresses and conveys a belief in own ability; prepared to take and support decisions; stands up to seniors; willing to take calculated risks; admits to areas of inexpertise.

Sensitivity to identify others' viewpoints

Listens to others' viewpoints; adapts to other person; takes account of others' needs; shows empathy in oral and written communications; aware of others' expectations.

Cooperativeness to work with other people

Involves others in own area and ideas; keeps others informed; makes use of available support services; utilizes skills of team members; open to others' ideas and suggestions.

Goal-orientation to win in the long term

Sticks to a plan; does not get side-tracked; sacrifices the present for the future; bides time when conditions are not favourable.

Figure 2.1 *A list of generic competencies*

Output / Competency	Strategic thinking	Problem solving	Persuasion	Staff management	Training and development	Customer service	Business development
Breadth of awareness	x	x		x			
Incisiveness	x	x	x	x	x		
Reasoning	x	x	x	x	x	x	x
Organization		x		x	x	x	x
Drive		x	x	x	x	x	x
Self-confidence	x	x	x	x	x	x	x
Sensitivity		x	x	x	x	x	x
Cooper-ativeness		x	x	x	x	x	
Goal-orientation	x		x	x	x	x	

Figure 2.2 *Grid relating competencies to roles*

piece of behaviour. In turn this will disrupt the validity of the assessment (Woodruffe, 1990).

The two variables of competencies and job roles must be kept separate, as shown for example in Figure 2.2.

Competencies and technical skills

Apart from the behavioural competency dimensions, the job analysis might also reveal specific technical skills, knowledge and abilities that are required for the job. Calling these 'competencies' is likely only to muddle the definition of a competency again, and it seems better to use a separate label. These technical skills and abilities apply particularly to those jobs with a professional component, for example the job of a solicitor. Many of the behavioural competencies in Figure 2.1 will be necessary to perform satisfactorily as a solicitor. In addition, there are the specific technical skills and knowledge such as knowing the law of tort and how to draw up a will.

Competencies and other person variables

To summarize thus far, competencies are different from aspects of the job. They are what the person brings to the job. The question then arises whether they are the same as other qualities of an individual, such as personality. The answer is a qualified affirmative. Competencies are indeed the same as aspects of personality such as traits and motives, but those terms are so poorly understood and agreed that to say that competencies are, for example, traits risks competencies inheriting the confusion that surrounds traits. Certainly it is unhelpful to the practising manager to define competencies in terms that are themselves frequently misunderstood.

Listing competencies

Having identified what a competency is, and is not, it is now important to ensure that it is presented in a format which can be *applied* and *used* by the practitioner.

1 **Focus on a level of generality**. It is pointless making distinctions between competency dimensions that are so fine they might be intellectually satisfying, but have no practical use. For example, assessors at an assessment centre might be unable to follow the distinctions being made: report writing and memo writing are often combined under written communication and speaking to meetings and speaking one-to-one put under oral communication. The trick is not to become so general that a competency dimension could be assessed at the same level in two people for very different reasons. It might seem sensible to combine oral and written communication under the umbrella of communication skills, but the difficulty is that some people are excellent at writing and not so good at oral communication. For others, the opposite applies. These two types of people could end up with the same score on the umbrella dimension of communication skills, and valuable information on their strengths and weaknesses would be lost. A second example of an umbrella dimension is one often labelled 'personal factors'. It is difficult to assess people under such a general title, because they can be strong on one personal factor yet weak on another.

2 **Visible dimensions**. The goal of the job analysis is to have a set of competency dimensions against which people can be assessed. They must be *observable*.

3 **Simplicity and brevity**. The number of competency dimensions must be kept within bounds. This is particularly vital when applying the competencies list to an assessment procedure. Gaugler and Thornton (1989) demonstrated that the accuracy with which assessors classify and rate people declines as the number of dimensions is increased. Indeed, Gaugler and Thornton argue for having between three and six dimensions because this is the maximum number people can, in practice, make use of in reaching decisions. In their support, Russell (1985) demonstrated that assessor ratings on 18 dimensions could be grouped into four factors, the most important of which were interpersonal and problem-solving skills. This research should be borne in mind if there is a temptation to produce a long list of dimensions. Probably 12–15 competency dimensions is the maximum for assessment purposes.

4 **User friendliness**. A competency must be phrased in plain English and reflect the language of the organization. This increases the ownership of the list and reflects the prevailing culture. For example, for Royal Insurance, Walkley (1988) describes how important it was that 'the jargon used was acceptable to non personnel staff and also helped to share ownership of the concept across the organisation'.

5 **Labelling the dimensions**. The competency dimension title must be backed up by behaviours that make up the dimension. In Figure 2.1 it can be seen that behavioural indicators such as 'gets a clear overview of an issue', 'grasps information accurately' and 'gets to the heart of a problem' have all been grouped under the dimension title of 'incisiveness'. The title is only the best summary term that can be found to describe the cluster of behaviours. The competency dimensions are derived by finding the behaviours, clustering these together, and giving the cluster an appropriate label. The order is not finding the dimension and then describing it in terms of behaviours.

6 **Discrete dimensions**. Spreading indicators across dimensions leads to ambiguity when assessment procedures are implemented. The acid test is to put yourself in the shoes of an assessor and imagine that you have seen a piece of behaviour. Will it be clear under which competency it is located?

7 **Future orientation**. Competency lists should look to the future, and not be based wholly in the past. We must get the best estimate of the future and what it will require of the people concerned. A system rooted in the past runs the risk of missing the changes in required competencies implied by changes in the organization and its environment. It is vital for the organization to keep the competency list under review, to ensure it continues to reflect the company's need (Greatrex and Phillips, 1989). Taking due account of the future is discussed in greater detail at the end of this chapter.

The competency list lies at the foundation of the assessment and development system. If the list is wrong it will raise problems for evermore. Apart from the organization failing to measure the things it needs, a poor list makes designing assessment procedures difficult, and will raise further problems at the time of assessor training. These problems will then follow through to any developmental workshops, etc. Really, it is a false economy to save time defining the competencies, and you must ensure they can stand up to even the most critical evaluation.

Generic competencies

At this point, it is tempting to ask whether the issue of specifying competencies could not be short-circuited. Is there a need for different lists for different organizations? Could there not be a list of universal competencies?

For example, the list in Figure 2.1 represents a summary of my own experience working with competencies for senior and middle managers. Undoubtedly there are generic management competency dimensions. Another list formulated by Thornton and Byham (1982) aims to encompass all the competencies relevant to 'top management' (Figure 2.3).

Oral presentation	Negotiation
Oral communication	Analysis
Written communication	Judgement
Organizational sensitivity	Creativity
Organizational awareness	Risk taking
Extra-organizational sensitivity	Decisiveness
Extra-organizational awareness	Technical and
Planning and organizing	professional knowledge
Delegation	Energy
Management control	Range of interests
Development of subordinates	Initiative
Sensitivity	Tolerance of stress
Individual leadership	Adaptability
Group leadership	Independence
Tenacity	Motivation

Figure 2.3   *Universal competencies for 'top management'*
Source: Thornton and Byham, 1982

Middle management competencies have been the focus of Dulewicz's (1989) research. He calls these supra competencies. Although not in their final state, these comprise four clusters, divided into a series of competencies (see Figure 2.4).

Intellectual	• Strategic perspective • Analysis and judgement • Planning and organizing
Interpersonal	• Managing staff • Persuasiveness • Assertiveness and decisiveness • Interpersonal sensitivity • Oral communication
Adaptability	• Adaptability and resilience
Results orientation	• Energy and initiative • Achievement motivation • Business sense

Figure 2.4   *Supra competencies*
Source: Dulewicz, 1989

Other lists that are worthy of comparison are those presented in *Personnel Management* during 1989 by major UK organizations. The summary lists are presented in Figure 2.5.

Without passing judgement on the merits of these various lists, there is clearly much overlap that supports a belief in generic competencies. However, there are also organization-specific competencies, and, most important, there is the problem of choosing between competencies in a generic list. The difficulty with generic lists is that they will be seen as applicable in their entirety. They also assume a uniformity of job titles.

Company	Cadbury Schweppes	WH Smith	BP	Manchester Airport	National Westminster
Author	T. Glaze (1989)	R. Jacobs (1989)	J. Greatrex and P. Phillips (1989)	L. Jackson (1989)	A. Cockerill (1989)
	Strategy	Written communication	Personal drive	Critical reasoning	Information search
	Drive	Oral communication	Organizational drive	Strategic visioning	Concept formation
	Relationships	Leadership	Impact	Business know-how	Conceptual flexibility
	Persuasion	Team membership	Communication	Achievement drive	Interpersonal search
	Leadership	Planning and organizing skills	Awareness of others	Proactivity	Managing interaction
	Followership	Decision making	Team management	Confidence	Developmental orientation
	Analysis	Motivation	Persuasiveness	Control	Impact
	Implementation	Personal strength	Analytical power	Flexibility	Achievement orientation
	Personal factors	Analytical reasoning skills	Strategic thinking	Concern for effectiveness	Self-confidence
			Commercial judgement	Direction	Presentation
			Adaptive orientation	Motivation	Proactive orientation
				Interpersonal skills	
				Concern for impact	
				Persuasion	
				Influence	

Figure 2.5 *Competency lists*
Source: Personnel Management, 1989, various issues

Organizations do not give the same title of seniority to the same approximate job level. One organization's director is another's manager.

It is difficult to make just minor adaptations to a provided list. Starting with a fresh sheet to derive a list that really does fit the particular job in a particular organization should be viewed as the optimal approach. Generic lists such as those shown in Figures 2.1, 2.3 and 2.4 might, however, be used as a check, against which the organization's own draft list can be compared.

Although generic competencies are usually second-best, generic competencies for the main job levels within an organization are essential. As Laupetre (1990) observes: 'it is rarely possible to analyse all the positions within an organisation and most of all to maintain such documentation'.

A recent contribution to the lists of generic competencies has come from the Management Charter Initiative (MCI). Their aim is to ensure a national development of managerial competence and so a national generic list is vital. The list must act as a common denominator for all organizations, large and small, and should indicate what is of particular relevance to different types of firm/industry.

The greatest publicity has been given to the MCI list of standards, which is based on functional analysis. Hornby and Thomas (1989) describe how a CMED working party asked companies about 'the kinds of things they would expect a graduate trainee to be able to do after a year or two in the organisation' (p. 52). The resulting list is comprised of units and elements, in specification of national standards of managerial competence. It is important to be clear that this MCI list deals with areas of competence and not competencies. Indeed, MCI are careful to separate the list of standards from the 'personal competences'. The standards include, for example:

Unit	*Elements*
• Recruit and select personnel	• Define future personnel requirements
	• Determine specification to secure quality people
	• Assess and select candidates against team and organizational requirements
• Seek, evaluate and organize information action	• Obtain and evaluate information to aid decision making
	• Forecast trends and developments that affect objectives
	• Record and store information

These are very different from what the manager needs in order to be competent. The 'to do' list of MCI standards seems far harder to agree about than a 'to have' list of competencies. The 'to do' list will vary much more between jobs and organizations than the 'to have' list of personal competencies. The risk is that the person who achieves the MCI standards may not need a good number of them in a particular managerial job, but may need additional areas of competence not covered by the standards.

The MCI list is tied to a three-stage qualification (certificate; diploma; MBA). Whether it is based on the MCI or another list, it is vital to remember that a qualification of competence does not mean that the person is fully equipped for all time for management within a particular organization. There will always be a need for honing and augmentation for a particular organization.

Clustering competencies

For some purposes it might be helpful to group competencies. For example, there might be groupings of types of competencies by domain, such as cognitive and interpersonal competencies to help in the presentation of developmental opportunities. For the same purpose, competencies might be grouped under the particular roles to which they are relevant, such as the competencies relevant to leadership.

One recent, superficially attractive, distinction was made between hard and soft competencies (Jacobs, 1989). Jacobs sees soft competencies such as creativity and sensitivity as conceptually different from his hard competencies, like organization. He seems to suggest that soft competencies are personal qualities that lie behind behaviour. However, soft competencies are really no different from hard competencies. They are all descriptions of regularities in behaviour, and none of them explains behaviour. In short, although at first sight attractive, the hard–soft distinction proves on reflection to be artificial.

Classifying competencies

Another contrast was made by Boyatzis between threshold and performance competencies. Threshold competencies are basic requirements to carry out the job, but do not differentiate between high and low performers. On the other hand, performance competencies do differentiate between levels of performance. Presumably, the threshold competency list need not include competencies that are so mundane they can be guaranteed at the level of focus. For example, while it would be realistic to include basic literacy and numeracy in the competency list of supervisor's jobs, they would be laughable in the list for a senior manager's job.

A problem with the distinction between threshold and performance competencies is that a good proportion of competencies for a job are both threshold and performance. People need a certain level even to start the job, but any extra is welcome. This is true both of cognitive and interpersonal competencies. Put more generally, the distinction between threshold and performance competencies seems to be a matter of degree, rather than of category. Normally a competency will tend towards threshold or performance rather than being absolutely one or the other. People should be assessed on all competencies relevant to the job and should be given the opportunity to develop all of them.

The danger of oversimplification that comes with categorizing competencies into threshold and performance is also inherent in other categorizations. For example, some competencies in a list might be described as more important than others, and labels such as core and peripheral are used. The danger in practice is that organizations will concentrate exclusively on those that are labelled more important and disregard those described as less important. Less important becomes unimportant. Furthermore, competency lists usually need to be taken as a whole. They provide balances to each other. For example, in the list in Figure 2.1, self-confidence and sensitivity are both required in equal measure. A sensitive person who is not self-confident would be a pushover. A self-confident person who is not sensitive runs the risk of being seen as lacking rapport.

Two categorizations that might be useful are those based on time and seniority. First, time. The competencies in a list must be reviewed to decide which are likely to remain important, which are likely to increase in importance and which are likely to become less important over time. This makes sense if the job analysis has concentrated on both present and future requirements. For most purposes it is better to concentrate on the future. After all, the organization is assessing and developing managers of the future, not of the present. Categorizing competencies in terms of seniority will show which are core throughout a person's career, which drop out with seniority, and which become salient only with seniority. This seems perfectly legitimate, and is based on comparing competency lists at different levels. The risk comes from extending the process to include those competencies that become more and less important with seniority. Again, the tendency is for the less important to be relabelled unimportant.

Determinants of competencies

To decide whether competencies can be developed, it is necessary to know what determines them. The issue is important both at selection and development. If competencies are hard to improve upon, then you can be less forgiving of a deficiency spotted at selection and obviously less optimistic about development.

Here it is important to remember that competencies are dimensions of behaviour, and so we are seeking to specify the causes of behaviour. Returning to the earlier discussion, it is not helpful to say a trait lies behind the behaviour or competency. The trait is only another word for the competency. For example, behaving with self-confidence might be a competency for a particular job. It does nothing to add that this behaviour is caused by a trait of self-confidence. However, it is helpful to look at what lies behind the behaviour that is summarized by the competency or trait.

Behind self-confidence lies the person's history, both distant and recent (Nelson-Jones, 1990). Certainly, the exact determinant of a particular person's competency will be specific to that person. What causes one person to lack self-confidence will be different from what causes another person's lack. Without going into all the possibilities, it can be seen that exploring the antecedents of competencies is a matter for the competent psychologist. This person should be able to advise on what has contributed to a particular person's level on each competency and to suggest the most productive programme for competency development.

The example of self-confidence illustrates the role of experience in determining a competency. It also points up that development might not be particularly easy. For some competencies, particularly some in the cognitive area, it does not seem too contentious to suggest that the possibilities for development will be quite limited. For example, it is probably harder to develop incisiveness than organization.

Future orientation

Competency lists can add real value by looking to the future. They should not be based in the past. We must get the best estimate of the future and what it will require of people, and ensure that the competency list is kept under review. A system rooted in the past runs the risk of missing the changes in required competencies implied by changes in the organization and its environment.

There are two aspects to looking to the future. The first is the need to include the competencies of change, and the second aspect is to include the changing competencies. First, to deal with the competencies of change: It is now a cliché to say that organizations and the people working for them must be flexible and able to change. Essentially, what is required are the competencies of 'changeability'.

For example, Pascale (1990) describes how Japanese companies have orchestrated a tension between opposites, rather than seeking to reduce ambiguity and paradox. Lorenz (1988) talks of the tight-looseness of the network organization and the need for leaders to mix the styles of management encapsulated in motivational theories such as X and Y (McGregor, 1960). Ashridge Management College (Barham, Fraser and Heath, 1988) say the need for change requires:

- Sensitivity to external influences. The manager needs the breadth to know how external political and economic factors affect the business.
- Ability to energize and mobilize other people.
- Public awareness acumen.

Sissons (1989) observes that for the flexible firm there is a need to establish a framework of creativity, and get away from control. It must have:

- Sophisticated employee relations
- Good external relations in the market place.

Specific competencies could be derived from observations such as these on what is required by changeability.

Apart from including the competencies of change, the organization's list must be flexible and able to reflect changes in the organization's direction. For example, Gerstein and Reisman (1983) described the different competencies salient for organizations in different business conditions. As conditions change so do the competencies. A more recent example is the organization going into Europe. Wood (1990) states that Euro managers must channel and manage diversity. Guptara (1988) talks of the need for:

- Observation—to spot differences between nationalities
- Curiosity to understand national differences
- Ability to gather information informally on people
- Analysis of data
- Tolerance of cultural differences

The need for an orientation to the future makes very questionable those competency lists that are based exclusively on comparing current high and low performers. They risk specifying the competencies up to today rather than those from tomorrow. It seems vital to build in the more speculative approach taken by, for example, Prentice (1990) who looks at the different management styles and associated competencies appropriate for the organization of the future. Such an organization, he says, will emphasize management by persuasion and consent.

Nevertheless, studying current high and low performers might well be part of the competency analysis. It means agreeing a definition of high performance. The best option is to define performance in terms of outputs, that is performance in roles, and at functions or tasks. However, converting this option into a practical measure is far from straightforward. One possibility is to index overall performance in the role, for example, performance at marketing or staff development. The index might best be a 'bottom-line' definition. For example, it might be a measure of sales performance or of the degree to which staff have been developed by the manager.

Rejecting competencies

Some people reject the competency approach, ridiculing it as trying to build an identikit manager. Iain Mangham of Bath University is particularly associated with this criticism. He says that, among other things, the competency lists fail to take account of the person's fit within the culture of the organization. This does not seem a disabling criticism. Of course, the person must want to fit into the organization's culture, but that is not an end to the competency approach. For example, Mangham says that people with a bank's competencies would not necessarily be good university administrators because they are not sympathetic to the university culture. This does not alter the fact that university administrators would be far better with many of the bank's competencies than without them. Of course, there is more to being a good manager than a set of competencies. However, they are a large part of the recipe.

In addition to the cultural extra, it is possible to be sidetracked by a 'Factor X', such as the charisma that makes some people absolute stars.

Management developers cannot give up because there happen to be a few charismatic people at the top of a few organizations. We have to improve the overall competence of the estimated two million people in the UK involved in management, and not be transfixed because they will not all be media stars.

Summary

The key point that this chapter has conveyed is that competencies are dimensions of behaviour which are related to superior job performance. They are ways of behaving that some people carry out better than others. The reasons for the differences between people's competency levels lie in the past and might be more or less easy to overcome. However, traits or dispositions do not belong among these reasons for competencies. They are in fact just another name for the competency dimensions.

It is vital that organizations ensure that their competency lists are well researched and robust. Unfortunately, there are many organizations with lists that make little sense. A particular problem is confusing competencies with job roles. Another is relying on the present and past to define competencies. Competencies must be oriented to the future and not a mechanism for cloning the past. It is also most important that organizations do not simply accept the generic list of a persuasive consultant. They must go to the effort of gaining a list over which they feel a sense of ownership. This might become a particular problem if the MCI list is seen as a definitive list of personal competencies which all organizations feel themselves obliged to adopt. The MCI list or a comparable generic list might, however, be used as a check on the organization's own research.

References

Barham, K., J. Fraser and L. Heath (1988) *Management for the Future: How leading international companies develop managers to achieve their vision*, Berkhamsted: Ashridge Management Research Group, March 1988.

Boyatzis, R. (1982) *The Competent Manager*, New York: Wiley.

Cockerill, A. (1989) 'The kind of competence for rapid change', *Personnel Management*, 21 (9), September 1989, 52–6.

Dulewicz, V. (1989) 'Assessment centres as the route to competence', *Personnel Management*, 21 (11), November 1989, 56–9.

Gaugler, B. and G. Thornton (1989) 'Number of assessment centre dimensions as a determinant of assessor accuracy', *Journal of Applied Psychology*, 74 (4), August 1989, 611–18.

Gerstein, M. and H. Reisman (1983) 'Strategic selection: Matching executives to business conditions', *Sloan Management Review*, Winter 1983, 33–49.

Glaze, A. (1989) 'Cadbury's dictionary of competence', *Personnel Management*, 21 (7), July 1989, 44–8.

Greatrex, J. and P. Phillips (1989) 'Oiling the wheels of competence', *Personnel Management*, 21 (8), August 1989, 36–9.

Guptara, P. (1988) 'How to shape up for 1992', *Personnel Today*, 14 June 1988, 24.

Hornby, D. and R. Thomas (1989) 'Towards a better standard of management', *Personnel Management*, 21 (1), January 1989, 52–5.

Jackson, L. (1989) 'Turning airport managers into high-fliers', *Personnel Management*, 21 (10), October 1989, 80–5.

Jacobs, R. (1989) 'Getting the measure of managerial competence', *Personnel Management*, 21 (6), June 1989, 32–7.

Krampen, G. (1988) 'Toward an action-theoretical model of personality', *European Journal of Personality*, 2, 39–55.

Laupetre, J. (1990) 'Methodological problems related to the assessment of the impact of new technologies on employment and qualification in the banking sector: A case study', *Applied Psychology: An International Review*, 39 (2), 15–167.

Lorenz, C. (1988) 'Nostrums fall from favour', *Financial Times*, 15 February 1988.

McGregor, D. (1960) *The Human Side of Enterprise*, New York: McGraw-Hill.

Nelson-Jones, R. (1990) *Human Relationship Skills: Training and Self-help*, 2nd edn, London: Cassell.

Pascale, R. (1990) *Managing on the Edge*, Harmondsworth: Penguin.

Prentice, G. (1990) 'Adapting management style for the organisation of the future', *Personnel Management*, 22 (6), July 1990, 58–62.

Russell, C. (1985) 'Individual decision processes in an assessment centre', *Journal of Applied Psychology*, 70 (4), 737–46.

Sissons, K. (1989) (ed.) *Personnel Management in Britain*, Oxford: Blackwell.

Thornton, G.C. and W.C. Byham (1982) *Assessment Centres and Managerial Performance*, New York: Academic Press.

Walkley, J. (1988) 'The use of assessment centres in management succession', *Banking and Financial Training*, 4 (3), September 1988, 17–18.

Wood, L. (1990) 'Is it a myth or a real Superman?' *Financial Times*, 14 February 1990.

Woodruffe, C. (1990) *Assessment Centres: Identifying and Developing Competence*, London: Institute of Personnel Management.

3 Identifying competencies

Rajvinder Kandola and Michael Pearn

The identification of competencies involves the use of one or more of a large family of job analysis methods. Even a cursory look at Sidney Gael's (1989) *Job Analysis Handbook* reveals at least 40 different job analysis techniques which can lead directly or indirectly to the formulation of competencies (see also Pearn and Kandola, 1988). These range from highly task-oriented methods, focusing on precise definitions of the tasks to be carried out, to psychologically oriented methods focusing on the human qualities (expressed in terms of knowledge, skills and other attributes) required to perform the job.

The most important step in the whole process of using competencies is the competency analysis. Elaborate management development systems, however expensive, will be built on foundations of sand if the competency analysis has been incomplete. The busy manager or personnel specialist could easily be bewildered by the variety of methods with which to obtain reliable data to formulate competencies; many of the methods give the appearance of using a sledgehammer to crack a nut. However, it is important to remember that the tasks of gathering data, carrying out an analysis, and formulating competencies that accurately reflect the components of successful job performance are not to be underestimated.

Data gathering

Data gathering, the first step to identifying competencies, is essentially a form of research activity. Data can be gathered 'blindly', in order to maintain a neutral stance, or it can be hypothesis- or values-driven so that a particular or desired outcome is achieved. Both approaches are acceptable forms of research. In the first case the context is likely to be stable without significant change in future. In the second case, the values determining the data gathering could stem directly from a newly created vision which expresses the future in new corporate values such as increased autonomy, commercial responsiveness and flexibility. For example, there may be an increased emphasis on decentralized or localized activity as opposed to highly centralized control. This would clearly have implications for the kind of data sought as well as their interpretation when determining the managerial competencies.

Another important consideration is how the competencies will be used. If the main use is to be specification of training standards and formalized assessment criteria, then it is quite likely that a neutral rather than a values-driven approach would be appropriate. This approach is currently being adopted in the development of competence-based national vocational qualifications and also the early lower level specifications of the Management Charter Initiative.

By contrast, many organizations attempting significant organizational renewal, or culture change, seek to identify competencies within a framework of values consistent with desired outcomes expressed in mission statements of organizational values. A good example of this can be seen below in the from–to cultural statements from ICL.

From	*To*
Technology-led	Marketing-led
Tactical and short-term	Strategic, long-term
Internal focus	External focus
Try to do everything	Specialized target markets
Parochial outlook	Company commitment
Procedure-bound	Innovative and open-minded
UK focus and export	Global competition

Choosing a method

When choosing a method or technique the user needs to consider a number of factors. It should be stressed that many writers on job or role analysis have argued that one source of data is probably insufficient as each method has its strengths and weaknesses. A multiple method approach will enable the strengths of one method to counterbalance the weaknesses of another. They key considerations are:

- worker or task orientation
- level of sophistication required of user
- level of quantification
- predetermined or user-determined structure
- closeness to job
- range of convenience
- sensitivity
- capacity to generate usable outcomes
- cost
- timescale
- computer assistance
- do-it-yourself, or the packaged approach

Orientation

Most job or role analysis methods can be divided into whether they are primarily focused on defining the precise tasks which need to be performed or the psychological factors that are necessary for their performance. Some methods fall between the two. In the context of competency analysis a single technique which combines both definition of task and the psychological characteristics required for the performance of tasks will be preferable to a technique that is primarily task- or worker-focused.

User sophistication   This can be an important consideration as some techniques require a very high level of statistical know-how and specialist computer support, whereas others are relatively straightforward and make fewer demands of the user.

It may sometimes be necessary for a large amount of data to be gathered and for complex statistical techniques to be used, such as factor analysis, but this would be rare. The system approach requiring the highest level of sophistication on the part of the user is probably the PAQ (Position Analysis Questionnaire), discussed later in this chapter.

Quantification   Most methods require a degree of quantification, whether in the form of simple rank ordering of statements, ratings, or other systems of number allocation. However, a great deal can still be achieved by intuitive interpretation especially within the context of values-driven data gathering. This is particularly appropriate where a specialist group has been brought together to evaluate and interpret the data that have been gathered.

Numbers in and of themselves can be misleading as they can create the impression that the data gathering and the interpretation is more objective and scientific than it really is. It is quite easy to build an impressive set of quantitative data that is subjected to complex statistical treatment and yet the whole process could be based on false assumptions.

Structure   Many of the methods available offer a predetermined structure for the user, e.g. PAQ and WPS (Work Profiling System) (Saville and Holdsworth, 1988), whereas others, such as critical incidents method or repertory grid, allow users to formulate their own structure which may be more relevant to their particular needs. Predetermined structure offers convenience as well as the likelihood that the structure has been derived and tested statistically. However, it can be too crude or general for a particular context and user-generated structure is preferable. There is then, of course, a need to test the structure for reliability and validity.

Job proximity   An important consideration is the extent to which the data were obtained indirectly, e.g. by descriptions provided by job holders, or directly, e.g. by observations or participation. The latter are very close to the job whereas checklists and interviews are indirect methods which gather only reported views and information. It is important to combine direct with indirect methods of data gathering and to obtain further evidence that establishes the validity and reliability of the indirect methods used.

Convenience   Some established methods of analysing jobs or roles are more appropriate to certain kinds of jobs. Other methods have a very wide range of convenience both in terms of jobs covered and range of outcomes that can be generated.

Sensitivity   An important consideration for a user is the extent to which the method or methods employed will enable the identification of less obvious, subtle but none the less critical, aspects of tasks or job performance. Some methods by their very nature are general in application and have a predetermined content and structure which, if used alone, might fail to detect critical aspects that should be embodied in any competency statement. This could be one of the strongest arguments against the sole use of commercially available systems for identifying competencies. The particular competencies that might be identified as relevant to, say, air traffic controllers (e.g. the capacity to maintain a mental picture of aircraft in their area) may not be revealed by the more general systems.

User outcomes   The systematic approaches tend to be associated with the capacity to offer computer-generated user outcomes such as employee specifications, job descriptions, comparative profiles, test specifications, etc. The methods that are primarily data gathering, such as checklists, questionnaires and diaries, still pose the problem of translating information which is essentially an objective description of the tasks involved into statements about the human attributes, skills and values required. Some methods try to combine the two processes (Fleishman's Ability Requirement Scales or Levine's Combination Job Analysis Method) while others leave it to a more intuitive interpretation (critical incidents or behavioural event interviewing) (Levine, 1983).

Cost   The cost of using a method often depends on the number of analysts that are required, the time it takes and level of computer-processing costs. Once again the advantage of the proprietary systems is that they are relatively cheap compared to the benefits derived.

This has to be offset against the efficiency with which they would identify the particular and precise needs in a given situation. A typical study could range in cost from a few thousand pounds to well in excess of £100 000, depending on the size of the project and the particular methods that are employed.

Timescale   Closely associated with cost is the time that a particular research approach or methodology requires in order to be fully pursued. The fully fledged critical incident technique and its derivative, behavioural event interviewing, can quite easily span periods in excess of a year to obtain the desired outcomes, but smaller-scale exercises of less complexity can be achieved easily within a few months. Once again, the range of packaged systemic approaches has the advantage of speed over other more intensive but possibly more specific and accurate methods.

Computer assistance   Some approaches, such as critical incidents or repertory grid, can be carried out quite effectively with the minimum of computer assistance but they can also be highly computerized, particularly when it comes to the processing and interpretation of hundreds of task or behavioural statements. By contrast other methods, e.g. PAQ or WPS, can only be used through the computer programmes of the commercial operator. Other approaches such as Sidney Gaels' WPSS (Work Performance Survey System) offer computer programmes for analysing data derived from ratings of task statements and behaviour statements which are uniquely generated by the user.

Do-it-yourself or packaged system?

Reference has already been made to the advantages and disadvantages of the packaged systemic approaches that are available. While it is recognized that under certain circumstances these approaches will meet the requirements of the user, it is unlikely that one method or approach will be capable of meeting all user needs under all circumstances. Consequently it may be appropriate, in certain situations, to use a combination of different approaches that are specifically put together by the user or to follow the guidelines and supporting material offered by a number of authors (e.g. the Versatile Job Analysis System, VERJAS, of Bemis, Belenky and Soder, 1983, and Levine's, 1983, combination job analysis method, C-JAM).

Competency identification

Clearly, the choice of data-gathering methods and interpretative tools will depend on the objectives of the user and other constraints such as size of organization, size of relevant populations, timescales and budgets. No one methodological approach or technique deserves more serious attention than others and none can or should claim to be the one and only way of identifying competencies.

As a generalization, competencies derived for use in vocational or training standards are more likely to place emphasis on the relationship of tasks and outcomes than on the behaviour and other attributes required. Management competencies, on the other hand, are much more likely to focus on the generic human attributes (incorporating skills, values and knowledge) that are judged necessary for the achievement of organizational objectives, particularly as translated into personal goals and objectives.

For example, the British Psychological Society has identified the competencies required of occupational test users. A checklist of competencies is provided that describes specifically what the person must be able to do, for example:

- Explain what a work sample test is and how it is used.
- Construct a frequency distribution (histogram or frequency polygon) from a sample set of raw scores.
- Describe the relationship between reliability and validity.
- Collect all materials when each test is completed.

On the other hand, within a London local authority, 11 competencies were identified as being relevant to managers. Two of them are given in Figure 3.1. In contrast to those above, these are a combination of skills, knowledge and values which are necessary for senior managers to be effective. These can then be tailored for individual objective setting and development within each of the departments of the council.

Having made the commitment to undertake some form of competency analysis, two dilemmas need to be resolved. These are, first, whether to

---

Managing people

Senior managers must be able to establish an atmosphere of participation, accountability and teamwork, engendering commitment and support.

The must be able to develop the staff who report directly to them and should identify overlapping organization and individual needs for special attention. They should take a broad approach to staff development rather than viewing it as purely sending people on to courses. They must also facilitate development opportunities for lower-graded staff by allowing job rotation, transfers, project work, etc.

Client/customer relationships

Managers need to have a service orientation towards their clients/customers. They need to implement marketing initiatives based on a thorough analysis of the market data and to evaluate the effectiveness of the initiatives. Senior managers need to be aware of and actively seek out client needs in developing policy/strategy. They will seek out client needs by direct contact with community representatives and by contact with their staff.

Figure 3.1   *Two competencies relevant to managers*

concentrate on jobs as they are currently done or as they might or should be done; and, second, whether to focus on jobs performed at an average level or to concentrate solely on the performance of above-average performers.

It is a relatively straightforward matter to analyse the tasks and behaviour required to achieve certain outcomes within a job. It becomes more complex when the job itself is unfolding and changing over a period of time as a result of changes occurring in the organization, the market or the general environment. Some roles may be undergoing a significant change which may not be entirely understood by many of the current job holders. For example, a brewery decided to change the role of its sales managers away from encouraging sales from its publicans towards a more business advisory service to publicans. This represents a change from a reactive sales-oriented and administrative approach towards one that is more consultative and entrepreneurial.

This is an example of a values-driven approach to the identification of competencies. In such cases it may be that only some of the data can come from existing job holders. Other data may have to come from those who have a view of the future role. This could include subject matter experts who would be used to discuss and interpret the findings. If the focus of the subject matter experts is too narrow, it can be balanced by 'visionaries' or others who have a strong grasp of the need for, and likely shape of, the future role.

One of the risks of the neutral approach to data gathering is that it reflects a status quo that may not be the most appropriate for the achievement of corporate goals. Several organizations, undergoing renewal and revitalization, have used competency statements, incorporated into assessment and development centres, as a way of communicating the new forms of behaviour required. To reinforce this, the competencies are utilized as the key elements in training and development, appraisal and performance-related pay.

Each of the methods described later will provide a particular perspective on a job role and consequently will make certain contributions in terms of deriving, defining and describing competencies. For these reasons it is often useful to use a combination of structured and semi-structured techniques. Figure 3.2 shows how they can make unique contributions to the competency analysis.

	Examples of techniques	*Contribution to competency analysis*
Structured	Position Analysis Questionnaire Work Profiling System	• Structure of aptitudes, personality and other character-istics required • Broad-brush picture of role
Semi-structured	Critical Incidents Technique Repertory Grid	• Highlights particularly important areas • Differentiates good from less good performer • Development of behavioural indicators

Figure 3.2 *The contributions techniques make to competencies*

Another consideration is who takes part in the analysis. This will depend on the focus on the outcomes. If it is essentially concerned with clarifying the competencies associated with a *particular* role then the key people to be talked to will be the job holders and their supervising managers. If, however, a more fundamental organizational review of the role is being undertaken then representatives of other key groups will need to be involved. If, for example, the change in job role is to be linked with management development, then senior management together with others involved with corporate strategy will need to be included. Essentially, the broader the perspective of change and the greater the impact, the wider the range of people needed to provide data at the competency analysis stage.

Competency analysis methods

Brief descriptions are provided here of some of the main job analysis methods that can be used to formulate competencies. These are:

• observation

- diaries
- interviews
- critical incident technique
- repertory grid
- checklists and inventories

This is not intended to be a comprehensive list. Descriptions of further job analysis techniques can be found in Gael (1989) and Pearn and Kandola (1988).

Observation As a means of obtaining background information and as a systematic data-gathering tool, observation is indispensable in many studies. Informal or structured observation will yield information on general context, variety of tasks, possible stress or pressure points, general operating atmosphere, etc. Although these things can often be directly reported in interviews or by means of questionnaires, their significance may become more apparent when observed during work.

Where time is limited the people observed should be those judged to be good at their work. Where there is more time available a comparison could be made of the differences in behaviour observed between good and less good performers, which obviously requires the use of a structured rating observation form (see Figure 3.3).

	Behaviour sequence												
Establishing needs	1	2	3	4	5	6	7	8	9	10	11	12	13
Benefit statement		|							|				
Feature statement			|								|		|
Supporting					|	|	|	|					
Disagreeing				|								|	
Seeking information	|										|		

Figure 3.3 Sequence behaviour analysis of a salesperson at work

A job analysis study carried out by one of the authors on foreign exchange dealers revealed many of the critical aspects of performance through individual interviews and group discussions, but other aspects only became significant to the job holders themselves when more probing questions were raised after a period of systematic observation by the analysts. What can seem normal and routine to a highly experienced person can be picked up by a trained observer and may well, after further discussion, be identified as a more critical aspect of the job.

A variation of direct observation, with or without a structured framework for recording, is the observation interview where the analyst sits by, or accompanies, the job holders as they go about their business. This enables the analyst to experience something closer to 'a day in the life' of the job holder and it also enables the analyst to ask questions to clarify why the job holder carries out activities in a particular way. One of the obvious disadvantages of direct observation is that it could influence and distort the way in which the job is carried out, thus resulting in biased data. Another disadvantage is that it may not be possible to observe all the important or critical aspects of a job directly, such as creating a mental picture.

Observation is probably at its most powerful when a behavioural framework is used to record systematically all the categories of activity that the person engages in during a specified period. It can also be useful to test out the difference between perception and reality, for example, in terms of perceived or judged percentage of time devoted to particular kinds of activities against the actual time.

It is important that those carrying out the observations receive training. They must be clear about their role, the objectives of the project, how they should carry out the observations, what to note down and how. This guidance and instruction will lead to more systematic gathering of data.

Diaries The advantages of observation are similar to those obtained by the use of various means of self-description, personal diaries and worklogs which are completed by job holders. This approach tends to concentrate more on tasks than behaviour though it can involve both. It does not readily lend itself to a high level of quantification, although it is possible. The approach tends to be unstructured except in terms of time or task sampling. It has the advantage of being quite closely related to the job as it is performed and can be applied to a wide range of jobs where the job holder is able to write or dictate comments on what they have been doing. For some jobs it may be possible to write a brief account every half-hour and for other jobs only at the end of a working day.

The chief advantage of the diary approach is that it is flexible, easy to use, close to the job and, at the same time, can generate very useful information that can be subjected to quantitative analysis. Ideally, job holders completing diaries should be trained and should use a structured framework to ensure that their accounts are not too variable and that important features are not left out. A large number of people can be involved in the data gathering, which can yield a great deal of information very quickly, in a way that does not significantly interfere with their carrying out of the job.

An example of output from diaries is provided in Figure 3.4.

Interviews Interviews are probably the most frequently used form of gathering data. They can be conducted with job holders and others who have relevant information or viewpoints. The interview can be used with equal

8.00–10.00 am	Arrived in office 9.00 am. Examined correspondence —sorted into things to be done today and ones which could wait. Met secretary. Discussed plans for the day—any important messages from day before.
10.00 am–noon	Most of morning spent looking at monthly monitoring data. Did an initial analysis of some of the trends and produced summary report. Wrote most of the important correspondence.
Noon–2.00 pm	Meeting with my team at 12.15. Established how current recruitment campaign is developing and what the next stages are.
	Lunch—30 minutes—grabbed a sandwich.
2.00–4.00 pm	Management team meeting. Updates on what is going on and how the business is progressing. At end of meeting returned calls that accumulated during the day.
4.00–6.00 pm	Read through summary report and made alterations. Packed bags with work for the weekend.
After 6.00 pm	

Figure 3.4 *Example of output from diaries*

ease to focus on specific tasks or to identify worker characteristics. It does not require a high level of sophistication on the part of the user though it is essential for trained interviewers to be used. The job analysis interview is just as susceptible to the sources of bias and distortion that plague every other kind of interview, particularly where the focus is on obtaining evidence.

In itself the interview process is not quantified but the outcomes of interviews can be subjected to statistical analysis. The interview approach has the slight disadvantage that it is not as close to the jobs under study as the diary and observation methods but, by trialling and careful sampling of job holders and supervisors, a reasonable degree of proximity to the job can be obtained. Almost all job analysis interviews are structured in some way and these can vary from relatively simple structures with four or five broad topics to highly proceduralized and detailed interviews which form the basic ingredient of systems such as the PAQ. A very simple but none the less effective structure for job analysis interviews, particularly with managerial, supervisory or professional grades, is shown in Figure 3.5.

Interviews as a form of data gathering have a high degree of flexibility but do require trained interviewers. They have the added advantage of being potentially sensitive to unusual or subtle aspects of the job which may be critical to performance but easily missed by more standardized approaches.

1 What do you understand to be the purpose of this job? What role or roles do you carry out?
2 What are the main activities you are involved in and what is your estimate of the percentage of time involved in each one?
3 Which of these activities do you consider to be most important and why?
4 What do you consider to be the most difficult things to achieve in your job and why?
5 How can you, or others, tell if your role is being satisfactorily carried out?
6 What do you consider to be the most important knowledge, skills or other attributes that are required for successful performance of this job?
7 What are the main challenges facing you now and in the immediate future (i.e. within the next two years)?
8 What are the main challenges facing you in the longer term (i.e. 3–5 years)?

Figure 3.5 *Example of a simply structured job analysis interview*

A variation of the one-to-one interview is the group discussion or group interview. As with the interview there is a need for a clear view of the kind of data sought and the way the group discussion is structured. Results can easily vary from one group to another according to the composition of the group and it can require skilful facilitation.

None the less, it can be a very useful way of combining different viewpoints and establishing greater credibility by involving a larger sample of job holders and relevant others.

Critical incident technique

This is one of the longest established formal procedures for systematically identifying the worker characteristics or psychological factors which contribute to effective job performance. It is not a method that would be used to identify the precise activities and tasks to be performed. However, it is still widely used today, almost 50 years after it was originally developed by J.C. Flanagan. The method is highly flexible and requires only a moderate level of sophistication on the part of the user, though this can increase substantially if high levels of statistical analysis are used. One advantage of the method is that it can be qualitative in terms of the data yielded or it can very easily be turned into a highly quantified approach. It is moderately close to the job in that it relies on the ability of job holders and supervisors or others to generate 'critical incidents', i.e. accounts of observed behaviour or activity that can be shown to be critical to either effective or less effective performance. To qualify as an incident, two criteria have to be met. First, the incident has to be observable in some way and, second, there should be little reasonable doubt about its relevance to effective or less effective performance.

The orthodoxy of critical incidents interviewing has been described in detail by Flanagan, but the essence of the data-gathering stage is as follows:

1 A job holder, supervisor or some other relevant person is asked to describe an incident which did or did not meet a particular job objective.
2 They are then asked to describe what led up to the particular incident.
3 They are then asked to describe what the person did (i.e. the actual behaviour displayed) and to say why it was or was not effective in meeting that particular job objective.
4 Some reference to place and time should be given.

This process is repeated until the interviewee can no longer think of new incidents. Clearly, there is an important role to be played in preparing interviewees for this kind of interview. Figure 3.6 provides an example of part of a critical incident interview. It would be wrong to generalize from one such incident, but let us assume that a number of similar incidents, reflecting both good and poor behaviour, had been obtained. The relevance of this type of behaviour for managers would then be seen to be important. Further analysis would show whether and how this information should be interpreted into a competency framework.

Interviewer	Can you think of an occasion when you did something extremely well, which meant that you met an objective, or, conversely, an occasion when you did something badly which meant you failed to meet an objective?
Manager	There was an occasion recently. We have been working on a project internally for a while now. We had set our deadline for it a few months previously. The deadline was approaching and the bulk of the work had been carried out. However, there were still some tasks left to do. We discussed it at the meeting and the view of some people was that we couldn't meet the deadline and we should extend it. I would not consider that and instead looked at how tasks could be allocated. This was done and the project was completed on time.
Interviewer	Can you tell me what you did that was good?
Manager	Primarily, I refused to budge from the deadline unless a very strong reason could be given, but also explained the importance of the project. If we get into the habit of routinely pushing them back we would never get anything finished. I also managed to get people to agree to undertake specific tasks by a particular time. It wasn't an easy meeting but we got through it and the project was completed on time.

Figure 3.6   Example of a critical incident interview

The data generated can be analysed in a variety of ways. The simplest approach is for a team of experts to content-analyse the incidents and the behaviours they describe and try to reach conclusions about general trends and clusters. Alternatively, and of course this is a more rigorous approach, a list of activities and behaviours can be derived that can be developed into a checklist or rating form. This can then be given back to a larger sample of job holders, supervisors, etc. who rate the items on a number of criteria that could include criticality to overall performance, frequency, consequence of error. The orthodoxy, as laid down by Flanagan, involves the creation of hundreds of incidents in order to achieve a comprehensive analysis of a job.

A variation of critical incident technique is behavioural event interviewing, which was the prime method used in the analysis of general managerial competencies carried out by Boyatzis (1982) for the American Management Association. The main difference in the approach is that the incidents, or in this case the behavioural events, are analysed in much greater detail so that a smaller number of 'incidents' is obtained but in much greater detail. For example, an interviewee may be required to recall if possible the actual words used by someone in an incident that they are recounting, so that the analyst has almost enough information to be able to recreate the situation or event under examination. Behavioural event interviewing, and variations of it, is probably more suitable for generating managerial competencies than the traditional critical incident method which can achieve comprehensive coverage at the expense of depth.

These approaches are likely to be useful in generating information that is relevant to the identification of competencies. There is still, of course, a gap to be bridged between long lists of discrete behaviours and the identification of the core behaviours and competencies underlying job effectiveness and which are judged to be critical. There is thus an extrapolitive leap from the long lists of behavioural events or critical incidents to the formulation of the underlying competencies. It can be achieved by asking different analysts to categorize the incidents, and the categories produced can then be shared and discussed. By these means, a set of agreed competencies can be produced. This is obviously a subjective process, but by having a number of analysts involved it can lead to a robust set of competencies being produced. Alternatively, the ratings from checklists can be subjected to statistical analysis such as factor analysis.

Repertory grid   One of the advantages and attractions of the repertory grid approach is that it attempts to go straight to the underlying behaviours and skills which distinguish between effective and less effective job performers. It achieves this at the expense of a systematic and detailed picture of the actual tasks to be carried out or the objectives to be met. Such information must be obtained by other means.

The repertory grid approach derives originally from George Kelly's Personal Construct Theory. The ways in which we view the world are known as personal constructs and the way these constructs are elicited is through the repertory grid interview. The interview has to some extent become detached from Personal Construct Theory and is now widely used as a versatile and flexible data-gathering technique where the objective is to elicit different ways of construing and interpreting things, some of which the individual may not be conscious of and may only be able to articulate or describe as a result of the repertory grid interview process. A self-administered approach to repertory grid is outlined in Chapter 5.

The more traditional form of repertory grid interviews would be conducted with the supervisor or manager of a group of people. The manager would be asked to focus attention on the people supervised—in the language of Personal Construct Theory, these people become the elements. To elicit the constructs the procedure should be as follows:

• The manager writes the names or initials of the people supervised on separate cards, one for each person;
• The cards could be separated into two piles, those who are good at their work and those who are less good;
• The manager takes two cards from one pile and one from the other. The interviewer then asks in which ways are the two similar to each other and different from the third;
• A construct such as 'dealing with figure work' may emerge, i.e. the two are good with figures and the third is not, or vice versa. The next step is to probe this further, known as laddering. The interviewer should ask 'How can you tell if someone is good at figure work?' or 'What would the signs be that someone is good at figure work?' This enables behavioural statements to be obtained for each of the constructs.
• The cards would then be replaced and the process repeated. If the same cards are chosen the interviewer would ask, 'Can you think of another way in which these two are similar and different from the third?'
• This process is repeated until no new constructs emerge.

This process not only enables the most important constructs to emerge, but the process of laddering enables observable and measurable behaviours to be identified which can be used as indicators (positive or negative) for a particular competency. An example of the process is given in Figure 3.7.

The data can be analysed by content analysis or it can be developed into a grid (see Figure 3.8). Here the various aspects of the construct have been turned into a kind of questionnaire. A group of people are assessed on each of the constructs; each person, or element, has been given a rating on a seven-point scale. The data can be analysed manually but also by computer.

A variation of this would be to use as elements different aspects of a person's job. This would enable an analysis to be made of how a person or group of people view their work.

The chief value of the repertory grid approach is that it is flexible and relatively easy to use, and can generate data of a kind that is often difficult to find by other means. It deliberately allows the individual or groups

Interviewer	Please tell me one thing which the two people you have chosen have in common and which is different from the third person in terms of the way they carry out their work.
Manager	These two believe in team work and this one is inclined to go off on his own.
Interviewer	How can you tell that someone believes in team work?
Manager	Well, they regularly attend team meetings and willingly ensure that key information is communicated to others in the team and they are prepared to help out others who may be under pressure. They also show an interest in the projects that others are working on.
Interviewer	Thank you. OK, then, how can you tell that someone does not believe in team working?
Manager	Essentially they work on their own much of the time and always see themselves as in competition with other members of the team. They are less prepared to help out others but would expect others to help them. Finally, they would show little interest in the projects of others.

Figure 3.7 *Example of a repertory grid interview*

	Nick	Susan	Navneet	Jim	
Attends team meetings willingly	7	4	7	7	Attends team meetings unwillingly
Communicates important information	4	6	6	6	Withholds important information
Helps others under pressure	2	5	7	7	Does not help out others
Shows interest in others' progress	5	4	5	6	Little interest in others' progress

Figure 3.8 *Example of a repertory grid completed by a manager supervising four people*

under study to describe ways by which they typically understand, compare and contrast things in their sphere of work. The repertory grid interview, as a basis for data gathering and data interpretation, should never be used alone. It is a powerful and useful adjunct to other sources of job information that can be used to identify, define and establish behavioural indicators (or anchors) for underlying job competence.

Checklists and inventories

After the use of job analysis interviews, probably the second most used form of data gathering and interpretation are checklists and inventories of one kind or another. They can range from straightforward lists of activities and/or behaviour, produced by a manager or group of managers, to highly standardized and elaborate inventories involving several hundred items that have to be computer analysed.

Checklists and inventories can be highly task-focused or entirely worker-focused; they can vary considerably in the sophistication required of the user and have considerable potential for quantification and statistical analysis. Their one possible limitation, particularly in the case of the standardized inventories, is the reduced degree of proximity to the jobs under study. Because they have been designed to be usable across a very wide range of jobs, generic inventories may lack specific detail and data gathering is constrained by the predetermined structure. The considerable advantages in terms of convenience and, possibly, cost saving must be weighed against the relative loss of sensitivity associated with the more generic approaches.

To overcome some of the practical disadvantages associated with the development of company-specific inventories, a number of analysis methods have been developed with computer programmes to facilitate the user in the formulation of job-specific checklists and inventories and in the analysis of the data generated.

Descriptions of three job analysis systems using this inventory format are given below. These are:

- the PAQ (Position Analysis Questionnaire)
- the JCI (Job Components Inventory)
- the WPS (Work Profiling System)

Position Analysis Questionnaire

The Position Analysis Questionnaire is a job analysis inventory containing 194 items, or elements, which is widely used throughout the world. In the United Kingdom it can be obtained from Oxford Psychologists Press (OPP). Although it is called a questionnaire, it is more accurately an inventory that requires a trained interviewer to rate a job on each of the 194 job elements by interviewing job holders and others. The PAQ offers a predetermined structure of underlying job dimensions (see Figure 3.9) which were derived from a large-scale factor-analytic study. The information, provided by job holders and others, is interpreted by comparing their ratings and scores on these dimensions with the world of work in general, using a massive database containing results of similar analyses from thousands of studies covering almost all jobs in the economy.

The PAQ offers a very high degree of statistical data processing but is unlikely to be effective in identifying competencies that are unique or unusual but which may, none the less, be critical to successful job performance. It can be used to paint a broad brush picture which can then be used to compare the job under study with other jobs. Its greatest strength lies in the range of data-processing options that are available and the wide range of computer-generated applications of the data obtained. Overall, the PAQ may have limited value in developing a unique competency profile for a job, but it can be useful to cluster very diverse jobs into job families that are similar in terms of the human or psychological demands made on the job holders.

OPP have recognized the complexity of the PAQ and it is issued by them only to those who have undergone suitable job analysis training.

Information input
1 Interpreting what is sensed
2 Using various sources of information
3 Watching devices/materials
4 Evaluating/judging what is sensed
5 Being aware of environmental condition
6 Using various senses

Mental processing
1 Making decisions
2 Processing information

Work output
1 Using machine/tools/equipment
2 General body movements
3 Controlling machines/processes
4 Skilled/technical activities
5 Manual/related activities
6 Miscellaneous equipment/devices
7 Handling/related activities
8 General physical coordination

Job context
1 Stressful/unpleasant environment
2 Personally demanding situations
3 Hazardous job situations

Relationships with others
1 Communicating judgements
2 General personal contacts
3 Supervisory/coordination/ related activities
4 Exchanging job-related information
5 Public/related personal contacts

Other job characteristics
1 Non-typical vs. day schedule
2 Businesslike situation
3 Specified vs. optional apparel
4 Salary vs. variable basis
5 Irregular vs. regular schedule
6 Job demanding circumstances
7 Unstructured vs. structured work
8 Being alert to changing conditions

Figure 3.9 *PAQ dimensions*

Job Components Inventory

Another inventory that has application to a range of jobs up to supervisory level is the Job Components Inventory (JCI). It was developed by MRC/ESRC Social and Applied Psychology Unit at Sheffield University for the Manpower Services Commission (as it was then known). It is divided into six broad sections covering:

- tools and equipment
- physical and perceptual skills
- mathematical skills
- communication skills
- decision making and responsibility
- conditions under which the job is performed

It is an essentially worker-oriented method that requires only a moderate level of sophistication on the part of the user. It is amenable to statistical analysis and is well structured to enable it to be used with a wide range of jobs. It differs from the PAQ in not being backed up by a powerful set of data-processing programs and computer-generated outcomes. However, it is a useful alternative to the PAQ when a more straight-forward method is required. The JCI was deliberately designed to be less complicated in structure so that it could be used with relatively little training or instruction.

Work Profiling System   The WPS was developed in 1989 by Saville and Holdsworth Ltd, and is an integrated job analysis system that consists of three separate questionnaires, each one looking at different types of jobs:

- managerial/professional
- service/administrative
- manual/technical

The administration of the questionnaire is unusual in that it is a combination of self-completion by the job holder or supervisor, followed by an interview with the analyst. The interview is described as a validation interview where the analyst seeks to identify whether the questionnaire has been completed correctly, i.e. that the respondent has understood the questions and is rating the items reliably.

The WPS is primarily a worker-oriented system, although it can be used for producing job descriptions. It provides a comprehensive coverage of jobs, and the information is computer analysed. Its uses include profiles of jobs, tasks and human attributes. It also provides recommendations on the assessment methods that can be used.

As with other inventory-type systems, it provides a framework around which clearly defined competencies can be developed and would be most effective when used in conjunction with other job analysis techniques that are less structured, e.g. critical incidents techniques, repertory grid. Although people do not have to be trained in its use, it is a complex instrument and a fuller and deeper understanding of it and the uses to which it can be put would be obtained through training.

Conclusion

This brief overview of job analysis methods provides an indication of the breadth of techniques which are available. No one technique will be sufficient on its own to develop a set of competencies that describes what is required of job holders. The best approach will often be one that combines methods that are quantitative and qualitative, direct and indirect, standardized and flexible. A comprehensive study could include, for example:

- observations
- documentation analysis
- structured interviews using the PAQ
- critical incident discussions

If data are collected by these different methods it is likely that a more complete picture of the competencies required for any job can be developed.

References

Bemis, S.E., A.H. Belenky and D.A. Soder (1983) *Job Analysis: An Effective Management Tool*, Washington, DC: BNA.

Boyatzis, R. (1982) *The Competent Manager: A Model For Effective Managers*, New York: Wiley.

Fleishman, E.A. (1975) 'Towards a taxonomy of human performance', *American Psychologist* 30, 1127–49.

Gael, S. (1983) *Job Analysis: A Guide To Assessing Work Activities*, London: Jossey-Bass.

Gael, S. (1989) *The Job Analysis Handbook for Business Industry and Government*, 2 vols, Chichester: Wiley.

Levine, E.L. (1983) *Everything You Always Wanted To Know About Job Analysis*, Tampa, Florida: Mariner.

Pearn, M.A. and R.S. Kandola (1988) *Job Analysis: A Practical Guide for Managers*, London: IPM.

Saville, P. and R. Holdsworth (1988) *WPS Manual*, Esher: SHL.

4 Assessing competencies

Mike Smith and Ivan Robertson

Once competencies have been defined, the next stage is to measure the extent to which they are held by existing managers and personnel. Sometimes this is called a competency audit. It aims to establish the existing situation which can then be compared to the required situation. The differences between the two is termed the 'competency gap'. Much of the activity of human resource managers is aimed at bridging the gap. Many of the techniques used to do this are described later in this book. Briefly, they consist of motivational methods such as appraisal and goal setting, procurement approaches such as recruitment and selection, and developmental approaches such as training and career planning.

Whichever method is used, there is one crucial fact: unless the initial levels of competence are determined with reasonable accuracy, there is likely to be waste and the objective may not be met. A construction engineer who does not establish the start position of the bridge runs the risk of making it too long, too short or in the wrong direction. He might also be blissfully unaware that a parallel bridge already exists only a few yards upstream.

The construction engineer is fortunate because there are one or two accepted methods for establishing the start point. The human resource manager is in a less fortunate position. Many more methods of establishing 'the start position' are available but there is much less consensus about which of these are acceptable or appropriate to a given situation. This chapter aims to indicate the range of available methods, to indicate their accuracy and to suggest situations in which each method may be an appropriate technique.

The methods available can be categorized into four main headings:

- **analogous approaches**, where the aim is to copy key aspects of the job. The common thread in all these methods is that they try to create, in miniature, one or more aspects of the job;
- **analytical approaches**, where the aim is to set up 'abstract' tests that apply to people in general. The activities may be quite different to those performed on the job;
- **reputational approaches**, which involve relying on the judgements of others;
- **miscellaneous approaches**.

One method, interviewing, that is often used in human resource management will not be discussed under any of the categories given above. Although interviews are widely used, their potential value in the accurate assessment of competencies is limited. In view of the material available elsewhere (e.g. Eder and Ferris, 1989; Dipboye, 1990), our attention has been concentrated on other methods.

Analogous approaches

Analogous approaches to assessing competencies try to use activities that are directly and obviously related to the job concerned. They try to encapsulate, in a simplified situation and shortened time frame, the main elements. In technical terms, there is 'point-to-point correspondence' (Asher and Sciarrino, 1974) between the assessment process and the work involved. If challenged, an assessor would be able to take each aspect of the assessment procedure and identify parallel job behaviours that are important to successful performance. Wernimont and Campbell (1968) made the rather emotionally loaded distinction between using *samples* and *signs* as methods of assessing competencies. Analogous methods are synonymous with the 'samples' approach. Analogous methods are synonymous with the term 'work samples'.

Over the years a great many analogous exercises have been devised. Ideally, they should be based on a thorough job analysis or competency determination. In practice, the analogous methods may be categorized into seven main types:

- group exercises
- in-tray exercises
- role play (counselling) exercises
- presentations
- written reports
- psychomotor tests
- trainability tests

Some assessors try to establish the competencies that are involved in each of these exercises. For example, the group exercise may be intended to measure competencies such as leadership, interpersonal relationships, problem solving and motivation. In theory, there are many advantages in this approach. By using a common denominator of competencies, it is much easier to ensure that a series of exercises cover all the main competencies required by a job. Further, using competencies as a common denominator should allow judgements to be made for different jobs. For example, an in-tray exercise relevant to an accountant involved with auditing company accounts is, on the basis of the principle of 'point-to-point correspondence', almost useless in assessing someone's competence as a branch manager in a bank. However, if the in-tray can be said to measure the ability to handle paperwork, then it might be useful in assessing competencies in other jobs. Unfortunately, there is evidence (Sackett and Dreher, 1982; Robertson, Gratton and Sharpley, 1987) that, in practice, assessors find it difficult, if not impossible, to make independent assessments on competencies. Using a small number of clearly defined competencies may help to improve assessors' judgements (Gaugler and Thornton, 1989).

Group exercises   Analyses of managerial work (e.g. Mintzberg, 1973, and Stewart, 1967) show that the largest part of most managerial jobs, especially middle management jobs, involves meetings and working in group situations. Consequently, it is almost mandatory to have some element in the assessment procedure for managers which requires the candidate to perform in a group setting. Usually, they are called group exercises or leaderless group discussions (LGDs) and their importance has been recognized for more than 50 years.

A part of the War Office Selection Board (WOSB) and the selection procedure for the Office of Strategic Services (OSS) included a group exercise. Typically a potential recruit was asked to build a bridge over a torrential stream using two barrels, a plank, a rope and a tarpaulin. To assist, he had two helpers who were, in reality, confederates of the assessors: one was so bright he had a new and interesting idea every 10 seconds, the other was so dim that he was thicker than the two planks!

The problem with this type of exercise is that there is very little point-to-point correspondence. The vast majority of group exercises utilize more realistic scenarios. At the most basic level, a group of assessees, such as graduate applicants, are assembled around a square or equal-sided table and asked to discuss a neutral, general topic such as 'the monarchy in British society', 'the legalization of prostitution' or 'the world in the year 2000'. Typically, there will be six to eight assessees and three or four observers. While group exercises of this kind may be useful, they still do not meet the requirement of point-to-point correspondence. More recently, group exercises have been divided into two generic types: cooperative and competitive.

Cooperative exercises   Probably the vast majority of group exercises are cooperative. In terms of game theory, they represent non-zero sum games where everyone benefits from working together. Initially, these exercises involved childish activities.

> *For example*: a group of managers would be given a supply of Lego bricks and observed while their team attempted to build the highest possible tower. A slight variation on this theme was to see which team could build the highest tower using Sellotape and string.

Better cooperative exercises have a higher level of point-to-point correspondence with everyday managerial tasks.

> *For example*: the Civil Service selection board in the 1950s used an 'island brief' exercise in which candidates were given a dossier containing details of a colonial island that had been granted independence. The assessee had to produce a plan to implement the decision. A similar exercise concerned the 'decentralization brief' where a scenario was constructed in which a large government department was to be moved from London to a provincial centre. Each candidate was given a dossier about the department, its equipment or staff, and details of the new site. Once again, the assessee had to produce a plan to facilitate the move.

The 'island brief', the 'decentralization brief' and other kinds of cooperative exercises share three features:

- They are obviously related to the type of work undertaken by senior civil servants—there is clear point-to-point correspondence.
- The topic is neutral in the sense that most people would be able to contribute to the exercise and a particular background would not confer a marked advantage. It should be noted that there is often an antagonism between correspondence and neutrality—the greater the correspondence to specific situations the more likely it is that the scenario will favour some people more than others.
- Candidates are provided with material that makes the situation more realistic and also provides the opportunity for deeper and more complex competencies to emerge. Fourth and fifth features of all good group exercises are the existence of clear standards for evaluating the actions of assessees and the training of the observers in the use of the standards.

Competitive exercises

Competitive group exercises are, in game theory terms, zero sum situations where one person's gain must be obtained out of another person's loss. They are particularly relevant to jobs where there are limited resources and where other organizations are likely to compete for these limited resources.

> *Example*: typical competitive group exercises are the budget meeting and the selection meeting. In the budget meeting, each of, say, eight assessees is allocated a role such as head of the production or personnel function. Each role has its brief outlining a laudable project that will cost 1 000 000 ecus. Unfortunately, only 6 000 000 ecus are available in total. The assessees are told that they are a part of a budget group that needs to resolve the problem and allocate the 6 000 000 ecus, preferably in a way that ensures their allocation is higher than that of their competitors' function. In the selection scenario, an important job such as assistant to the chief executive is described. The assessees are told that the job has fallen vacant and there have been eight applicants, one of whom is expected to be helpfully disposed towards them and their department. All assessees are given the application forms of the candidates but they are expected to argue in favour of the candidate who is likely to be favourably disposed to them. In some situations the assessees are asked to nominate the person who is to be offered the job and in other situations they are asked to arrive at a short list of four candidates. Often the short list version is preferred because it is more realistic and because it can give information about competencies such as coalition building and compromising.

Other examples of leaderless group discussions are given by Dulewicz and Fletcher (1982), and LGDs are discussed at length by Bass (1974), Ungerson (1974) and Feltham (1989).

Competencies measured by group exercises

There is no empirically established list of competencies that are reliably or validly measured by group exercises but the following list may be useful in the absence of anything better:

- Social skills in dealing with others
  —spoken communication and listening skills
  —interpersonal skills
  —conflict resolution skills
  —dominance, leadership, etc.
- Planning and organizing

Guidelines for producing a group exercise

The production of a group exercise takes about four days' work but this may be reduced if suitable material is readily to hand.

Stage 1   The first stage is to analyse the type and frequency of the group work that is involved in the job. If, as in most management jobs, there is a great deal of group work, both a competitive and a cooperative exercise would be justified. The scenario chosen should be relevant to the job but it will probably be necessary to simplify a real scenario and to alter it in a way that makes it fair to all candidates.

Stage 2   Once the scenario has been determined, the dossier for each candidate should be prepared. The size of the dossier will depend on the time available. For a 30-minute exercise, the dossier should not be much more than two sheets of A4 paper otherwise too much time will be taken in reading information. For a half-day exercise, a dossier of 10 or more pages is usual. It is important to design the exercise in such a way that it can be used by groups of varying size—it is rare for exactly the expected number of participants to materialize!

Stage 3   Once the dossiers and scenario have been established, the scoring system should be developed and observers trained. A 'materials pack' for a group exercise will consist of:

- A log sheet showing
  —names of participants and observers. It should be worked out in advance which observers are 'shadowing' which participants;
  —room layout—so that no participant is seated in an advantageous position;
  —instructions for administering the exercise—including the standardized verbatim instructions to be given to participants, and the timing for the exercise or parts of the exercise, if necessary;
  —list of materials;
  —duties of assessors. One of the assessors should be specifically nominated as senior assessor;
- A scenario sheet for each participant;
- A dossier of information for each participant.

Psychometric aspects of group exercises

Two types of reliability are important to group exercises: inter-rater reliability and inter-exercise reliability. Inter-rater reliability concerns the consistency of the marks given by assessors who observe the same group. This kind of information should be routinely available though relatively few studies have been published (e.g. Jones, 1981). However, some estimates of inter-rater reliability may be inflated because marks are awarded after discussion among the assessors. Gatewood, Thornton and Hennessey (1990) obtained a mediocre reliability of 0.7 where there was no discussion between assessors. Inter-exercise reliability is probably more important because it will indicate the stability of results from group exercises in general. Here, the findings of Gatewood et al. are discouraging. The median of their 10 reliability estimates is only 0.44—in other words, about 81 per cent of the variance in group exercises is random.

There is little information concerning the validity of group exercises but the low reliability indicated by Gatewood et al. sets a low ceiling on the validity. The interactive nature of group exercises could lead to low expectations of their validity. To a large extent, an individual's performance on a group exercise depends on the other members of the group— a good candidate will have difficulty in showing his or her ability in a group where all the time is 'hogged' by seven other boring and dull candidates, whereas, in another group, a poor candidate may be stimulated into saying something intelligent by the brilliance of the seven other people in the group. Unless there is some way of ensuring that the group membership is typical of the groups in the organization, this effect will reduce validity. A theoretical, but practically unheard of, possibility would be to standardize the groups by having only one true candidate in each group and using actors for the other members. Robertson and Kandola (1982) found a reasonably good median validity coefficient of 0.34 for group exercises.

In-tray exercises   According to analyses such as Mintzberg (1973) a manager will spend about one-fifth of his or her time dealing with paperwork. In-tray exercises, or in-basket exercises as they are sometimes called, are an attempt to sample this type of work (see the example on p. 56).

This basic design for in-trays was developed by Frederiksen, Saunders and Wand (1957) but many people felt that it was too static to give true point-to-point correspondence with the way that managers actually dealt with paperwork. Several people, including Lopez (1966), tried to impart dynamism by arranging telephone calls and extra messages to be given. Unfortunately, however these innovations make the in-tray a very cumbersome technique and, in practice, these innovations are rarely used.

Example: Almost inevitably, candidates or assessees are presented with the following type of scenario:

It is now 10 a.m. on Saturday 1 April. It has been a hectic 24 hours. At 5.25 p.m. yesterday (Friday) your boss fell, or was pushed, under the proverbial bus. The chairman of the organization has telephoned to ask if you would do your boss's job until a permanent appointment is made. Your boss has a very efficient secretary who keeps all outstanding paperwork in an in-tray. On Saturday morning there is no one else around to help. You decide to spend the time doing some of the paperwork. A taxi has been ordered for 10.45 a.m. to take you to the airport to catch a plane for a three-day conference which *you cannot miss or postpone*. As there is no one around, you must write all your comments and instructions on the appropriate items in the in-tray. To help you, there is an organization chart and a diary, and the secretary has included some helpful notes.

The assessee is then given a pile of items which are a representative sample of letters, reports, messages and other material. An in-tray scheduled for 30 minutes will have about 15 short items. An in-tray scheduled for half a day will have about 25 longer and more complex items. The items may appear to be a random collection of paperwork. In fact, it should be carefully assembled to resemble the paperwork encountered in an organization but also include items of differing importance, urgency and complexity. A good in-tray will also require candidates to spot links that allow an underlying issue or problem to be identified. When time is up, candidates are often given an extra few minutes to clip the items together in the order of their importance.

The candidate's responses are then compared with a carefully worked out scoring system. Usually, this system compares the candidate's order of priority with the order recommended by experts. The responses may also be scrutinized to see whether the underlying problem has been identified, whether the communication is clear and polite, whether there are actions that would upset others and whether the responses are well coordinated and organized (e.g. there are no double bookings of diary dates).

Guidelines for producing an in-tray

The production of an in-tray takes about five days.

Stage 1   Initially, there is a survey of the paperwork encountered in the organization. During this survey examples of actual paperwork are collected.

Stage 2   On the basis of the survey, the structure of the in-tray in terms of the type of item and the competency required is determined.

Stage 3   Next, a subset of items that fulfil the structure is extracted. Often these items will need modification by shortening or removal of technical and confidential detail so that there is no unfair requirement for specialist knowledge.

Stage 4   Finally, the scoring system needs to be devised.

The complete in-tray pack will contain:

- a log sheet showing names and seating of participants, name of administrator, verbatim instructions and introduction, statement of time limits, list of materials;
- scenario sheet for each participant;
- diary sheets for each participant;
- in-tray materials;
- marking scheme.

Competencies measured by in-trays

The competencies measured by in-trays will depend to a great extent on the type of item included, but the following list should be appropriate to most in-trays:

- analysis and problem solving
- organization, planning and scheduling
- organizational awareness and 'political' skills
- sensitivity
- written communication
- delegation and control
- flexibility
- stress tolerance
- initiative
- decisiveness
- reading and understanding

Psychometric aspects of in-trays

Relatively little seems to be known about the psychometric properties of in-trays. A tiny study by Gill (1979) indicates that participants find in-trays one of the most acceptable methods of determining competencies. Tett and Jackson (1990) have provided some data on the reliability of in-trays. They found that inter-rater reliability was reasonable (averaging about 0.8) but the data for internal consistency were lower and ranged from 0.42 to 0.79). Robertson and Kandola (1982) found a median validity coefficient of 0.28 for situational exercises, many of which were in-trays.

Role play exercises (counselling)

Many jobs involve a one-to-one interaction with others and it is fairly easy to develop analogous exercises to measure these activities. It is easy to ask a potential salesman to act out a scene with a 'customer' and it is easy to ask a potential nurse to give medical attention to a 'patient'. Probably the most frequent role play of this kind is the counselling role play. A fundamental part of most managers' jobs is to mentor subordinates in order to improve their performance and it is easy to capture these activities in a simulation.

> *Example*: a candidate is given the personnel file of an imaginary subordinate whose performance is not acceptable. The candidate is asked to plan and conduct a counselling interview which is observed and scored. The role of the subordinate is usually played by a confederate and it is possible to brief the confederate in a way that both standardizes the procedure and elicits a range of competencies. The nature of the underlying problem may also be varied. In some cases the problem may arise from a personality clash, in others it can arise from a domestic problem or a misunderstanding.

Guidelines for producing a role play exercise

Counselling exercises are fairly easy to develop, needing about three days' effort.

Step 1   Several hours need to be spent researching the type of problem most frequently encountered in an organization.

Step 2   About half a day is spent with a small panel of subject matter experts in order to define an appropriate scenario.

Step 3   About a day will be required to produce a personnel file plus the brief to the confederate.

Step 4   The final step involves a further meeting with subject matter experts to refine the brief and produce a marking scheme.

Competencies measured by role play exercises

Depending on the exact scenario, counselling exercises may measure:

• problem solving and analysis
• oral communication
• emotional stability
• interpersonal skills

Presentations

Many jobs require the incumbents to give a talk or presentation to others. This is particularly true of jobs that focus on liaison or public relations activities. Presentations are the easiest type of analogous measure to prepare and they fall into two categories: free choice and imposed choice. With free choice presentations the assessees can choose any topic they wish. All the assessor has to do is decide on an appropriate time limit and prepare some kind of scoring scheme. In general, however, free choice presentations are to be avoided because at least some participants will choose subjects that are unrelated to the work situation or unsuitable for presentations.

It is generally much better if candidates are allowed to choose from a range of work-related topics of approximately equal difficulty. Sometimes it is advisable to invent a background scenario giving details of the type of audience, the context and the aim of the presentation. All this information, together with the topic choices, can usually be contained on one page that requires only an hour or so to prepare. Production of a scoring scheme might require another half day.

Competencies measured by presentations

Depending on the scenario and the topics chosen, presentations can gauge:

- oral communication
- planning and organizing
- emotional stability

Written reports

For jobs that require incumbents to write reports, manuals, or any substantial document, it may be worth measuring competencies by asking candidates to prepare a written report. These are usually best if specific, work-related topics are given as the subject for the report. It is also advisable to provide a brief containing a scenario (e.g. a report for the board, an information leaflet to salespeople or, say, a part of a staff manual) plus several pages of data and background information. Written reports consume a great deal of candidates' time and little can be achieved in less than an hour. Some reports can be scheduled to take eight or nine hours which the candidate has to organize in time periods when no other activity is scheduled.

A useful general purpose brief is to ask assessees to produce a 'handover brief'. A typical scenario is as follows:

Example: You have been appointed as head of the production unit in Glossop and must take up that post straight away. The replacement for your present post will not arrive until next Monday when you will not be available to brief him or her.

Consequently, you must write a memo, about 2000 words long, informing your replacement about the job he or she has taken over. Try to be as helpful as you can and include tips or any other information that might be helpful. Base your comments on your present job.

In some cases, candidates are asked to prepare the handover brief in advance and to bring it with them when they attend for other exercises. In this situation, the handover brief helps to gauge competency in mobilizing resources and help from others in order to achieve an important objective.

Competencies measured by written reports

In general, written reports may be used to measure:

- written communication
- analysis and problem solving
- organizing and planning

Depending on the scenario chosen, they can also be used to measure competency in empathizing with the positions of others.

Psychomotor tests

Analogous work-sample tests have been widely used to assess a range of psychomotor competencies. Probably the best known and most widely used psychomotor work-sample test is the typing test. However, the typing test is just one example and employers have developed psychomotor tests for occupations such as engineering, technical drawing, and driving heavy vehicles. Like all work-sample tests, psychomotor skills tests need to be based on point-to-point correspondence between the job and the test.

Guidelines for producing a psychomotor skills test

There are several examples in the literature showing how psychomotor skills tests may be developed. One clear exposition is provided in Campion (1972). Campion's procedure involved four main stages:

1 Use job experts to obtain tasks.
2 Identify the major competencies that discriminate between effective and ineffective performers and identify behavioural examples relevant to each competency.
3 Using the information from stages one and two, select representative tasks that provide a basis for assessing candidates' competencies.
4 Design scoring procedures.

Competencies measured by psychomotor tests

Psychomotor analogous tests can provide information on a number of competencies including:

* eye-hand coordination, which may form the basis for many more precise, job-relevant competencies
* keyboard ability
* error correction

Robertson and Kandola (1982) obtained a median validity coefficient of 0.39 for psychomotor tests.

Trainability tests

Trainability tests are, despite their name, analogous measures of the competency to learn new things. They attempt to set up point-to-point correspondence between the assessment situation and the training situation. In essence, trainability tests have four stages:

1 A task is explained to assessees, they are asked to perform the task without help, and the attempt is scored.
2 They are given a short period of instruction, say 20–30 minutes.
3 They are asked to attempt the task again and their efforts are scored.
4 The initial scores and the later scores are compared to gauge how much the assessee has gained from training.

Example: The classic trainability test is probably the 'bags test' used in the textile industry to assess the suitability of applicants for training to use a high-speed sewing machine. In essence, applicants are given two square pieces of cloth. They are asked to place them together and sew around three sides to form a bag. Their efforts are scored according to the straightness of the seams, the neatness of turning corners, the neatness with which the seam is finished off, etc. They are then given a short period of instruction in which the machine, maintaining straight seams and turning corners is explained to them and they are allowed to ask questions. Then the candidates are given more squares of cloth and asked to produce bags. The key features are scored and the two sets of scores are compared.

Trainability tests were pioneered by Downs (1968, 1989). The basic procedure has been used with a wide range of occupations including fork-truck drivers, welders, carpenters and managers (Gill, 1982; Robertson and Downs, 1989).

Guidelines for producing a trainability test

The development of trainability tests is a resource-intensive activity that is only justified when it is necessary to screen a large number of potential trainees or where the cost or consequences of training are high. The procedure, especially development of scoring methods, can take considerable time and is described in Downs (1989).

Competencies measured by trainability tests

A trainability test can be constructed to measure almost all the sub-competencies (e.g. ability to understand instructions, ability to identify errors, etc.) that are components of competency in learning new things. Essentially, their main use is to assess candidates' potential to develop job-specific competencies.

Robertson and Downs (1989) found a wide range of mean validity coefficients for trainability tests. The mean correlations were between 0.20 and 0.57.

Scoring methods for analogous approaches

The accuracy of analogous methods of assessing competencies depends to a considerable extent on the development of accurate scoring methods. Careful preparation of exercises can be ruined by sloppy scoring methods. At the other extreme, scoring can be tried and tested as thoroughly as the scoring of psychometric tests. However, in the majority of circumstances, any given exercise will be used on less than 100 people and the resources needed for extensive field trials are not available. It is usually possible to construct a reasonable scoring system by adapting the following method.

A group of subject matter experts (SMEs) is assembled. Twelve is a good size because, should the method be challenged in a court of law, the sample could be defended as being at least as rigorous as the court's own methods. The SMEs should be drawn from a wide range including technical experts, superiors and job incumbents. It is also advisable to include SMEs who have no vested interest in the procedure and who can provide a wider perspective. For these reasons, some of the SMEs are usually external to the organization.

The SMEs are usually convened for a meeting lasting a half or a whole day. In preparation for this meeting, the exercise needs to be piloted on, say, 12 'guinea pigs'. An excellent way to achieve this is to ask each SME to try the exercise on two people, one of whom could be expected to be very good and one of whom is expected to be poor—perhaps someone new to the job or in a lower grade. The object of the meeting would be to generate responses that can serve as performance standards. The precise method will depend on whether scoring is to be by exercise or by competency. If the exercise as a whole is to be scored then perhaps four examples of each scoring category (exceptional, very good, good, adequate, poor, etc.) will be needed. If competencies are to be scored, then two examples of each category for each competency will be required from each SME.

The examples should consist of between two and six sentences describing unambiguous, observable behaviours. Often, they can be cast into the form of a nine-point behaviourally anchored rating scale (BAR). In most appraisal systems, the bottom two points of a rating scale are rarely used. Consequently, a nominal nine-point scale becomes, in practice, a seven-point scale. There are considerable data which show that ratings on a seven-point scale can be made easily and reliably. The examples can be used as anchors at alternate points (1, 3, 5, 7, 9) so responses that fall in between the examples can be accommodated.

Often it is best to divide the SMEs into three groups. During the first part of the meeting each group generates its own set of examples. Later, the SMEs give independent ratings for each example. After the meeting it is easy to calculate the average rating given to each example and the spread of opinion (e.g. the interquartile range) among SMEs. Those examples which duplicate a level of difficulty and the examples with a wide spread of marks are discarded. The results are formatted and collated in a small booklet ready for use. If SMEs can subsequently be used as assessors, less effort will be needed for assessor training.

Analytical methods

Analytical methods try to isolate the key aspects of competencies in terms of generic human qualities and test these in general terms. The approach is equivalent to Wernimont and Campbell's (1968) term 'signs'. Point-to-point correspondence with the actual work undertaken in a job is not necessary. Indeed, on the surface, there may appear to be no connection between the activities involved in the measurement and the activities involved in the job. Perhaps a good example of the distinction between analogous and analytical methods would be the competency of intelligence. The analogous method of measuring intelligence would be to present someone with a work-related problem such as determining the type of clothing a retail clothes shop should stock in summer. Analytical tests present an abstract problem such as 'swimsuit is to summer as anorak is to . . . . . .'. Clearly, the analogous approach is much better PR since it is easier to explain. But, is it more accurate? In theory, the analogous approach should be more accurate because it 'captures' both the generic abilities of intelligence and the more specific aspects of a particular job.

In practice, the superiority is less clear. Because analogous methods must have point-to-point correspondence with a specific job or a specific group of jobs, they can only be used with a restricted number of people. A direct consequence is that organizations are unlikely to provide enough resources for their development and standardization. Further, the point-to-point correspondence anchors analogous methods into specific jobs to the detriment of wider and longer-term considerations. For example, an in-tray for junior managers might be quite predictive of performance at junior management level, but will it be predictive at subsequent stages of a managerial career or in several years' time when, perhaps, the nature of the junior management job has changed and there is no point-to-point correspondence with the in-tray that was administered five years ago? The point-to-point correspondence has a further disadvantage because the connection works the other way. Thus people who have had some experience of the job will have an advantage. Analogous measures will therefore tend to perpetuate the *status quo* and be unfair to people with ability who could learn the job quickly, but who have no experience of the work itself.

Perhaps the issue is best resolved by reference to the literature. Hunter and Hunter (1984) conducted a meta-analysis of several methods of assessing competencies. One of the methods was work samples (analogous method) and another was ability tests (analytical method). They analysed both methods in identical ways and obtained mean validity coefficients (which were adjusted for statistical artifacts) of 0.54 for work samples and 0.53 for ability tests. Thus it seems that there is little difference, but analytical methods may be the better choice if:

- a wider range of jobs needs to be considered at subsequent stages;
- longer-term performance (after training?) is important;
- there are limited resources for development of measures;
- public relations and user acceptability are not crucial issues.

Many writers (e.g. Smith, Gregg and Andrews, 1989) divide analytical measures into three categories: ability, temperament and motivation. A further issue concerns the use of computerized tests.

Ability tests

Ability tests have been used at least since the start of this century and have been developed to a reasonably high level of accuracy and sophistication. They are of two main kinds: mental ability and physical ability, but psychologists usually focus on mental ability tests. Such tests were the centre of considerable controversy in the 1930s and 1940s but now there seems to be a consensus that mental ability is a general trait (Spearman's 'g') and that specific abilities, while present, are less important. What this means is that if you are good at one type of problem there will be a strong likelihood that you will be good at other types of problem (see, for example, Gottfredson, 1986). Under some circumstances, especially in a 'tight' labour market, it may be desirable to use tests that measure specific abilities such as numerical ability, verbal ability, spatial ability and mechanical ability.

Competencies measured by ability tests

Many tests of ability exist. The competencies measured by the main ones are shown in Figure 4.1.

There are also tests which are said to measure diagramming, fault finding, following instructions, spatial checking, word processing, etc. A fuller list can be obtained from test publishers such as Saville and Holdsworth, ASE or the Psychological Corporation. Competencies measured by tests of manual ability are:

- visual acuity

> * *General intelligence*: the ability to identify the key aspects of a problem, see how these key features relate to each other and then anticipate what will happen next. Many good tests exist including Weschler Adult Intelligence Scale (WAIS), Raven's Progressive Matrices, the AH series of tests. In some circumstances, it is best to choose tests according to the level of personnel being assessed. For example, the Advanced Progressive Matrices might be more appropriate when selecting postgraduate students, and Saville and Holdsworth's Advanced Test Battery might be more appropriate to measuring competencies of senior managers. There is little evidence to suggest that new tests are any better than older ones *provided* standardization has been kept up to date—i.e. up-to-date comparisons can be made.
> * *Numerical ability* is often a by-product of tests of general intelligence such as WAIS but, if this competency is important, it is usually better to use a specific test such as the Numerical Reasoning Scale from the Differential Aptitude Test Battery (DATB) or one of Saville and Holdsworth's Numerical Reasoning Tests.
> * Similar comments apply to *verbal ability*. A 'golden oldie' measuring verbal ability is the Mill Hill Vocabulary Scale. An alternative choice would be a verbal concepts test.
> * *Spatial reasoning* is an important competency for professions such as architect or design engineer. There are many tests of spatial ability including the Minnesota Form Board, or the Spatial Reasoning test from the DTB.
> * *Mechanical reasoning* tests need to be chosen with care because many seem to be more related to a knowledge of GCSE physics. The Vincent Mechanical Reasoning and the Macquarrie tests are well established.

Figure 4.1   Competencies measured by ability tests

* finger dexterity
* hand-eye coordination
* ability to use hand tools (spanners, screwdrivers)

Guidelines for using ability tests

Ability tests are sold only to qualified users who hold a relevant occupational position and have had a minimum of one week's training in their use, although they can be administered, but *not* interpreted, by clerical staff with one or two days' training. It is difficult to measure ability in much less than 30 minutes and most ability tests require 30–50 minutes. Adequate precautions to ensure the confidentiality of tests must be taken. Other aspects in choosing and using ability tests are given by Bethell-Fox (1989).

Psychometric properties of ability tests

The psychometric properties of reputable ability tests are better than most other ways of assessing relevant competencies. Reliability is almost universally high: above 0.7 and usually 0.8 or 0.9. Validity is harder to assess because it depends on the use to which a test is put (a good test used for a stupid purpose has no validity). For most jobs the validity coefficients of ability tests vary between 0.2 and 0.5. Further, most tests are fair to women and minority groups. Evidence from the United States suggests that, if anything, tests of ability tend to favour minority groups slightly (Hunter, Schmidt and Hunter, 1979).

Temperament tests   Many people confuse the terms 'personality' and 'temperament'. Personality is the sum total of characteristics that make up a person. It includes abilities, motives and temperament. Temperament is a narrower concept. Many of the so-called personality tests are in fact tests of temperament. In the past, psychologists have devised quite whacky ways of measuring temperament—looking at ink blots, listening to jokes. Many temperament tests were developed for clinical uses rather than for assessing occupational competencies. Some of today's tests are appalling—often because they try to do too much in too little time. A main cause is using too few questions. It is a well established principle that, up to a certain point, the more questions you ask the more accurate the final score. This is because each individual has his or her own set of experiences and consequently any question will mean different things to different people. Given a reasonable number of questions, these differences will cancel out and give a fairly accurate picture of the person. With only a few questions, the incidental differences are less likely to cancel out and misreading a single question will have a disproportionate effect on the results. A good first sieve of a personality test is to ask how many scores it produces. Then establish the number of totally *independent* questions it asks (this is not the same as the number of marks—a question that gives four alternatives and asks you to mark the most and the least like you is only one independent question). Divide the number of questions by the number of scores. If there are fewer than nine or ten questions per score, beware! Ideally, the manual of the test should be consulted to obtain the exact levels of validity and reliability.

One of the reasons why tests with too few items per scale were produced was theoretical confusion. There was no agreed set of dimensions for competencies so designers often tried to measure everything they could think of. Fortunately, however, in the last few years five major factors of temperament have come to be accepted (Digman, 1990). They are:

- extroversion–introversion
- stability–neuroticism
- agreeableness–toughness
- openness to experience (intellect)–restriction of experience
- controlled–expedient

There are very few tests that meet the three simple criteria of being suitable for occupational use, having enough items per score and being able to represent (perhaps after statistical amalgamation of other scores) the 'big five' factors of temperament. Some well known tests which reach these standards are:

- 16PF forms A, B, AB
- OPQ Concept 5
- NEO Five Factor Inventory (Costa and McCrae, 1989)

It should be noted that these comments relate to specific versions of tests. There are several versions of all three tests above but, for example, versions C and D of the 16PF would not qualify because there are too few items per scale. Other tests give an adequate view of some of the components of temperament. For example, the Eysenck Personality Questionnaire gives an adequate view of the first two (possibly three) factors.

Competencies measured by temperament tests

Most temperament tests measure the five factors of personality outlined above. Many tests also yield scores at a more detailed level. For example, the 16PF divides extroversion into outgoingness, enthusiasm, venturesomeness and group orientation.

Guidelines for using temperament tests

The guidelines for using temperament tests are similar to those for using ability tests. The training required to become a registered user is much longer—a minimum requirement is the successful completion of a course lasting about two weeks. Interpretation of results is more subjective and the use of temperament tests is much more controversial.

Psychometric properties temperament tests

In general, the psychometric properties of the personality tests quoted here are not as good as those of ability tests, but they are better than those of many other ways of assessing competencies. For example, the reliabilities of forms A and B of the 16PF for the 'big five' factors are all 0.9 (Krug and Johns, 1986). However, for the individual 16PF scales reliabilities are lower but still acceptable (0.75+) except for the scale measuring intelligence. The validity of temperament tests is much harder to establish. A single scale chosen from a miscellaneous battery of tests will probably produce a correlation of about 0.15 (Schmidt, Gooding, Noe and Kirsch, 1984). By combining the results from several scales, slightly higher validities should be obtained. However, a crucial issue is whether temperament tests add to the predictive validity of ability tests. There is some evidence (Day and Silverman, 1989) that temperament tests do have some incremental validity of this kind.

Motivation and interest tests

Tests of motivation attempt to measure the 'psychic energy' people will put into achieving certain goals. Interest tests attempt to measure people's liking for certain types of activity and it is assumed that people are motivated to perform activities that interest them. Few tests of motivation are available but there are many interest tests.

Probably the most widely used test of motivation is the Picture Story Exercise which was derived from the Thematic Apperception Test (TAT). People are shown vague pictures and asked to tell stories about them. The stories are scored according to a complex scheme to reveal the person's motives (McClelland, 1963). Usually, three needs are scored: the need for achievement, the need for affiliation and the need for power. Research suggests that the need for achievement is related to entrepreneurial activities while the pattern of high power/low affiliation/moderate achievement motivation is related to success in large organizations.

The concept of 'locus of control' is sometimes used to select people who believe that they personally control the events that happen to them. The assumption is that these people are more likely to take responsibility and push proposals through. The original locus of control scale is not very suitable for occupational use but a version by Spector (1988) seems to hold promise.

Many interest tests are available and the 'golden oldies' are the Strong-Campbell Interest Inventory and the Kuder Personal Preference Inventory. In terms of competency determination, probably the most useful tests are Saville and Holdsworth's Advanced Occupational Inventory and the Management Interest Inventory.

The purchase of interest tests is not strictly controlled. Completion time is usually about 20 minutes, but, almost universally, interest tests are excruciatingly tedious to score. The use of interest tests in the context of selection and assessment needs care because the purpose of the tests is often very transparent and probably easy to fake.

Competencies measured by tests of motives and interest

Most definitions clearly include motives as competencies. The main motives measured are achievement, power, affiliation and internal locus of control. Under some circumstances, appropriate interests can also lead to superior performance and may also be viewed as competencies. The interests most frequently measured are shown in Figure 4.2.

Computerized testing

A relatively recent development is to use a computer to administer and score tests. The initial development was to take existing tests and transfer them to a computer. The advantages of this are dubious. Licences to use the computer programs are no cheaper than supplies of test booklets and answer sheets. The capital cost of providing a computer is substantial and prohibitive for large numbers, the medium is less portable and there is no great saving in administration time. However, there is a notable saving on the time taken to score and analyse the results. If image is important, computer-administered tests tend to project a more techno-logical and up-to-date image.

This view of computerized testing does not apply to future uses with purpose-designed tests exploiting the full potential of computers. A whole new genre of tests will be developed that involve real time action as things appear, move and develop. For example, it is possible to think of a new test of strategic thinking. The computer would give the candi-date certain resources to achieve certain goals. Initially, the candidate would be presented with a 'steady state' in which the resources need to be deployed. Gradually, the speed of action could be increased and the task made more complex by the addition of options and difficulties. All the time the computer will be recording the actions taken and assessing the effectiveness of the candidate's strategy and his or her ability to adapt.

Reputational approaches

The use of reputational approaches to assess competencies is common. Examples of reputational procedures include references, supervisors'

General interests	Advanced interests	Managerial interests
outdoor	medical	production operations
mechanical	welfare	technical services
computational	educational	research and development
scientific	control	distribution
persuasive	commercial	purchasing
artistic	managerial	sales
literary	administrative	marketing support
musical	legal	personnel and training
social service	financial	data processing
clerical	data processing	finance
practical	information	legal and secretarial
medical	media	administration
	art and design	collecting information
	physical	processing information
	biological	solving problems
	process engineering	making decisions
	mechanical engineering	modelling
	electrical engineering	spoken communication
	construction engineering	written communication
	caring	organizing things
	influencing	organizing people
	procedural	persuading
	non-verbal	developing people
	verbal	representing

Figure 4.2   *The most frequent interests measured by tests*

assessments and assessments provided by colleagues or peers. In one sense, almost all the assessment procedures described in this chapter rely on the judgements of third parties to provide information about assessees. The unique feature of reputational methods, as classified in this chapter, is that the judgement is derived from everyday contact with the candidate, rather than observation of behaviour on a set piece exercise (e.g. an in-tray or group discussion). This distinctive feature highlights one of the main advantages of reputational methods: there is no need to take assessees away from their normal job, and there is no need for the time-consuming and expensive work involved in developing tests or exercises to measure competencies. These obvious advantages are balanced by disadvantages. The first and most obvious disadvantage is that it is impossible to assess competency on tasks that are not part of the assessee's current job; related to this is the fact that many kinds of reputational assessments can only be collected for internal assessees (i.e. those already working for the organization).

Since reputational methods are based on observation of assessees during their everyday work there may be some reason to hope that the longer observation period involved will lead to greater accuracy. While this may be a reasonable hope, in practice it is balanced by the loss of stand-ardization and precision provided by properly designed analytical or analogous tests.

It is probably obvious by now that the success or failure of reputational assessments depends on the adequacy of the procedures used to elicit information from judges. The adequacy of the elicitation procedure is, in turn, broadly dependent on two things: the technical soundness of the measurement process (e.g. rating scales used, anchor points) and the readiness of judges to provide accurate information.

As far as the measurement process is concerned, occupational psychol-ogists have devoted a great deal of attention to developing measurement procedures based on scales of one kind or another. This research has produced some fairly clear results showing that well-designed scales can and do display adequate psychometric properties. One of the most use-ful procedures for rating scale design involves the development of behaviourally anchored rating scales (BARS, Smith and Kendall, 1963). Unlike traditional graphic scales (e.g. 1–poor, 2–adequate, 3–good, 4–excellent) BARS provide much clearer definitions of scale anchor points. The steps involved in constructing BARS are time-consuming but there is good evidence that, if the steps are followed, the resulting scale will be reliable and valid. An outline of the steps involved in developing BARS is:

Step 1   define competencies,
Step 2   generate several examples of high, average or low perform-ance behaviour for each competency,
Step 3   using an independent group of SMEs, match the behaviours with the competencies,
Step 4   using another, independent group of SMEs, derive scale values for the behavioural examples under each competency.

The readiness of judges to provide accurate information will depend on many things including the adequacy of their training (there is clear evi-dence to show that training improves rating accuracy), the adequacy of their briefing and their beliefs about the use to which the information they provide will be put.

Reputational judgements can be obtained from people in a position to observe the assessee. The main possibilities are the assessee (self-ratings), subordinates, colleagues (buddy ratings), and superiors. In some cir-cumstances, it may be appropriate to obtain judgements from clients or customers. The use of self-assessment is particularly interesting since both the advantages and disadvantages of reputational methods are par-ticularly clear. On the one hand, self-assessments are constructed on the huge database held by each individual on himself or herself. On the other hand, there could be large 'leniency' effects.

Competencies measured by reputational methods

In principle reputational methods can be used to provide measures on any job-related competency, but care needs to be exercised in selecting competencies that will not be better measured by alternative means.

Validity of reputational methods

As far as validity is concerned reputational methods cannot be considered together. The research evidence suggests that both supervisors' ratings and peer ratings provide quite good predictive validity (see Schmitt et al. 1984; Hunter and Hunter, 1984; Reilly and Chao, 1982). By contrast, references have not generally been found to show good levels of predictive validity. The data concerning the validity of self-assessment is more promising. Recent work on self-efficacy has adopted rigorous procedures and produced quite acceptable results (e.g. Lee and Gillen, 1989) but further evidence is needed before self-assessment can be used with any confidence to assess competencies.

Miscellaneous approaches

There are many other approaches to identifying competencies, including the ancient approaches of astrology, palmistry, phrenology and graphology. They are rarely used in the UK but graphology is widely used in France. These techniques tend to be reliable but there is very little evidence to suggest they are valid. However, three methods—biodata, accomplishment record, and future autobiography—need serious consideration.

Biodata

Biodata is a way of making predictions from biographical data. Insurance companies and credit companies have used the technique for many years. By asking for biographical data such as age, sex, years of driving experience, past claims and area of residence, motor insurers are able to calculate the probability of further claims. The use of the technique in human resource management is much more recent and there is much less consensus on which questions to ask and the way in which the replies should be weighted.

A typical biodata project will start with a large survey of 300 or more people. The sample will be confronted with a large questionnaire of, say, 60 questions. There will be 'hard questions' that could be verified by other sources, e.g. age, number and types of jobs, length of tenure, educational qualifications, place of residence, etc. There may be intermediate questions which are fairly objective such as newspapers usually read, involvement in pastimes, family background. There may also be 'soft' questions such as favourite subjects at school, liking of television programmes, etc. Soft questions are essentially subjective and are different from many of the questions in tests of temperament.

A statistical analysis then reveals the combination of answers which best predicts success in a job. A shorter questionnaire containing only the important questions is given to applicants and their replies are scored using the 'key' produced by the statistical analysis. Biodata methods of this kind are rarely used to identify specific competencies but they have been quite successful in predicting global job success. Generally, validities of about 0.4 have been obtained.

Unfortunately, biodata questionnaires have a number of difficulties. It is not inevitable but there is always the danger that some questions or combinations of questions will discriminate against minority groups.

Further, the scoring 'keys' are not very stable and will not 'transport' across jobs or organizations—they need to be established afresh in each situation. Finally, the scoring systems tend to go out of date quite quickly and need to be verified at least every two years.

Accomplishment record

The accomplishment record (Hough, 1984) is a new approach that has not been tested very thoroughly; in some ways it is similar to a flexible and open-ended biodata system. A job is first analysed into the main competencies needed. Candidates are asked, for each main competency, to state their previous accomplishments that have used that competency. Finally, their replies are scored according to a carefully worked out scheme.

Future autobiography

The future autobiography was suggested by Tuller and Barrett (1976). It is one of the few methods of assessing competencies that is future-oriented. It is based on the notion that people have ideas about how they would ideally like to be and that they tend to work towards their ideals. It would follow that, if we wish to know what someone will be like, we should find out about their ideals. In the future autobiography, candidates are asked to imagine themselves at a period, say, five years in the future and to write a biography of what they have achieved or done in the five years. These accounts can then be scored according to a set of competencies that have been derived from a competency analysis.

Assessment centres

It is highly likely that more than one method will be needed to assess all the competencies demanded by a job. Rather than disrupt individuals by asking them to complete one method today, another in a week's time and yet more later still, it is probably best to have one large event. These events are usually called assessment centres.

A typical assessment centre lasts two days and involves eight candidates, four assessors and often an occupational psychologist. In the classic design, using dimensions (competencies), a matrix is constructed with dimensions across the top (it also helps if they are arranged in order of importance) and potential exercises down the side. A combination of exercises is then chosen so that each competency is gauged by at least two different measures. A slightly more sophisticated approach is to gauge the important competencies by, say, four exercises and the less important ones by two or three. Designing an assessment centre based on the exercises model boils down to using a systematic sampling procedure to make sure that the combination of exercises provides a reasonable reflection of the tasks of the job. At a slightly more sophisticated level, the tasks would be weighted by their importance. For example, a panel of subject matter experts (SMEs) would be given a list of all the tasks involved in a job. Each task would then be rated on, say, frequency of occurrence, difficulty and criticality. Using a formula derived by Levine (1983) an index of a task's importance may be derived. The exercises for the assessment centre could then be chosen on the basis that the tasks high on the list should receive proportionately greatest attention.

Guidelines for using assessment centres

Assessment centres require a great deal of preparation and are resource-intensive. To construct a two-day assessment centre *de nouveau* will require about 20 person-days, plus three days' assessor training (with four assessors and a psychologist, the total required is 15 person-days) plus two days' assessment centre (total 10 person-days), plus one day for the evaluation of results (five person-days). The resources for one assessment centre are about 50 person-days plus expenses. However, the marginal costs are much lower—about 15 person-days , plus expenses for each additional centre.

Benefits of assessment centres

The benefits of assessment centres are:

- greater clarity in the organization about the competencies it requires and should be building. This may lead to a clearer and better organizational culture;
- better competency determination (but see below);
- involvement of senior management in an essential organizational function. Their training as assessors will have a spin-off in many other areas;
- feedback to other assessment systems in the organization. Managers receive feedback on their subordinates and this may help to establish standards which can be used when appraising other subordinates. Employees will feel that the system is fair because it is clear that everyone is faced by the same exercises and their results will be evaluated in the same way;
- training and self-evaluation by the assessees. Attendance at an assessment centre is probably the first time that the competencies demanded by the organization have been made clear to the assessees. They also learn from doing the exercises and from seeing how they are tackled by other candidates. Often assessees maintain contact with each other and the informal communication network that is set up is beneficial to the organization.

It is sometimes contended that the non-assessment benefits are of equal or greater value than the benefits derived from assessing competencies.

Psychometric properties of assessment centres

Research suggests that assessment centres provide good predictions of many aspects of job performance and are even better at predicting which assessees will obtain good ratings for their management potential. Gaugler et al. (1987) suggest that when the data are corrected for statistical artifacts, the validity of assessment centres lies between 0.33 and 0.53. However, this information needs to be treated with caution. Like most other methods, assessment centres predict some criteria better than others.

Development centres

Often, participants at an assessment centre report that they have learnt a great deal from attendance and that attending the centre was a significant influence on subsequent development of managerial competencies.

Several organizations therefore changed the focus of the centres to concentrate on what was originally a by-product. At first, the changes were fairly superficial but, for full exploitation of the developmental potential of assessment centres, the design needs considerable modification. One of the best descriptions of these differences is given by Kerr and Davenport (1989). In essence, there are six main differences:

1 Development centres are usually at least twice as long so that participants can complete an exercise, receive feedback and attempt a similar exercise a second time, perhaps experimenting with a different approach. Usually, development centres also measure a bigger range of competencies.
2 There is a climate where it is okay for participants to make mistakes.
3 The programme includes review time and participants are given feedback *during* the centre.
4 Observers act as facilitators and mentors rather than as detached assessors.
5 Exercises of moderate rather than high difficulty are used.
6 The centre ends with a substantial section containing counselling and personal development planning.

Conclusion

Competencies are the underlying qualities that provide the basis for successful job performance. This chapter has reviewed all the major methods available for assessing individual competencies. Analogous (work-sample) approaches to assessing competencies have been shown to provide consistent evidence and can provide a good indication of likely performance across a range of occupational areas and different kinds of competencies. Analytical methods for assessing competencies are less consistent, although several useful measures are available for the assessment of cognitive abilities. Personality (temperament and disposition) tests provide an approach to the assessment of competencies that is attractive to many practitioners. Evidence shows fairly modest validity for these tests and further work to explore fully the potential of these approaches is much needed. Reputational approaches show reasonably good validities, except for references which, although widely used (see Shackleton and Newell, 1991), have not been found to display acceptable levels of validity.

References

Asher, J. J. and J. A. Sciarrino (1974) 'Realistic work sample tests: a review', *Personnel Psychology*, 27, 519–33.

Bass, B. M. (1974) 'The leaderless group discussion', *Psychological Bulletin*, 51, 469–92.

Bethell-Fox, C. E. (1989) 'Psychological Testing', in Herriot, P. (ed.) *Assessment and Selection in Organisations*, Chichester: Wiley.

Campion, J. E. (1972) 'Work sampling for personnel selection', *Journal of Applied Psychology*, 56, 40–4.

Costa. P. T. and R. R. McCrae (1989) *NEO PI/FFI Manual Supplement*, Odessa, Florida: Psychological Assessment Resources.

Day, D. V. and S. B. Silverman (1989) 'Personality and job performance: evidence of incremental validity', *Personnel Psychology*, 42, 25–36.

Digman, J. M. (1990) 'Personality structure: emergence of the five factor model', *Annual Review of Psychology*, 41, 417–40.

Dipboye, R. (1990) *Selection Interviews*, Cincinnati, OH: South Western.

Downs, S. (1968) 'Selecting the older trainee: a pilot study of trainability tests', *National Institute of Industrial Psychology Bulletin*, 19–26.

Downs, S. (1989) 'Job Sample and Trainability Tests', in Herriot, P. (ed.) *Assessment and Selection in Organisations*, Chichester: Wiley.

Dulewicz, V. and C. Fletcher (1982) 'The relationship between previous experience, intelligence and background characteristics of participants and their performance in an assessment centre', *Journal of Occupational Psychology*, 55, 197–207.

Eder, R. W. and G. R. Ferris (1989) *The Employment Interview: Theory, Research and Practice*, Newbury Park, CA: Sage.

Feltham, R. T. (1989) 'Assessment Centres' in Herriot, P. (ed.) *Assessment and Selection in Organisations*, Chichester: Wiley.

Frederiksen, N., D. R. Saunders and B. Wand (1957) 'The in-basket test', *Psychological Monographs*, 71, 9, whole number.

Gatewood, R., G. C. Thornton and H J. Hennessey (1990) 'Reliability of exercise ratings in the leaderless group discussion', *Journal of Occupational Psychology*, 63, 331–42.

Gaugler, B. B. and G. C. Thornton (1989) 'Number of assessment centre dimensions as a determinant of assessor accuracy', *Journal of Applied Psychology*, 74, 611–18.

Gaugler, B. B., D. B. Rosenthal, G. C. Thornton and C. Bentson (1987) 'Meta-analysis of assessment centre validity', *Journal of Applied Psychology*, 72, 3, 493–511.

Gill, R. W. T. (1979) 'The in-tray (in-basket) exercise as a measure of management potential', *Journal of Occupational Psychology*, 52, 185–97.

Gill, R. W. T. (1982) 'A trainability concept for management potential and an empirical study of its relationship with intelligence for two managerial skills', *Journal of Occupational Psychology*, 55, 139–47.

Gottfredson, L. S. (1986) 'The g factor in employment', *Journal of Vocational Behavior*, 29, 293–450.

Hough, L. M. (1984) 'Development and evaluation of the Accomplishment Record method of selecting and promoting professionals', *Journal of Applied Psychology*, 69, 1, 135–46.

Hunter, J. E. and R. R. Hunter (1984) 'Validity and utility of alternate predictors of job performance', *Psychological Bulletin*, 96, 72–98.

Hunter, J. E., F. L. Schmidt and R. R. Hunter (1979) 'Differential validity of employment tests by race: a comprehensive review and analysis', *Psychological Bulletin*, 86, 4, 721–35.

Jones, A. (1981) 'Inter-rater reliability in the assessment of group exercises at a UK assessment centre', *Journal of Occupational Psychology*, 54, 79–86.

Kerr, S. and H. Davenport (1989) 'AC or DC?: the experience of Development Centres.' In S. Jefferies (ed.) *British Telecom Occupational Psychologists: developing the developers*, Derby House, Bletchley, MK2 2DQ: British Telecom.

Krug, S. E. and E. F. Johns (1986) 'A large scale cross validation of second order personality structure defined by the 16PF', *Psychological Reports*, 59, 683–92.

Lee, C. and D. J. Gillen (1989) 'Relationship of Type A Behaviour Pattern, self efficacy perceptions on sales performance', *Journal of Organisational Behaviour*, 10, 75–81.

Levine, E. L. (1983) *Everything You Wanted To Know About Job Analysis*, Tampa, Florida: Mariner Publishing Co.

Lopez, F. M. (1966) 'Evaluating executive decision making: the in-basket technique', *AMA Research Study 75*, New York: American Management Association.

McClelland, D. C. (1963) *The Achievement Motive*, New York: Appleton Century-Crofts.

Mintzberg, H. H. (1973) *The Nature of Managerial Work*, New York: Harper and Row.

Reilly, R. R. and G. T. Chao, (1982) 'Validity and fairness of some alternative employee selection procedures', *Personnel Psychology*, 35, 1–62.

Robertson, I. T. and S. Downs (1989) 'Work sample tests of trainability: a meta-analysis', *Journal of Applied Psychology*, 74, 402–10.

Robertson, I. T. and R. S. Kandola (1982) 'Work sample tests: validity, adverse impact and applicant reaction', *Journal of Applied Psychology*, 55, 171–83.

Robertson, I. T., L. Gratton and D. Sharpley (1987) 'The psychometric properties and design of managerial assessment centres: dimensions into exercises won't go', *Journal of Occupational Psychology*, 60, 171–83.

Sackett, P. R. and G. F. Dreher (1982) 'Constructs and assessment centre dimensions: some troubling empirical findings', *Journal of Applied Psychology*, 67, 401–10.

Schmidt, F. L., R. Z. Gooding, R. A. Noe and M. Kirsch (1984) 'Meta-analyses of validity studies published between 1964 and 1982 and the investigation of study characteristics', *Personnel Psychology*, 37, 407–22.

Shackleton, V. and S. Newell (1991) 'Management selection: a comparative survey of methods used in top British and French companies', *Journal of Occupational Psychology*, 64(1), 23–36.

Smith, J. M., M. Gregg and R. Andrews (1989) *Selection and Assessment: A New Appraisal*, London: Pitman.

Smith, P. C. and L. M. Kendall (1963) 'Retranslation of expectations: an approach to the construction of unambiguous anchors for rating scales', *Journal of Applied Psychology*, 47, 149–55.

Spector, P. E. (1988) 'Development of the work locus of control scale', *Journal of Occupational Psychology*, 61, 335–40.

Stewart, R. (1967) *Managers and their Jobs*, London: Macmillan.

Tett, R. P. and D. N. Jackson (1990) 'Organization and personality correlates of participative behaviours using an in-basket exercise', *Journal of Occupational Psychology*, 63, 175–88.

Tuller, W. L. and G. V. Barrett (1976) 'The future autobiography as a predictor of sales success', *Journal of Applied Psychology*, 61, 3, 371–3.

Ungerson, B. (1974) 'Assessment centres: a review of research findings', *Personnel Review* 3, 4–13.

Wernimont, P. F. and J. P. Campbell (1968) 'Signs, samples and criteria', *Journal of Applied Psychology*, 52, 372–6.

PART TWO

Issues and practice

5 The first step on the ladder— a practical case in identifying competencies

Peter Honey

As outlined in Chapter 3, there is a whole library of job analysis methods which can be used to identify competencies. This chapter will focus on one such method, the repertory grid (Repgrid). The aim of the chapter is to provide a worked example of the Repgrid in action. The step-based guide should enable any practitioner to explore the Repgrid and begin to utilize it as a means of identifying competencies.

Why choose the Repgrid?

- It is an excellent means of surfacing people's perceptions, attitudes or concepts in an uncontaminated way.
- It is a flexible tool that can be self-administered as well as administered by the practitioner.
- It is equally valid whether used on a small population or applied to a very large group.
- It provides a competency description in both effective and less effective terms.

There are, however, a number of problems when applying the Repgrid: it is difficult to explain, lending itself most favourably to demonstration; and it is a difficult technique to interpret. Various computer programs exist to interpret Repgrids (such as Flexigrid[1]) but:

- Most of the printout displays need a lot of explanation before anyone can find their way around them;
- Unless you are 'on time' there is a delay between the completion of the Repgrid and the arrival of the printout;
- The computer 'does it all' and potential insights are missed because it deprives people of the need to work through the data themselves.

This chapter aims to overcome these obstacles by providing an easy-to-follow format through the use of a worked case study for administering and interpreting the Repgrid data.

The case itself

Background   The client was a successful manufacturing organization interested in moving from an autocratic to a more consultative/participative way of managing. There was some previous history of in-company management training, particularly at foreman and supervisory levels, but none aimed at developing people skills. The organization, some 4000 strong, had a reputation for putting people under pressure but paying them over the odds. They had tight control procedures with daily reporting systems. Managers right up to the top were expected to know in detail exactly what was happening on their patch.

The organization wished to establish the development needs of its staff in connection with people skills. To do this it had to focus on establishing what was effective and ineffective behaviour when managing people. A competency-based approach was therefore ideally suited to meeting their needs. On establishing a competency profile it was possible to have a bench-mark against which individuals could be reviewed and their training requirements evaluated. The use of competencies also enabled the organization to establish its vision of the participative/consultative manager.

Methods of developing staff once a competency profile has been established are discussed in detail in Chapter 7. This chapter therefore focuses its attention on establishing the competencies needed for an 'effective people skills' manager. It is important to note that in this case only a subset of competencies is being tapped—those concerned with people skills—rather than a desire to identify a comprehensive competency profile of a manager.

Methodology   The Repgrid was administered in a group setting. Typically this was done by visiting the manufacturing location for a day and administering the Repgrid three times to three groups of eight or so people. The format followed for the administration is outlined in Figure 5.1.

The participants were asked to think of nine managers in the organization, three who were viewed as good at handling people, three who were viewed as poor, and three who were felt to be average. The names of the managers were jotted down on slips of paper and numbered 1 to 9. Having shuffled these, the participants then extracted three slips and had to consider the question:

When it comes to handling people, which two are most alike and different from the third?

They write down whatever it is that the pair has in common in the left-hand column of the Repgrid form and whatever it is that makes the single-ton different in the right-hand column. They then return the slips to the pile and rate all nine managers on a scale of 1 to 5, where a rating of 1 indicates a manager who is most like the left-hand description and a rating of 5 to the manager who is most like the right-hand description. Ratings of 2, 3 and 4 go to managers in between these extremes.

What you say:

The session has been arranged to pick your brains about people-handling in this organization. The idea is to find out *your* views so that competencies can be defined and development programmes devised to help managers build their skills.

The survey will eventually assemble opinions from 70 or 80 managers at all levels in different parts of this organization.

Some reassurances about this process:

First, the whole survey is being conducted anonymously. You will not be asked to put your name on anything.

Second, your ideas will be put into the melting pot along with everyone else's. After analysis, the results will be fed back, initially to top management and then to you all. Everyone who takes part will receive a summary of the main findings and news of the decisions that were taken on the strength of them.

Third, even though in this session you will be asked to centre your thoughts on real-life managers in this organization, you will not need to divulge at any time or to anybody who you based your ideas on.

Finally, this isn't an exam or test of any kind. Even though your views will be canvassed there are no right and wrong answers. Your opinions are as valuable as anybody else's.

Before introducing you to the method, are there any questions you would like to ask about the exercise in general?

Well, let's move on to the survey itself. Most people find this survey method interesting and a rather novel way of collecting views on people-handling. There isn't a questionnaire to complete but there is a simple form for each of you to fill in.

Before we come to the form itself, however, you need to select nine managers in this organization to focus your thoughts on. It is important to select:

- three managers who, in your opinion, are 'good' at handling people
- three who you think are 'bad' at handling people
- three who are 'average' at handling people.

The managers you select must be, or have recently been, in this organization. They can be at any level in the management hierarchy but you must have first-hand knowledge of the way they handle people.

Figure 5.1   Commentary for administering Repgrids

1, 2, 3	4, 5, 6	7, 8, 9
1, 4, 7	2, 5, 8	3, 6, 9
1, 5, 9	2, 6, 7	3, 4, 8
3, 5, 7	1, 6, 8	2, 4, 9

Figure 5.2   Ordering for the manager comparisons

The slips are selected on an ordered basis (see Figure 5.2). This ordering produces a total of 12 poled statements and 12 sets of ratings. An example of a completed Repgrid form is reproduced in Figure 5.3.

The final part of the process is to rate all nine managers for overall effectiveness and in terms of most autocratic and most democratic.

Since the organization was interested in moving from autocratic to more democratic management styles the survey wanted to see what tie-up, if any, there was between this and the effectiveness ratings.

Each session was concluded by asking participants to complete three supplementary sentences:

- I would be better at handling people if . . .
- My boss would be better at handling people if . . .
- In my opinion, the biggest single improvement in handling people in this organization would come about if . . .

Generally, the timing for the administration procedures is 1 hour 45 minutes (see Figure 5.4). A final question and answer session can be valuable as a means of handling concerns or confusion over the analysis of the forms.

When it comes to handling people, what do the pair have in common?	1	2	3	4	5	6	7	8	9	When it comes to handling people, what makes the other person different?
Good style and approach in handling people	1	5	4	1	5	2	1	5	5	*Not always involved with subordinates*
Good listener. Change their mind if something better comes up	1	1	2	1	5	2	1	4	4	*Too dogmatic. Always right*
Prepare statements with care and adequate research	1	3	2	1	2	3	1	5	5	*No preparation when making statements. No attempt to assemble relevant facts*
Pleasing personality. Pleasant manner when involved with subordinates	2	2	1	2	1	3	1	5	4	*Aloof. Not prepared to understand people's strengths and weaknesses*
Show confidence in teamwork and getting harmonious relationships	1	1	3	1	1	2	1	5	5	*More likely to deal with people on an individual basis. No teamwork*

Figure 5.3 *A completed Repgrid form*

Delegate responsibilities to subordinates	1	2	1	2	3	1	1	4	5	Poor delegator. Does not give subordinates enough information
Use experience at handling people to full advantage	1	3	2	1	1	2	1	5	5	Inexperienced at dealing with people effectively
Encourage cooperation between people	1	1	3	1	5	1	2	4	2	Tends to go own way and keep people divided
Consistent when disciplining subordinates	2	3	1	1	1	3	1	5	4	Inconsistent in applying discipline procedures
Organize their work load—approachable at all times	1	2	5	2	2	3	1	5	4	Always too busy. Not approachable
Positive commitment to day-to-day situations	1	3	2	1	2	1	1	5	4	Shows little interest in day-to-day matters
Good sense of humour —plenty of laughs	1	1	2	1	2	1	1	3	5	Takes everything seriously
MOST EFFECTIVE AT HANDLING PEOPLE	1	3	2	1	2	2	1	5	5	LEAST EFFECTIVE AT HANDLING PEOPLE
MOST AUTOCRATIC	2	2	1	5	1	3	3	1	3	MOST DEMOCRATIC

Figure 5.3 *cont'd*

Time	Activity
15 mins	Initial introduction, reassurances and answers to general questions about the Repgrid approach and the purpose of it.
5 mins	Selection of 9 managers and raising slips.
10 mins	Taking them through the Repgrid routine.
45 mins	Completing the Repgrid form.
10 mins	Completing the three supplementary sentence-completion items.
20 mins	Question and answer session.
1 hr 45 mins total	

Figure 5.4 *Timing of Repgrid activities*

Analysis and results   Analysing the Repgrid forms is the most crucial phase in the whole exercise. Just to put the task into perspective, the survey produced 73 completed Repgrid forms. Each form had space for 12 poled attitudes. Furthermore, each person had been given two additional items (most effective—least effective/autocratic—democratic) giving 14 sets of ratings per person, a total of 1022 sets of ratings. No shortage of data! But how to set about making sense of it?

The following seven-step procedure is recommended:

1   Number the forms   Before you do anything, give each form a code number—especially if the survey was anonymous. How sophisticated your coding system is depends on how many subgroupings are involved. You might, for example, want to sort the data by seniority or by function as well as by location. Once the forms are safely coded, you can sort them into as many different groupings as you wish.

2   Score each form by establishing differences between each set of ratings (including those for autocratic–democratic) and the ratings for effectiveness (most effective at handling people—least effective at handling people).

For example: Establish the differences between the effectiveness ratings and all the other sets of ratings recorded in the middle panel of the form. A convenient way to do this is to note the overall ratings on a spare piece of paper and use it as a mask. Simply align it with a set of ratings, establish the differences (no need for minus signs or anything like that), record the difference in the margin on the right-hand side of the form under total difference and move on to the next set (Figure 5.5).

Low-scoring differences such as 0, 1, 2, 3 or even 4 indicate views that are closely associated with judgements about effectiveness. High-scoring items, anything scoring 12 and above, indicate one of two things:

- either the high-scoring items are not closely linked with the judgements of effectiveness; or
- the left-hand and right-hand descriptions might need to be switched round. Check this by re-scoring the items but this time with the overall effectiveness ratings reversed.

So the effectiveness of ratings of

       1   3   2   1   2   2   1   5   5

become

       5   3   4   5   4   4   5   1   1

and you use the reversed ratings to re-score all the other sets of ratings.

Whenever you find that the new score (using the reversed ratings) is lower than the previous score, it indicates that the left and right-hand descriptions need to be switched.

It takes about five minutes to score each form manually in this way.

When it comes to handling people, what do the pair have in common?	1	2	3	4	5	6	7	8	9	When it comes to handling people, what makes the other person different?	Total difference
Good style and approach in handling people	1	5	4	1	5	2	1	5	5	*Not always involved with subordinates*	7
Good listener. Change their mind if something better comes up	1	1	2	1	5	2	1	4	4	*Too dogmatic. Always right*	7
Prepare statements with care and adequate research	1	3	2	1	2	3	1	5	5	*No preparation when making statements. No attempt to assemble relevant facts*	1
Pleasing personality. Pleasant manner when involved with subordinates	1	3	2	2	1	3	1	5	4	*Aloof. Not prepared to understand people's strengths and weaknesses*	4
MASK { MOST EFFECTIVE AT HANDLING PEOPLE	1	3	2	1	2	2	1	5	5	LEAST EFFECTIVE AT HANDLING PEOPLE	

Figure 5.5 *Scoring the Repgrid form*

3 Extract the 'top' data Extract the four lowest-scoring items from each form. The lowest-scoring items are the ones most closely associated with the 'most effective/least effective' judgements. This creams off the top third of the data, in our case a total of 292 items. This is referred to as the 'top' data. It is best to type these out—with double-double spacing between each item for reasons that will become obvious in Step 5.

Prepare statements with care and adequate research.	No preparation when making statements. No attempt to assemble relevant facts.
Use experience at handling people to full advantage.	Inexperienced at dealing with people effectively.
Positive commitment to day-to-day situations.	Shows little interest in day-to-day matters.
Show confidence in teamwork and getting harmonious relationships.	More likely to deal with people on an individual basis. No teamwork.

Figure 5.6 *Examples of the 'top' data*

4 Extract the 'tail' data Now do the same but the other way up to get the 'tail' data (because in effect we are 'topping and tailing' the data).

Extract the four highest-scoring items from each form. These are the items least associated with the 'most effective/least effective' judgements. The routine is precisely the same as in Step 3. Steps 3 and 4 have split the data into thirds:

- Top data: 33⅓ per cent of data compiled by extracting the four lowest-scoring items from each form;
- 33⅓ per cent of data untouched—this is the middle wadge;
- Tail data: 33⅓ per cent of data compiled by extracting the four highest-scoring items from each form.

5   Sort and categorize the data   This step is less routine and absolutely crucial to making sense of the data. The 'top' and 'tail' data need to be sorted (separately) into families or categories of competencies. Start with the 'top' data first. Cut up the typed items so that each occupies a separate strip. Each strip needs to be durable enough to survive being sorted along with 291 others on a table. If the strips are too thin and flimsy they'll drive you mad! This is why I suggest double-double spacing when the items are typed out.

Start with no preconceived ideas about categories and sort them, tentatively at first, into piles of similar-seeming items on a large table top. You will soon become more confident and allocate items of a similar sort to the appropriate pile more quickly. When a pile gets too big, go back through it to see if it can be subdivided in any obvious way.

When you are satisfied with the categorizing into competencies, simply paste the strips onto sheets of paper under competencies headings. This is a permanent record of the sorted data and if necessary can be photocopied. Then repeat the whole process for the 'tail' data.

Clearly, this sorting/categorizing process has its dangers. There is a risk of imposing an order on the raw data that wouldn't otherwise be there. This is truly dangerous because one of the strengths of the Repgrid is that it is a technique that collects uncontaminated data. If we now proceed to contaminate it by forcing items into categories for our convenience, this is a serious distortion of the data.

The category headings used should only be seen as an initial 'sorting' term. Once categories are coherent then the titles used need to reflect the culture of the organization and the flavour of the behavioural indicators (see Craig, Chapter 7 in this book).

Safeguard yourself against these temptations in two ways:

- Always be prepared to have miscellaneous items that don't fit main competency headings. The items come first and categories second. This means being prepared to have as many categories as it takes to accommodate the data. Never set any kind of limit on the number of categories and never have preconceived ideas about what the categories will be.

- Invite at least two other people to sort the data into categories quite independently. Provide them with photocopies of the 'top' and 'tail' data (warning them to keep them separate), give them a pair of scissors and leave them to it.

When they have finished, compare your competency headings with theirs. This may help you to change your mind either about the title for a category or, more fundamentally, about which items belong where.

It is, therefore, highly recommended that you involve at least one other person in an independent check on the way you have sorted the data. It may be less convenient than doing it on your own but it helps to safeguard the data against unwitting distortion.

Sorting and categorizing the data is not only the single most important stage in the analysis process, it is also the most time-consuming. You need to set aside the best part of a day and be relatively free from interruptions for this stage of the analysis.

6 Compare the 'top' and 'tail' data The penultimate step is to compare the 'top' and 'tail' data. In particular, look for similarities within the two sets of data. Similarities tend to indicate that there isn't a clear consensus on what constitutes effective people handling. If, for example, a high percentage of 'top' data indicates that democratic managers are most effective and this is echoed in the 'tail' data, it suggests that at least as many people think that democratic styles of management are important as think them unimportant when it comes to handling people. This puts the 'top' data into perspective.

Taken by itself, the 'top' data would have shown a strong link between democratic styles and effectiveness and autocratic styles and ineffectiveness. The 'tail' data may warn us that this is by no means the whole story since there is a similar number of items that are 'neutral' about the tie-up between democratic/autocratic styles and effectiveness.

You may be tempted to skip both the categorizing of 'tail' data in Step 5 and comparing it with the 'top' data in this step. It certainly saves time and quite a lot of effort if you just concentrate on analysing the 'top' data and produce the competencies from that alone. The comparison is helpful, however, in making sense of the 'top' data. A case in point was an apparent contradiction between two of the main 'top' data categories: 'empathy' and 'firmness/toughness'. A similar number of items went into these two categories at 15 per cent and 13 per cent respectively.

This suggests that there are strong attitudes associating effective people management with empathy and almost as strong associations between effectiveness and toughness. Examination of the 'tail' data gave valuable interpretive assistance for none of the 'tail' data items fell into the 'empathy' category but as many as 21 per cent came under the 'toughness' one. This means that we are probably correct in concluding that there are strong attitudes associating empathy with effectiveness. The conclusion about attitudes associating toughness and effectiveness is not so clear-cut, however. The 'tail' data warn us that more people are relatively neutral about it than those that hold strong views. Comparing the 'top' and 'tail' data doesn't take long once they have all been categorized in Step 5.

7   Product the list of competencies and behavioural indicators   This is the final step. Summarize the 'top' data, taking the findings from Step 6 into account, to produce lists of competencies together with their behavioural indicators. The categories arrived at as a result of Step 5 are the competencies. The behavioural indicators can be extracted from the items on the forms that fell under that heading. For example:

Competency : Empathy

Behavioural indicators : Listens to people. Always approachable. Asks questions about people's personal circumstances, family, etc. Says things like 'I can see it from your point of view' and 'I understand how you must feel'.

Conclusion

The Repgrid is an excellent way to 'surface' people's perceptions and thus arrive at competencies and behavioural indicators. The advantage of using the Repgrid routine is that there is no need to design a questionnaire. The disadvantage is that the data are a great deal messier to analyse and interpret!

Note

1. John Porter, Flexigrid
   Peter Smith, UMIST (for the Micro)
   Laurie Thomas, Brunel University (for the Apple)

6 Using competencies in selection and recruitment

Rob Feltham

The early chapters of this book have dealt with the issues of defining and identifying competencies, and with techniques for assessing them. The present chapter looks at how these various strands can be drawn together in selection and recruitment.

A competency-based approach can contribute to the effectiveness of selection and recruitment in three main ways. First, the *process* of competency analysis helps the organization to identify what it needs from its human resources, and to specify the part that selection and recruitment can play. Second, the *implementation* of competency-based recruitment and selection systems results in a number of direct practical benefits. And third, where systems are linked to competencies, aspects of fairness, effectiveness and validity become amenable to *evaluation*.

Each of these three areas will be examined in more detail.

Process

Before a selection or recruitment exercise is begun, it is important to be clear about what new recruits will be expected to contribute—why their roles are necessary, how their work will change over time, and, in the case of managerial selection, what they will add to the development of the organization. Competency analysis can help in this by identifying what it is that the organization needs, and how recruitment can make its optimum contribution.

The primary focus should be *business strategy*. People are the seedcorn of organizational growth. But the natural and understandable bias of line managers tends to be to concentrate on meeting today's needs. One of the disciplines of competency analysis is to encourage those responsible for recruitment to think forward about the kinds of people who will be required in, say, five or ten years' time, and to link competencies to overall market positioning. For example, the financial services sector has undergone considerable change in recent years, with factors like client skills and entrepreneurial orientation coming much more to the fore. Technical competence tends no longer to be sufficient.

Business plans need also to take account of changes in the labour market, particularly demographics. For example, in recent years there have been shortages of graduates in key skill areas like scientific engineering and other applied sciences, partly because student preferences have swung away from such subjects towards business and related studies (Pearson and Pike, 1990). Also, women and mature students have a low representation in engineering and some of the applied sciences. Since these groups will account for a rising share of entrants to higher education in the 1990s, with overall student numbers remaining relatively static, it is likely that the supply of engineering and applied science graduates will continue to fall. Organizations need to be proactive in anticipating and planning for such changes.

A criticism occasionally levelled against the business strategy type of approach to human resources is that the future is unknowable. However, it is clearly sensible for organizations to make best guesses about emerging trends, and to try to position themselves accordingly. Particularly in graduate recruitment, organizations need to feel confident in finding people who will be able to ensure long-term business survival and growth. Also, by comparing future requirements with current competencies of managers—for example, through management audit—organizations can use recruitment as a change mechanism.

The focus on business strategy requires the involvement of senior policy makers in competency analysis. But it is equally important to involve those familiar with the day-to-day work of new recruits. This usually means job holders, their managers and occasionally other groups like subordinates or customers.

At the end of a competency analysis, one is seeking shared understandings of the kinds of people the organization needs. One of the major aims of competency analysis should be to gain the commitment of all interested parties to new policies and systems. So, for example, if an organization has a regional structure, it is important for managers and selectors in all geographic areas to feel they have been involved in the process. By involvement and consultation at each stage, it should be possible to win acceptance for new systems, something that is more difficult when change is simply imposed from the centre. This issue is brought into particular focus when organizations merge. Competency analysis can be an important element in bringing the organization together, and committing it to common objectives.

Once there is a shared understanding of the broad human resource requirement, decisions still need to be made about ways of achieving it. Recruitment is not always the answer. There is usually a variety of strategies for achieving a particular competency mix, and no 'right' solutions. For example, if specialist skills are scarce, an organization may choose to design those skills out through technology, or to train existing staff, or to hire specialist consultants when needed in preference to employment of permanent staff.

An example of an organization designing out skills through technology comes from IBM in the late 1970s. At this time IBM was faced with steeply rising salary costs of the maintenance engineers needed to repair circuits at the component level. The decision was taken to cut this salary cost by changing the kinds of maintenance engineers required. Products were reformated around multi-layer circuit boards, so designing out expensive 'component level' expertise, and reducing maintenance skill requirements to the level of 'board replacement'.

Once all the options have been considered, and the decision is to recruit staff, there are further choices about the level of education and experience required. The costs and benefits of hiring experienced people need to be compared with those of recruiting at more junior levels and investing in skills development. For example, Courtaulds have recently reduced their reliance on graduate intake, in favour of recruiting 'those with sound A-levels which fall short of university entrance requirements . . . The emphasis is then placed on training and personal development, in the context of the job' (Treadwell, 1989).

Essentially, the process of competency analysis is important in clarifying the role of selection and recruitment, gaining commitment to systems that are introduced, and enabling organizations to view selection and recruitment flexibly as one means of achieving business objectives.

Implementation

Once competencies are in place, the central thing that they bring to the actual practice of selection and recruitment is a visible set of *agreed standards* which provide a basis for systematic assessment procedures and for consistency among different individuals making hiring and promotion decisions.

Without agreed competencies, selection practices can be haphazard. In graduate recruitment, for example, there tend to be differences between individual selectors whose focus is effectiveness in entry-level roles, as opposed to those seeking to identify senior management potential. At more junior levels, recruiters may focus on a small number of obvious but limited criteria that are relatively easy to assess. A good example here is a food manufacturing plant, with massive turnover of operatives, where selection decisions were made largely on aspects of personal hygiene evident during interview, such as cleanliness of fingernails. While hygiene was a relevant factor, the structure that a competency analysis can provide was clearly required. Selectors need to know what to look for and to be armed with assessment methods (e.g. structured interviews or tests) that broaden the base of information on which decisions are made.

Once organizations take steps to put competency frameworks in place, they have a basis on which to improve the professionalism of a number of aspects of recruitment and selection. These aspects include targeting applicants, attracting applicants, realistic job preview, designing application forms, initial screening procedures, choosing assessment methods, assessment itself, and the automation of assessment. It is worth looking at each of these areas in detail.

Targeting   Use of competencies can make targeting applicants a more sophisticated and flexible process, by focusing attention on characteristics necessary to do a job rather than on factors like age and educational level which are only indirectly, if at all, related to job suitability. Better targeting helps employers in two main ways. It helps to overcome projected manpower shortages related to structural changes in the composition of the labour force. And it helps in addressing equal opportunities concerns.

As regards manpower shortages, recent demographic projections suggest that the UK will experience a long-term decline in numbers of young entrants to the labour market. Combined with increasing numbers of school leavers staying on into higher education, this means that employer competition for young people is on the increase.

One solution to the problem clearly lies in looking at other recruitment sources such as women returners, people with families who want to work flexible hours, older workers, and so on. At the same time as numbers of young people are declining the total labour force is likely to grow, mainly as a result of increasing economic activity among women and older people. As a result the UK will experience long-term structural change in the composition of the workforce. A similar pattern applies across the rest of Western Europe, and the industrialized world as a whole.

Employers should be focusing on competencies needed to do jobs, in order to free themselves from traditional stereotypes and to enable them to take advantage of growing recruitment sources. However, in a recent IMS survey, Pearson and Pike (1990) found that employers were responding very slowly. They concluded that competition will probably intensify in the 1990s as the majority of employers continue striving to maintain their intakes of young people. They found that only a minority were looking to new recruitment sources, and predicted that some young people would be diverted away from higher education.

So, plainly, there is still a good deal of blinkered thinking. Though the current economic downturn is providing short-term relief from labour shortages, the underlying trends are likely to re-emerge as the UK economy picks up.

There are, however, signs that more progressive employers have recognized the issues and are starting to address them. For example, some major retail organizations are now actively recruiting older workers to compensate for shortages of younger people.

A prime example of a forward-looking initiative comes from the cosmetics retailer, Body Shop, which in 1990 ran a successful experiment in recruiting homeless people into its London stores. Picking up on an Industrial Society scheme called LEAP (linked employment and accommodation project), Body Shop was able to offer a combination of accommodation and pre-recruitment training which resulted in the acquisition of some committed and hard-working employees. Interestingly, the failures were as informative as the successes. Body Shop commented that the scheme only really worked when the same criteria were applied at interview as with all successful employees.[1] This reinforces the message that employers should experiment with different recruitment sources, but be clearly focused on job competencies.

This example also shows that flexibility is not just a question of considering applicants from non-traditional sources when they happen to apply for jobs. It is more a question of identifying promising labour pools, and deliberately attracting applicants.

Employers will inevitably be forced to adapt to demographic changes. The question is how quickly they will adapt, and how many harmful side effects will be experienced along the way, in a fruitless struggle to maintain the *status quo*. The relevance of a competency-based approach is that it has in-built flexibility. When organizations are free of norms relating particular jobs to people with particular backgrounds, the process of adaptation becomes less painful.

The equal opportunities implications of all this are self-evident. Most major organizations nowadays are keen to be seen as fair employers, and particularly to avoid the distasteful publicity that can come from court or tribunal decisions going against them. The more an organization makes a practice of seeing jobs in terms of objective sets of competencies, the less likely it is to fall into the trap of treating individual job applicants or incumbents unfairly.

Attracting applicants

Once appropriate groups have been targeted, the task is to find and attract qualified applicants, through methods such as advertising, school/university liaison, executive search, and so on.

Whatever the method, when organizations begin the search for applicants they are engaging in a two-way communication process. Organizations should aim to convey relevant information about the job, and to create conditions for applicants to communicate relevant information about themselves. A focus on competencies helps to make the process more efficient and effective.

When writing an advertisement or job description, making a presentation about a job, or conducting an interview, recruiters should identify what it is that applicants need to know. The better that applicants are informed, the more likely they are to make rational choices about whether to continue with the process. It is obviously in the recruiter's interests to encourage less suitable applicants to self-select out early on, leaving more time to undertake detailed assessment of those better qualified.

The communication process is well illustrated in the business of advertising. Conveying accurate information about job requirements means detailing job demands, competencies required to cope with those demands, and as much relevant context as possible. Virtually every organization wants to paint a positive picture of itself, and the recruitment process is increasingly recognized as one of the ways in which corporate image is created. But it is also important in advertisements to draw attention to aspects that some may find negative. If a job necessitates frequent overnight stays away from home, for example, there is little point in interviewing candidates for whom this is a deterrent.

To illustrate these points, let us take a look at extracts from two separate advertisements for sales staff (see Figure 6.1). The advertisement for Organization A gives very little useful information, beyond the fact that ambitious people with sales experience are required to work for an enthusiastic company and contribute to sales strategy. The advertisement for Organization B, however, gives information about the roles (area sales managers), the type of selling (major accounts with a service

---

Organization A

Sales professionals

We are a large, very successful and diverse international organization with ambitious growth targets. We are currently setting up a new UK specialist manufacturing company and are seeking to appoint sales professionals who have a track record of successful selling in competitive industrial markets.

If you have drive together with the determination to develop your career through further sales success in an extremely enthusiastic company environment, then this could be the opportunity you have been waiting for.

You will also have the marketing and technical backing so essential for success, together with opportunities to influence sales strategy and the freedom to implement.

Organization B

Area sales managers

The task is to develop the company's established market position, and extend our penetration in Britain and Europe. Market potential is enormous, and this year we have almost doubled turnover. The sales role will be to sell to major accounts, providing customers with high and professional standards of service.

Those appointed will be energetic, but also meticulous in attention to detail and well organized. High quality sales experience is essential, preferably gained in selling to major companies. In addition, experience in the printing or packaging field will be especially useful. The ability to speak a European language other than English will be an advantage, and essential for appointments within Export.

Figure 6.1 *Excerpts from two recruitment advertisements*

component, UK and European) and some of the competencies required (energy, organizing ability and attention to detail), including desirable experience (selling to large organizations, knowledge of printing/ packaging, language capability).

Organization A's advertisement may fail to attract responses from some well qualified job seekers, simply because the relevant points about the role are not communicated. Of those that do apply, a high proportion may be inappropriately qualified.

Realistic job preview

Communicating competency-based job requirements to applicants through advertising is one type of 'realistic job preview' (RJP). This term is used to describe a variety of methods for giving candidates prior exposure to job content, enabling them to assess their own suitability for particular roles. RJPs take many forms, ranging from presentations and videos about jobs to actual job try-outs.

Some of the most effective kinds of RJPs are known to be job simulations and work samples (see Chapter 4). Where candidates are given the opportunity to discover, through practical experience, how they might fare in specific job situations, it seems they are more likely to self-select out before joining the organization, and less likely to resign after joining (Feltham, 1989).

However, not all kinds of RJPs have this effect. In the present writer's experience, the major weaknesses of advertising and other similar methods of RJP is that applicants tend to over-interpret what is spoken or written. Most people who have engaged in practical recruitment will be familiar with the phenomenon of applicants who are attracted to one or two words within a job description which they then take out of context to fit some idealized role, with the result that many key elements are ignored or misunderstood.

Makin and Robertson (1983) draw a distinction between experiential and vicarious methods of RJP. An experiential RJP is something requiring active participation, for example, a job try-out. A vicarious RJP is largely passive, for example, a booklet or a job visit. An advantage of the experiential approach is that the candidates learn not only about jobs, but also about their ability to cope in job-like situations; this appears effective in helping them make accurate decisions about whether or not they are suited to particular roles. However, the vicarious RJP assumes that individuals already have realistic assessments of their own abilities, and need only information about the nature of the job. This assumption appears to be mistaken in many cases, and there is evidence that vicarious RJPs have little effect on self-selection.

The language of competencies can be helpful in communicating job requirements to candidates. But the research on RJPs tends to suggest that the way in which competencies are communicated is crucial. Rather than say to a candidate, for example, that the job competencies include 'identification of customer requirements', it would be better to role play a customer meeting in which the candidate was fully briefed and tasked to achieve this objective.

Application form design

Another aspect of using competencies to enhance two-way communication in recruitment is through the design of application forms (AFs). Traditionally, AFs ask for details of candidate qualifications, job experience, reasons for job change, salary and other biographical information. This is usually supplemented with one or two catch-all questions which ask candidates to say why they want the job, or to give details of relevant qualifications or experience not mentioned elsewhere on the form.

With a competency framework, things can be made more specific. For example, if part of a customer service manager's job is to deal with serious customer complaints, it may be relevant to explain this on the form, and ask for details of any past experience in resolving conflicts.

However, there is danger in taking this to extremes. AFs which ask for too much detail may be cumbersome and off-putting for candidates, particularly those who are keeping their options open and responding to a large number of advertisements. The skill in designing an AF is to strike a balance between relevance and brevity. More detailed questioning can be left to later stages in the selection procedure.

In any case, use of AFs is far from universal. For many kinds of recruitment CVs tend to dominate. Where time is of the essence, these offer the obvious practical advantage of communicating information quickly to a prospective employer, without the intervening stage of sending out and completing an organization-specific form.

Initial screening

Clearly, information from a well-designed application form, when available, can be useful when making screening decisions. Though occasionally recruiters will interview everyone who applies for a job—for example, in selection of factory operatives where labour is scarce—the use of some kind of paper sift prior to first assessment is almost universal.

Paper sifting tends to be highly subjective, and governed by unspoken rules: applicants should complete the form fully, using all the space provided but no more; they should be neat and legible, and avoid spelling mistakes; they should indicate by their responses that they have read the organization's brochure, and that they are eager to work for it. Failure to stick to these rules makes rejection more likely (Herriot, 1989).

While factors like spelling may be relevant for some jobs, the danger is that screening decisions are made on such information regardless of the relationship to job requirements. Competencies can be used to make sifting somewhat more objective and consistent. Armed with a set of agreed competency headings and associated behaviours, those doing the sift can look for specific evidence in each category. For a trainee managerial role, for example, if 'drive and energy' was a competency evidence of active involvement in a range of spare-time activities might be classified as a positive indicator.

Assessment methods

Once candidates have been shortlisted, in-depth assessment is required. A competency approach can assist in selecting appropriate methods and techniques for this assessment. Chapter 4 has discussed the more valid and reliable techniques that are available. With a competency framework it is possible to choose techniques that will enable relevant attributes to be comprehensively assessed, and to check on any redundancy in the assessment process.

The contribution of a competency approach to the choice of assessment methods can be seen by way of an illustration. Figure 6.2 shows a grid similar to one recently used by a large public sector organization in its assessment for the role of divisional manager. The organization used 11 competency dimensions, grouped into four aspects of the managerial role—managing change, communication, decision making and implementation. The grid shows how four assessment methods—a group exercise, a battery of psychometric tests, an in-tray exercise and a situational interview—were mapped onto the competency dimensions. The solid blocks show methods *not* contributing to assessment of particular competencies. So, for example, evidence of creativity and innovation was obtained from the group exercise and the personality test in the psychometric battery, but not from the particular in-tray or structured interview used. Multiple assessment procedures of this kind are known as 'assessment centres'—defined and discussed in Chapter 4.

From the grid (Figure 6.2) it can be seen that assessment methods were chosen to provide adequate coverage of all competencies, with little redundancy or duplication of assessment except in the cases of leadership and sensitivity. Leadership is, in any case, a complex dimension for which it is arguable that assessment requires a broader base of information.

Once appropriate assessment methods have been identified, as in the example in Figure 6.2, decisions can be made about the stage at which they should be used. So, for example, analytical/intellectual abilities are most readily and reliably assessed by psychometric ability measures. These are cheap and quick, and can be administered and scored by clerical-level staff (with appropriate training). For this reason such tests are often used as the first stage of assessment, reducing the candidate field to a size where it becomes practicable to apply more time-consuming methods such as group exercises and in-trays.

While competencies provide a framework for coherent assessment procedures, it is necessary to sound a note of caution. Competencies aid, but are no substitute for, the use of job-related tests and exercises. As far as possible, tests and exercises should be directly representative of the more important job tasks and roles.

Job relatedness is especially important for simulations. While psychometric tests provide relatively pure measures of particular skills or psychological traits, job simulations are known to produce behaviour which is quite specific to clearly defined situations (Robertson, Gratton and Sharpley, 1987). So as well as providing opportunities for assessment of job competencies, simulations should, where possible, directly represent real job situations. For example, an in-tray used as part of the process to select police superintendents should ideally include typical items (e.g. memos, standard reports) adapted from real superintendents'

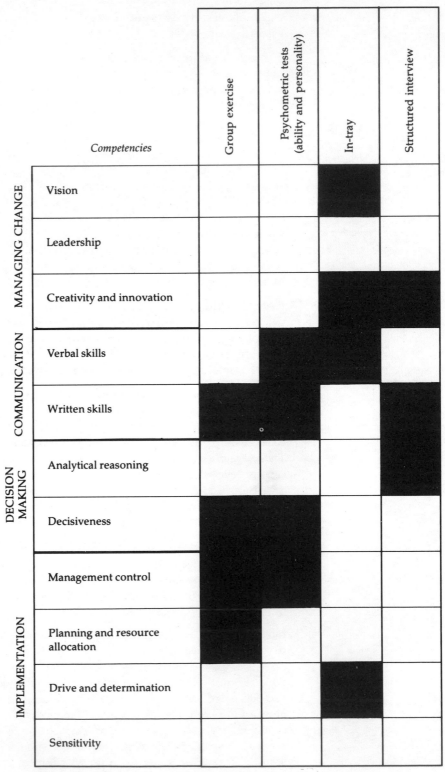

Figure 6.2 *Assessment of role of divisional manager*

in-trays. The only limitation is that exercise content should not be such as to give unfair advantage to candidates with detailed specialized knowledge.

Assessment Once assessment methods have been chosen and/or designed, the quality of selection decisions depends upon:

- pre-trial of assessment methods—particularly job simulations and structured interviews—to ensure that they operate as intended;
- clear guidelines for observing behaviour, for rating competencies and for assessing overall job suitability;
- careful selection and monitoring of assessors;
- training of assessors in observation and rating techniques.

The process of competency-based assessment is illustrated by extending the example of the divisional manager procedure given earlier. From Figure 6.2 it may be seen that one of the competencies assessed by structured interview was 'drive and determination'. Figure 6.3 shows a list of specific questions used to gather information about this competency.

COMPETENCY: *Drive and determination*

1 What motivates you about your current job?
 —what 'de-motivates you?
 —how do you know when you succeed?
2 Describe a major issue you have had to fight for.
 —how did you go about it?
 —why was it important to you?
 —what was the outcome?
3 How do you cope with unrealistic objectives?
 —what are your feelings?
 —what is your strategy?
4 What problems have you encountered where a solution was not possible?
 —how did this make you feel?
 —how did you react?

Figure 6.3 *Structured interview questions*

Once the interviewee's responses had been noted, assessors referred to guidance on specific points of evidence, as shown in Figure 6.4. Both positive and negative indicators were then taken into account in arriving at a rating of drive and determination on a scale of 1 to 5.

At the end of the full assessment centre, information from the different exercises was pooled. In the case of drive and determination, evidence from the interview was combined with evidence from the group exercise and relevant personality dimensions in the psychometric test battery (see Figure 6.2) to arrive at an overall rating for this competency. Finally, information from all competencies was reviewed and discussed by the assessment team in order to judge each candidate's suitability for the divisional manager role.

COMPETENCY: *Drive and determination*

Look for

- Sets high personal standards
- Undaunted by setbacks or criticism
- Fights for objectives
- Needs to achieve
- Looks for ways through—experiments

Contra-indicators

- Easily put off
- Little need for achievement
- Does not fight for own opinions
- Blames situation/other people
- Easily side-tracked
- Rationalizes failure
- Does not learn from problems/failures

Figure 6.4   Guidance for assessors

These observation and rating methods are fairly representative of those used in good-quality assessment centres, and the basic principles can be applied across a range of assessment methods. Performance in group exercises, for example, can be assessed in a way similar to that described for the interview, using positive and negative indicators that relate to each competency dimension.

Automation   Increasingly computers are being used to save staff time in the assessment and interpretation process. Automation issues are dealt with in detail by Mike Smith and Ivan Robertson in Chapter 4. However, one further specific point is relevant in the context of a competency-based approach to selection and recruitment. This is that computerization of psychometric tests can assist in relating them more directly to competencies, and linking them into overall decision-making frameworks.

So, for example, if creativity is a competency you wish to assess, and if you can demonstrate its relationship in a particular organization to, say, two personality dimensions and an ability measure, software can be written to produce an overall rating of creativity combining information from the different sources. This considerably assists the business of integrating psychometric test data with information from other assessment formats, and an increasing number of organizations are adopting this approach.

Implementation case study: Safeway

Many of the implementation issues that have been discussed are illustrated in the Safeway case study[2] (see Case Study One).

Evaluation   A major aim of this chapter has been to show that competency frameworks can greatly enhance the effectiveness of an organization's recruitment and selection system. However, it should be recognized that competencies also have a role to play in evaluating and justifying that system. Specifically, competencies help facilitate the evaluation of fairness, validity and cost benefit, each of which will now be briefly considered.

Fairness   As was pointed out earlier in the chapter, where recruiters' attention is focused on clearly defined job requirements, they are less likely to make the mistake of judging people on irrelevant personal characteristics. If organizations can show that their selection decisions are based on assessments of competencies, which have been thoroughly researched and form the basis of relevant assessment procedures, they have gone a long way towards meeting criteria laid out in UK equal opportunities legislation.

Commitment to equal opportunity is also good business because it means making the most of available human resources. Competencies provide the link between meeting business needs and assessing and developing people fairly.

Validity   Validity is related to fairness, to the extent that if assessment methods are not valid they are unlikely to be fair. A full description of validity would lead into a conceptual and technical discussion that is beyond the scope of the present chapter; such discussions can, in any case, be found in many other texts (e.g. Guion, 1976). But, in essence, the business of validating a selection test or assessment procedure is about checking whether it actually measures what it purports to measure. So, for example, a test designed for use in selection of clerical staff should discriminate between those candidates who will do well and those who will do less well in clerical roles; this is known as predictive validity.

In theory, competencies can be helpful when conducting validity studies, since the specific criteria used at the selection stage can also be used to assess the performance of people actually doing the job. So, to continue the clerical selection example, if a test was designed to assess a competency labelled 'speed and accuracy', scores on the test could be related to speed and accuracy as assessed for successful candidates six months into the job.

Unfortunately, this potential benefit of competencies tends not to be fully realized. In practice, it proves exceedingly difficult to obtain good differentiated measures of work performance.

Performance competencies are generally rated by line managers, who typically tend not to make fine differentiations among aspects of performance, even when quite sophisticated appraisal systems are used. Ratings of different and quite distinct aspects of work performance (for example 'energy' and 'oral communication') are usually highly correlated with one another, reflecting a predominantly uni-dimensional view of an employee's worth: 'good' versus 'bad'.

Despite problems of obtaining good job-performance criteria for validation, the results of research over a number of years are quite consistent in showing that particular kinds of assessment method—especially well-designed ability tests, simulations and work samples—are consistently effective in predicting quality of work performance. To the extent that competencies facilitate the design of good, job-related assessment procedures, they contribute to the validity of the recruitment and selection process.

Cost benefit analysis

Though competency-based recruitment procedures have many direct benefits, their introduction usually results in at least some additional expenditure over what has gone before, such as the costs of designing simulations and training assessors. While there is no avoiding this fact, it should be emphasized that spending on selection and recruitment is an investment. When considered against the potential (dis)benefits of selection decisions, a few hundred or even a few thousand pounds per recruit may not be excessive. This is particularly true for critical management positions, where headhunters typically charge around one-third of annual starting salary.

The claim that money invested in recruitment procedures is money well spent has been given empirical support by recent developments in a technique known as utility analysis. This is a method of investment appraisal by which the benefits of selection procedures, or other types of human resource intervention, such as training, can be estimated in money terms.

Evidence steadily accumulating from studies in a range of organizations suggests that any professionally designed assessment procedure should more than pay for itself through the subsequent performance of selected personnel (Boudreau, 1989). Usually, the investment in selection is returned several times over. Furthermore, the cost of the recruitment procedure appears to have a relatively small impact on the overall balance between costs and benefits. In effect, where you have a job with reasonable scope for above-average and below-average performance, and where you introduce a recruitment procedure that produces moderate improvements in typical job performance, the monetary benefits of using even expensive methods like good quality assessment centres, as opposed to unsophisticated methods like traditional interviews, are likely to be great. Typically, these benefits will be so large that the cost of the recruitment procedure *per se* is almost insignificant in relative terms.

When you realize that traditional methods of recruitment can be considerably improved even by the addition of short competency-related aptitude tests—cheap to administer and relatively simple to interpret—it is difficult to imagine any traditional recruitment situation where some intervention of this kind would not be of direct financial benefit to the employing organization.

This is, in fact, an appropriate note on which to conclude the chapter. It has been argued throughout that a competency-based approach to selection and recruitment is beneficial for organizations in virtually every respect—from responding to skills shortages and equal opportunities concerns, to identifying those individuals who can contribute most effectively to business objectives. But, in the final analysis, the concern of most organizations is that professional selection and recruitment will ultimately contribute to their bottom-line profitability. Good human resource practice must also be good business, and cost benefit analysis helps establish the link.

Notes

1 Information supplied by Trish de Spon, The Body Shop International plc.
2 Information supplied by Stephen McCafferty, Career Development, Safeway plc.

References

Boudreau, J.W. (1989) Selection Utility Analysis: a review and agenda for future research, in M. Smith and I.T. Robertson (eds) *Advances in Selection and Assessment*, New York: John Wiley.

Feltham, R.T. (1989) Assessment Centres, in P. Herriot (ed.) *Assessment and Selection in Organisations*, Chichester: John Wiley.

Guion, R.M. (1976) Recruiting, Selection and Job Placement, in M.D. Dunnette (ed.) *Handbook of Industrial and Organizational Psychology*, Chicago: Rand McNally.

Herriot, P. (1989) Social Processes in Selection, in M. Smith and I.T. Robertson (eds.) *Advances in Selection and Assessment*, New York: John Wiley.

Makin, P.J. and I.T. Robertson (1983) 'Self-assessment, realistic job previews and occupational decisions', *Personnel Review*, 12(3), 21–5.

Pearson, R. and G. Pike (1990) *The IMS Graduate Review 1990: IMS Report No 192*, Brighton: Institute of Manpower Studies.

Robertson, I.T., L. Gratton and D. Sharpley (1987) 'The psychometric properties and design of managerial assessment centres: dimensions into exercises won't go', *Journal of Occupational Psychology*, 60, 187–95.

Treadwell, D. (1989) 'How Courtaulds find graduates a material factor', *Personnel Management*, 21 (11) November, 54–5.

Safeway plc: Use of competencies in recruitment

Rob Feltham

Safeway plc is an organization firmly committed to the use of a competency framework as the foundation for recruitment, assessment and development of managers at all levels. The organization is also a key supporter of the Management Charter Initiative (MCI), launched by a group of employers in 1989 to increase general awareness of management development issues and to stimulate commitment to good practice. Competencies are at the heart of the MCI approach.

As a company, Safeway is one of the furthest advanced in implementing MCI guidelines, largely because thorough on-going use of competencies within the organization in many ways predates the MCI. A competency-based approach was first introduced in 1985 as the basis of Safeway's retail career development centre (RCDC).

The RCDC is a three-day assessment centre for existing Safeway staff, designed to assess and develop competencies required for effective performance in store manager roles. The programme is based on assessment of performance in simulated store management settings. The RCDC was originally developed by Safeway's one-time US parent company, and extensively validated in the US against measures of overall store performance and profitability. It was later developed in the UK, and adapted, on the basis of job analysis, to reflect the somewhat different retail environment.

Building from the beginnings in the RCDC, considerable work has been done recently to develop key competencies and to establish them organization-wide. Use of competencies has now been extended to include most aspects of management recruitment and development, including graduate selection and management career planning. Safeway's recent collaboration with the MCI has both contributed to the development of the guidelines, and helped Safeway upgrade and update its approach.

Competency classification

Safeway competencies are classified at three different levels of generality:

Major competencies   These are the broad areas of operation within which Safeway managers need to be proficient:

- Managing within Safeway environment
- Managing resources
  —people
  —finance
  —information
  —assets
- Personal effectiveness
- Professional competencies (job-specific)

Each major competency is then subdivided into 12 core competencies.

Core competencies   These are the particular areas of personal competence which are a prerequisite of effectiveness in the major competency areas:

- Problem analysis
- Decisiveness
- Problem solving
- Planning and organization
- Delegation
- Management control
- Leadership
- Oral communication and presentation skills
- Written communication
- Human relations skills
- Self-confidence
- Stress tolerance

Competencies   These represent functionally important combinations of core competencies together with elements of specific knowledge and skill. Two examples for the position of store manager are shown here:

- *Competence*: Monitor and maintain all cash-handling procedures to ensure accuracy. *Contributing core competencies*: Problem analysis, Problem solving, Management control.
- *Competence*: Ensure information required by head office is accurately transmitted on time. *Contributing core competencies*: Planning and organization, Management control.

These competencies are further specified for individual jobs in terms of very specific performance criteria. For example, for the competence 'monitoring and maintaining all cash-handling procedures . . .', one performance criterion is 'complete weekly cash results tables for district manager'.

An illustration of the relationship between the various levels of competency is shown in Figure C.1.

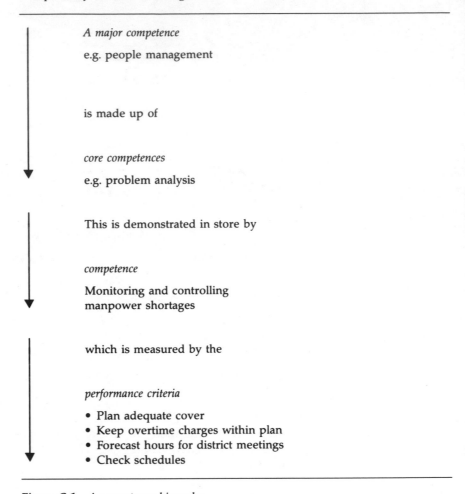

A major competence

e.g. people management

is made up of

core competences

e.g. problem analysis

This is demonstrated in store by

competence

Monitoring and controlling manpower shortages

which is measured by the

performance criteria

- Plan adequate cover
- Keep overtime charges within plan
- Forecast hours for district meetings
- Check schedules

Figure C.1   *A competency hierarchy*

That describes Safeway's broad approach to competencies. Now let us look at how it is applied to one particular category of recruitment and development.

Graduate recruitment and development

Safeway currently recruits around 100 graduates each year, to fill approximately 60 trainee posts in retail, and 40 in central headquarters functions. The typical career path of a graduate joining Safeway in retail is shown in Figure C.2. A graduate management trainee initially works in several different stores in a variety of different functions. As the person's career progresses, a planned series of managerial assignments is interspersed with off-the-job training specifically designed to develop required Safeway competencies. After five years' satisfactory performance, the graduate is assessed at the RCDC. This serves the dual purpose of assessing suitability for store manager level, and identifying any remaining development needs. After all development needs have been met, and the trainee has demonstrated the required generic management competencies, Safeway expects to be able to award the MCI Diploma in Management. The company is at present on the pilot programme.

Suggested progression

			Off-the-job management development courses
12 months	Management Trainee		
			Personal effectiveness
6 months	Dry Grocery Manager 1st Assignment		
		Certificate Level	
6 months	Dry Grocery Manager 2nd Assignment		
			Performance through people
6 months	Fresh Foods Manager 1st Assignment		
6 months	Fresh Foods Manager 2nd Assignment		
			Business awareness for retail managers
12 months	Deputy Manager 1st Assignment		
			Development of specific highlighted competencies
12 months	Deputy Manager 2nd Assignment		
Total – approx 5 years	RCDC (3-day Assessment Centre)	Diploma level	

The candidate will work in several different stores and will experience varying volumes of store trade and working environments. Following RCDC, there will be a period when the deputy manager will spend time working on particular development needs as highlighted by the assessment centre. This could take place while in a provisional store manager role. However, the candidate will not be considered to have qualified for Diploma status until all development needs have been met and competence has been demonstrated in all the generic management competencies.

Figure C.2   Scope of the certificate and diploma level awards

Safeway's competency framework is applied right throughout the graduate recruitment process. However, there is a recognition that not all the organization's competencies can be assessed at the pre-employment stage. So competencies like 'problem analysis' and 'human relations skills' are included, while others like 'management control' and 'delegation' are not. In all, eight of the twelve core Safeway competencies are assessed.

In line with most other major graduate employers, Safeway begins the recruitment process with annual advertising, milk round visits to universities, presentations, and professionally produced brochures. Promotional material illustrates early careers in some detail, and highlights some of the competencies required.

Since the retail industry is perceived by many graduates as less glamorous than areas such as oil and finance, a major aim at this initial stage is to sell the concept and benefits to potential applicants. For example, a career in store management can bring early responsibility for large numbers of people, and in large revenue-generating operations.

Once applications have been received, they are sifted prior to first interview. These interviews are conducted either at the place of study or at a local store by regional personnel officers who have attended a two-day introductory course on the use of assessment centres, followed by a one-day training session on the use of structured situational interviews. The interview centres on specific competencies. Candidates are given three situational questions and their responses are rated.

Those who are successful at this stage move on to the second stage which consists of an assessment centre (AC). Before the AC, applicants are required to visit a Safeway store. During these visits, applicants are set specific objectives to find out about particular aspects of store operation. This stimulates an active process of discovery about the organization, and serves as a realistic job preview. Also, candidates' understanding of what they have observed can be explored at the second assessment stage.

Assessment centre   The AC lasts one day. Typically, a group of about twelve candidates is assessed by a team of four managers.

For each candidate, the AC comprises a biographical interview, an in-tray exercise, two group exercises (involving six candidates at a time) and two psychometric tests. One of the group exercises is of the 'assigned role' type in which candidates have a specific brief to argue a particular case. The psychometric tests used are GMA Abstract—to assess non-verbal reasoning and flexible thinking—and Computer Rules—to assess aptitude for working with computer software.[1]

Each assessor observes every candidate in at least one exercise or interview. After each exercise, assessors take time individually to rate their candidates on the eight core competencies. Pooling and discussion of information is left to the end of the AC.

The design of the AC is based on the need to assess potential for a range of different management functions. For this reason, the AC exercises cannot be specific to any one part of the Safeway operation. (However, there are now moves to develop separate ACs for different career paths, which will probably result in exercises becoming more job-specific.)

An example of the AC exercises or simulations currently used is the in-tray, which makes demands typical of many junior managerial roles. The scenario is that the candidate is asked to organize a conference at very short notice, from a file of papers giving instructions and relevant information in the form of correspondence with speakers, hotel prices, and so on. The candidate is allowed 45 minutes to absorb a reasonable amount of detail, to suggest actions and list them in order of priority, and to make decisions about costs, venues, food, and so on. The exercise essentially tests organizing ability, with quite a high component of basic numerical calculation.

For this exercise, as for others, assessors are required to rate their candidates' performance on all eight core competencies, using a standard five-point scale. However, assessors are given the option not to rate a particular competency where no relevant information has been produced. For example, the in-tray will provide a lot of information for competencies such as 'problem analysis' and 'planning and organizing' but little, if any, for competencies such as 'human relations skills' and 'self-confidence'.

In rating performance, assessors are given, for each scale, definitions of the scale points coupled with pointers to 'positive' and 'negative' behaviours. For example, for problem analysis, positive behaviours include those in which the candidate 'recognizes important data and identifies causes of problems'; negative behaviours include those in which the candidate 'does not distinguish between important and trivial factors'. Under each competency heading, assessors note specific behaviours contributing to their ratings.

At the end of the AC, there is a round-up consensus discussion involving the four assessors and the coordinator, who is from Safeway's career development department. Each candidate is considered in turn. Competency ratings and associated observations of behaviours are pooled, and overall competency ratings are agreed, together with an overall rating of the candidate's potential for progression within Safeway.

Finally, each assessor individually ranks all twelve candidates from top to bottom. These ranks are discussed, and a final ranking agreed. This ranking forms the basis of job offers.

One critical element in all this is assessor training. In fact, Safeway operates a thorough training and development process for assessors. All are senior store managers or district managers who have been through a systematic three-day training programme, and who have had previous assessment experience in ACs run for existing staff (the RCDC). The view is taken that graduate assessment is an extremely difficult task, since so little is known beforehand about the candidates. Therefore, it is essential that assessors have had experience with existing managers before moving on to graduate assessment.

Rigorous training and development of assessors is a key element contributing to the overall professionalism of the AC process.

Note

1 Assessment procedures published by ASE, the business test division of NFER-Nelson Publishing Company Limited.

7 Using competencies in career development

Stephanie Craig

The focus of this chapter is on development for the future. This is distinct from development in the current level or position which should be encompassed by performance improvement. Many of the techniques referred to in the previous chapter will enable development in-post to occur. Career development, as addressed here, has a future focus. Realistically, this future focus tends to have an ever-expanding but limited horizon of about three to five years.

Why concern ourselves with career development when we all know that, in practice, career planning by organizations and by individuals tends to be dictated strongly by internal and external events? Total spontaneity does not work for either organizations or individuals. Planning for the future gives some predictability and, interestingly, increases both the organization's and individual's ability to be flexible in response to the ever-changing pattern of events. Organizations have a need for career development to ensure adequately skilled and trained individuals are promoted into key positions. A reservoir of developing talent gives confidence and flexibility to enable organizations to respond quickly.

Individuals need career development to obtain and increase levels of job satisfaction and reward. The needs of organizations and individuals are inextricably bound together and, when met, they combine to provide vitality and survival for both. There are two other reasons why career development should not be neglected. Organizations have a need to deliver on an often-stated commitment to development and individuals have a need for self-improvement. While these needs obviously vary markedly between organizations and individuals, both can have a powerful influence on events.

The competency-based approach truly comes into its own when dealing with career development. Many career planning decisions are made on the basis of *current competence*. The danger of this approach is that a level of incompetence is surely and inevitably reached, often with unfortunate consequences. While a career is progressing in a series of steps within a level it is possible to pinpoint and act on development needs using task performance and results as a measure. Once a career faces a 'bridge', such as movement from a technical or professional role into operational management, or a still later bridge of movement from operational to strategic management, the performance evidence gained from the current level ceases to be wholly relevant. It is difficult, if not impossible in some cases, to extrapolate from current performance to expected future performance in a new level or position type. Examples abound: salesperson to sales manager, scientist to project leader, senior lecturer to head of department, general manager to regional director and thence to chief executive. Practicality and the impact of failure on both the individual and the organization conspire to prevent career development taking place as a series of trial roles that would give actual performance information to guide career-planning decision making. However, the competency-based approach, using the sets of behaviour patterns needed to perform tasks and functions, can provide guidance on the likely performance at the next level. Competencies as needed at the next level or over the bridge can be measured with some accuracy, allowing career development decisions to be meaningful, planned and effective.

Competencies have a cyclical importance in career development. Their importance is vital prior to promotion but will gradually diminish as the individual progresses with planned development through the grade. Their importance increases again as the individual approaches the middle of the grade when both organization and individual should be preparing for movement towards the next grade. The flow is as follows:

• Competencies set standards for progression;
• Competencies provide the referent for assessment;
• Competencies, expressed in terms of strengths and development needs, set the referent for development;
• Competencies set standards for progression to the next grade.

While the methods of identifying and assessing competencies have been explored in depth in Chapters 3 and 4, the career development setting places certain demands and emphases on the nature and use of competencies. These particular aspects will be discussed under the following headings:

• Identifying and establishing competencies so that they are usable and acceptable for career development in an organization;
• Using competencies to achieve organizational and individual needs;
• Techniques for assessing competencies which are most frequently used within the development context;
• Managing the output of using competencies in development;
• Implementation issues that need to be resolved throughout the process.

Identifying and establishing competencies

Defining the scope

It is important to define the scope of any competency analysis before it begins. Competency analysis requires a focus or target. This can be a single key position or level or it can be a series of positions or levels. Either way, the scope needs definition and the design of the analysis needs to be planned accordingly.

The single position or level competency analysis is obviously the easiest to manage. The activities and roles of job holders can be described, as can the associated competencies. The resultant competency profile is clear, distinct and meaningful. The more difficult option is to conduct an analysis across functions and levels. The scope may encompass a whole department or a whole organization and within these there may be a large geographical spread.

Design of the larger-scope analysis must allow for comparisons to be made on competencies between levels, functions, geography and other variables which may be important in gaining credibility for the output. The major danger in the larger-scope analyses is that the resultant competencies are so generalized as to be meaningless for a specific level or function. The disagreement within the literature, on the usefulness or otherwise of generic managerial competencies, is an aspect of this problem.

An effective compromise position which many researchers adopt is to collect information on activities and competencies for bench-mark positions. This is often done in two stages: first, a qualitative information collection phase using job analysis interviewing techniques and, second, a quantitative phase using a role analysis questionnaire.

An analysis of the qualitative information will identify whether the competencies change in degree or kind by position, function or other relevant variables. A decision can then be made on how many role analysis questionnaires will be needed. If the competencies appear to apply in varying degrees across all the variables, then one role analysis questionnaire can be used. If, however, there is a change in the nature of the competencies, several role analysis questionnaires may be needed.

The questionnaire often takes the form of a matrix where the competency list is the same for all positions but the activity list will vary by position. This latter aspect enables comparisons to be drawn between positions, levels, functions and geography. If the scope is large, the sample size for a role analysis questionnaire likewise needs to be large to ensure that the results are giving a representative picture on each of the relevant variables. The output of this two-phase, large-scope analysis can provide meaningful and useful information for longer-term career planning and development. The bridges defined by differences in kind on the competencies become visible and provide a focus for planning individual development.

Once the scope of the competency analysis has been defined, other more detailed issues need to be addressed.

Defining target position

It is important to bear in mind the horizon most individuals have of their own development. We typically operate on a three to five year horizon which is constantly adjusted outwards. The target position, or that bench-mark role which has been chosen for analysis, needs therefore to be meaningful and achievable for those who are to be developed. Choice of a target position for detailed competency analysis needs to address two other points as well.

First, the position needs to be worthy of the effort that will be put in to achieve it. This means that the position should be visible, valued by the individual and others, and there must be openings available within the time frame. If effort is to be put into development the individual must be assured that there will be a reward at the end.

Second, the target position needs to have, between itself and the current position, some intermediate development positions. There should also be an alternative career path position for those individuals for whom the target position is inappropriate or unwanted. The intermediate development positions enable individuals to follow a staged progression where their efforts are successively rewarded and they are given the opportunity to practise newly acquired skills. The alternative career path is vital to prevent what is known as 'the walking wounded'. These are individuals who, through capability or interest, find they are not suited to the target position, and consequently feel as though they have failed. This is not healthy for the individual or the organization and usually means a waste of talent that could be redirected elsewhere.

Future orientation

Organizations are dynamic; positions defined in today's competency terms may have evolved considerably within the three to five year time frame. The dynamism is relative according to the nature of business and the target position. Even in the most dynamic of organizations, it is important to note that change may appear dramatic when viewed from a start to an end point, but has actually been a steady evolution. The competency analysis needs to tap into this evolution by incorporating the views of visionaries, those who are planning the future horizon and those who have succeeded through the dynamism of the past.

It is vital to include in the competency analysis those individuals who are shaping the target position for the future. These individuals will certainly include currently successful job holders and their bosses who are regarded as having achieved success through forward-looking strategies and actions. In addition, it may be necessary to interview more senior managers and perhaps corporate planners if the target position is likely to evolve rapidly in its tasks and functions. This is obviously necessary where structural or organizational changes are intended but not yet made public. It is also important where the target position itself is wide open to external influences such as the impact of economic downturn or upturn. The views of the future shapers and/or the forward looking can be built into both the interview or qualitative phase and into the questionnaire or quantitative phase. Having collected the future orientation information, it is vital to discuss the analysis results with the key people.

The emergent competency pattern needs to be 'felt right' in terms of the foreseeable future.

Involving influencers

To ensure later acceptability, commitment and enthusiasm for the competency-based approach, it is often useful and necessary to involve influencers at an early stage. These influencers are people whose views are respected within the organization and who can, by their understanding of and consequent support for the competency-based approach, influence others to a similar level of support.

Influencers can be involved within the competency analysis itself both in giving information and in discussion of the results. They can also be involved in the later process design and implementation. An obvious and potent example of the use of influencers in this way is to involve them in a design team for producing scenarios for a career development workshop and later as observers on the workshops. Involvement at this level of detail provides a great deal of understanding and appreciation of the method. With such knowledge and involvement, the influencers can radiate confidence in the process.

Often these same people are asked to assist in the communication process within the organization. They can host briefing meetings and in doing so remove any mystique or fear around the process. They are usually seen as having no hidden agenda and are therefore more trustworthy than perhaps internal or external consultants or human resources personnel, who may be seen as having vested interest or as wishing to use the process in ways not made explicit.

Ownership of competency labels

A well-designed competency analysis will provide several lists of indicators which describe what observable behaviours are included within each. These descriptive lists need titles or labels that are meaningful within the organization. The labels rapidly become a shorthand for discussions ranging across the whole spectrum of behaviour at work. The labelling will capture any cultural and change aspects of life in the organization. They will incorporate 'the way we do things here', a response given by a group personnel director when asked to define what the competencies meant for his organization. Given the potentially pervasive impact the labels can have, consultation with key parties is critical before the labels are set in print.

For example, many middle to senior positions have a set of indicators relating to achieving results. The labels produced can vary from the straightforward 'results orientation' to, in one company, the more evocative 'results getter'. Positioning messages can also be given, often around a competency such as business awareness. In some organizations where there is a need for all to recognize the strategic implications or pitch of this competency, the label will include 'strategic' as an adjective, or it may be described as 'business vision'. The message given through the label must be accurate in terms of the behavioural indicators. The labels should be evocative; they should contain meaningful images and messages for users that ensure consistency when they are used as a shorthand.

If the labels chosen are ambiguous or lack meaning within an organization, their usefulness as a shorthand diminishes, but most importantly there will be inconsistency in application. People will quickly give their own meaning to the labels and these meanings will vary as a multiple of the users. The value of the competency-based approach, with its improved objectivity and consistency, will be lost.

Technical/output implications

While it may seem premature, it is important to have an idea of how the competencies will be used in the development process before embarking on a time-consuming and visible competency analysis. Nothing is more depressing and more destructive of credibility than having to backtrack to collect more and different information because of the demands of the technique ultimately chosen. The extra information points needed, but frequently overlooked in conventional analyses, are given below.

If the assessment of strengths and development needs is to be made using 'scenarios' drawn from the roles or activities in the next level, then information needs to be collected on what people typically do at that level. The career development workshop technique is a good example. The most effective assessment will come from putting individuals into situations that have a point-to-point correspondence with the actual demands of the position. In order to do this, information on roles, responsibilities and critical incidents needs to be collected during the competency analysis.

It may also be important to gain a measure of the relative criticality of each competency for successful performance. This can be important for development as it can define which competencies are vital and which may be nice to have. The criticality of the competency will come from an assessment of how frequently it is needed, the consequence of error and its association with roles which are regarded as most vital. Distinguishing between frequency and association with a vital role can produce interesting results. For instance, the position may require the job holder to be skilled in social interaction and in incisive analysis. A frequency measure may show interpersonal skill to be high and therefore, one might assume, most important, yet incisive analysis may be low in frequency or rarely used but associated with one vital role, and this must increase its importance. The two competencies may need, therefore, to be given equal weighting during the assessment phase. Equal weighting, or equal consideration given to both, will take into account the *overall* importance of the competencies. On other occasions, one competency may be more frequently used *and* associated with the most vital role. In this case, it may be necessary to give a higher weighting in this assessment.

A less obvious technique implication relates to the provision of an alternative path for career development. Concentration on the competencies of the target positions only with no information collected on the alternative career path position may seriously hinder efforts to direct career planning. Assessment can only be made on 'fit' with the target position; no assessment can be made on the alternative career path position.

Having considered all the above aspects on identifying and establishing competencies, the next step is how to use the competencies to effect career development.

Using competencies

Succession planning

This is an organizational survival need. Many succession planning models that have apparent sophistication are computerized, and look good until you investigate the input data. Often they are based on the evidence of current performance or the evidence of performance at one or two highly visible events. Neither gives adequate evidence of potential and the latter is wide open to the 'halo' effect (where one positive piece of evidence bathes all other evidence in a positive glow) or the opposite 'horns' effect. All too often the input is subjective, lacks consistency and clarity of definition between raters, and becomes a globalized 'good person' measure. This leads to a perpetuation of old styles which may not suit a dynamic organization, or to the building of myths within the organization on how one progresses, and it can have serious equal opportunity implications.

How can competencies help?

- by defining what competencies are required at each level/position;
- by forcing evaluation on behavioural sets rather than on a globalized whole person;
- by developing individuals for a position before they arrive.

Definition of the competencies required at each level provides a set of standards for progression. Their very existence tends to focus minds on what is really needed at the next level, not what the evidence of today or the past may indicate. Behaviour observation is automatically lifted out of current performance and focused on the aspects that give evidence of potential. Planning is truly future-oriented.

The nature of competencies forces the observers, be they line managers or human resource managers, to look at aspects of behaviour. There is a constant questioning process of what evidence is available to indicate performance in this or that area. It reduces the tendency to globalize on performance ratings or descriptions. It forces specificity and a search for evidence. The 'good chap' syndrome is difficult to maintain across a set of competencies. The adequacy of the assessment technique used is obviously important but, even with those most open to halo and horns effect, improvement by using competencies is apparent.

Assuming that assessments of strengths and development needs in respect of the promotion position, or alternative career path position, are made periodically and that effort is directed towards developing the individual, then the organization gains major benefits. Talent is spotted early on in a person's career and that talent is developed so that they are ready to assume the additional responsibilities at the time of promotion. Too often a person is promoted, possessing the raw talent but lacking in developed skill. This can lead to becoming a 'victim of succession planning' as one high-flyer described himself. He was constantly promoted, at the point of having achieved the requisite skill for one level, into the next level and had to start skill acquisition all over again.

Using competencies within succession planning models ensures that the focus is on the needs of the next level, that evidence is objectively and systematically collected and that steps can be taken to spot and develop talent early on in individuals' careers.

Development planning

While planning development is centred more at the individual than the organizational level, it should be a tripartite responsibility involving not only the individual but also the line manager and the organization. For career development to be effective all three parties need information on what competencies are required to produce successful performance, how the individual matches against the standard and what they can do about it.

How can competencies help?

• by focusing aspirations and expectations;
• by allowing for the assessment of strengths and development needs;
• by enabling the production of personal development contracts and programmes.

The competency definitions can focus the aspirations and expectations of individuals. By reviewing what is needed at the next level, individuals can make informed decisions as to their capacity to achieve the requisite skill level and their willingness or motivation to embark on a development programme. Realism and determination will produce more effective development.

In order to plan development, individuals will be seeking knowledge of their strengths and development areas. The assessment process will have meaning and purpose for them; it will not be an imposed process providing the organization with knowledge to use as it sees fit. The individual will be a full and active participant in the process.

The output of the assessment, if handled well, can enable the individual in concert with his/her manager to produce a realistic and time-planned personal development action plan. The personal development plans of individuals will, if actioned and well managed, enable specific and progressive development to the satisfaction of both the person and the organization.

The next three sections address some of the specifics in using competencies in planning and actioning career development.

Assessment techniques

There are numerous techniques for assessing competencies. These are amply described in Chapter 4. The techniques more frequently used in career development tend to be:

- career review meetings
- accomplishment record and interview
- tests
- promotion centres
- career development workshop

Each of these is described in some detail below. A point common to all is that *the competency focus needs to be on the target position not on the current position.*

Career review meetings

This is perhaps the most popular technique of all as it closely resembles the appraisal meeting in structure and process. It has a familiarity about it. The advantages and disadvantages of the career review meeting technique are directly related to its familiarity.

The major advantage lies in familiarity making the technique acceptable and in it being seen as part of the normal process of manager–subordinate interaction. The disadvantages derive from its *sheer* familiarity. There is a danger that both parties concentrate on the competencies and results of current and past performance rather than the competencies of the next level. Additionally, there can be issues around rater bias as the manager may or may not feel comfortable with the idea of admitting his/her subordinate to his/her own or an even more senior position.

Some attempts have been made to capitalize on the advantages while diminishing the disadvantages. One such example involves preparation and form filling by the individuals and their direct supervisors, followed by a career review meeting with an 'uncle' who can be drawn from another section, region or department. The preparation involves the completion of potential assessment forms that seek ratings on the next level competencies and supportive examples of behaviour relevant to these competencies. The ratings and examples obviously come from current and previous performance but the behaviour referred to is relevant to the next, not the current, level. Behaviourally anchored rating scales (BARS) are used to ensure consistency and the examples provided by both parties provide the content for the 'uncle' to explore during the meeting. As with open appraisals, information is shared and explored, and ratings are agreed between the individual and the 'uncle'.

An additional technique is sometimes used in the career review meeting to cover those competencies where behavioural evidence from the current position is not so easy to recognize and define. The technique is akin to the structured interviewing found in selection interviews. The most commonly used approach is that of situational interviewing. Here the individual is presented with standardized scenarios drawn from critical incidents that appear in the next level position. The individual's responses are checked against answers and guidelines which have previously been tested out on high and low performers in the next-level position. Design of the answers and guidelines needs to follow sound psychometric principles.

The output of a career review meeting can be a set of ratings by next-level competency which define strengths and development needs. These should indicate the degree and type of development needed for progression to the next level.

Accomplishment record and meeting

This technique is new and relatively untested in terms of the literature. However, it has been used and in usage it bears remarkable similarities to the career review meeting format. The difference lies in how the individual prepares for the meeting. The accomplishment record is a form on which each next-level competency with its behavioural indicators is presented and the individual draws from his or her own life experiences to date, accomplishments or achievements which indicate use of the competency. The accomplishments typically refer to current performance incidents and can therefore be verified.

The accomplishment record is marked using predetermined and tested guidelines designed following sound psychometric principles. The accomplishment record is regarded by individuals as somewhat different, but seen as essentially fair because it taps into what they have done, their achievements to date. The results and marking procedure, plus the accomplishments themselves, become the subject for a discussion which again is similar in format and process to that of an appraisal or career review meeting. The output is also similar although sometimes more focused on what further experiences are necessary for the individual to develop.

Tests

The range of types and properties of tests is described in Chapter 4. The most widely used tests in career development tend to be temperament (or personality as they are most commonly called) and ability measures. Their usage tends to be *ad hoc*, often at the request of the individual, sometimes at the suggestion of the human resources manager. It is rare, in my experience, to find a battery of tests (other than proficiency tests) being used as the formalized and only assessment technique in career development.

Their *ad hoc* use, however, is quite frequent. The tests can be conducted in-house by a trained person or externally by an occupational psychologist. There are advantages and disadvantages to both. An in-house person needs not only to be qualified but also to have the appropriate level of *gravitas* to be acceptable. External consultants are often given these properties, deserved or not. Conversely, an in-house person has knowledge of progression possibilities, alternate career paths and barriers, secondment possibilities and suchlike, which are vital for career development to be effected. An external consultant can only elicit this information from the individual or from human resources.

Using tests effectively as a technique for assessing competencies requires, first, that the progression competencies are defined and, second, that the tests are chosen as best measures of those competencies. The report should synthesize the results under the competency headings to be most meaningful to the individual and his/her sponsor. The report needs to be discussed and the results translated into workplace activities and intentions. This latter aspect is the major disadvantage of using tests as the single technique in career development. They lack the point-to-point correspondence with workplace activities, may be seen as irrelevant by either party and are often difficult to tie into specific development intentions or actions.

Career counselling is an aspect of career development where tests have been found very useful. The more abstract nature of the test output does not detract so much from its usefulness. The output is often focused around job needs or those predominant aspects of a person that need satisfaction in a job. For instance, a high degree of sociability, both in need for people and skill in dealing with them, suggests a certain role requirement for interpersonal contact. Career counselling meetings are often conducted using the services of an external consultant and they are often confidential to the individual who may or may not share the information with a line manager or human resources manager. The purpose of the meeting is usually to give individuals information to enable them to make a fundamental review of their goals and objectives alongside their strengths and development needs.

Promotion centres

An often used and highly formalized process in career development is the promotion centre or assessment centre for promotion. The assessment centre model, whether used for selection or promotion, is a process that enables observations to be made on performance according to job-related criteria or competencies; it uses multiple assessment techniques and multiple trained assessors. The assessment centre approach tends consequently to be the most valid of all assessment techniques when viewed singly.

To the benefits can be added the job preview nature of a promotion centre. The exercises, designed to reflect actual activities in the promotion position, given attendees a flavour of what the job really involves. Attendees can thus add their own judgement as to whether this position or an alternative career path position is most suited to their capabilities and aspirations.

Career development workshops

A modification of the assessment centre approach, designed for specific use in career development, is the career development workshop. It is becoming the most frequently used technique in this area. It is similar to assessment or promotion centres in that its design enables observation of behaviour on the competencies, and multiple assessment techniques and multiple trained assessors are used. The differences lie in structure and process.

On a macro level, the structure needs to meet the objectives of both assessment and development. To be useful, participants must gain an understanding of their strengths and development needs. This is the assessment aspect. Participants also need, within the workshop, to be guided towards the next phase: that of planning how to action their development and plan for the future. This is the development aspect.

This balance can be achieved in a variety of ways, one of which is illustrated in Figure 7.1.

	Participants	Observers	Line managers
Day 1	Diagnosis of strengths and development needs	Observation of behaviour	
Day 2	Preparing for development	Observers' conference	
	Feedback	Feedback	
Day 3	Design of development plan	Briefing line managers	Briefing from observers
	Discussion of development plan		Discussion of development plan

Figure 7.1   *Career development workshop schedule*

Day 1 most closely resembles an assessment centre, with some differences at the micro level which are referred to later. Day 2 changes the process mode for the participants. From an information giving and collection phase, participants now move into exploring how best they can learn, what opportunities are available for development or learning and how to formalize their learning and effect full transfer to the workplace. The morning session is a participative workshop and it is followed by feedback from the observers. The observers, meanwhile, are involved in conference and in preparing for the feedback session.

Day 3 shows another mode change. Participants become involved in planning their own development by designing action plans or contracts. At the same time, each line manager is being briefed by the observer who managed his/her subordinate's feedback session. The briefing is on how the individuals performed in the workshop and on their preferred development activities. The line manager then works with the individual to finalize and agree on a plan and timetable for actioning development.

The differences at a micro level on Day 1 involve the way the exercises are handled. Each exercise is preceded by hints and tips covering what behaviours are being assessed and how they might be displayed. This ensures that all participants are equally knowledgeable on what is expected of them. Following each exercise, participants review their own performance and what, with hindsight, they might have done differently. This review provides excellent material for the feedback meetings and ensures that participants feel fully involved throughout the day.

One further difference between an assessment centre and a career development workshop relates to the semantic messages given. The whole process is called a 'workshop' not a centre, assessors are called 'observers', attendees are called 'participants' and development is usually referred to as 'learning'. These semantic differences may appear cosmetic but they serve to remind all who are involved that the purpose of the whole exercise is to ensure that effective career development occurs.

Managing the output

The preceding sections have dealt mainly with the identification and assessment of competencies. This does not produce career development. Identifying and assessing competencies merely provides the vehicle that enables career development to occur. The output of the assessment process must be well managed if development is to be effective. The effort and expense will have been wasted if the process stops dead after assessment. Expectations will be raised and if they are not met, to at least some degree, disappointment will rapidly become resentment and disaffection. Managing the output has three distinct strands which tie neatly into the responsibilities of the individual, line management and the organization, usually represented by the human resources department.

Preparing for development

The person most interested in developing is the individual. Without his or her motivation to develop, little or nothing will actually happen. The days of waiting to be dragged to the cavern of development are long gone. A useful process to introduce is that of self-managed development. Its purpose is to help individuals to prepare to take charge of their own development.

Preparing for development usually takes place in small peer groups. The content of the day is similar to that covered in Day 2 of the career development workshop described above. The day starts with an exploration of what it means to take charge of their own development, the blocks to development encountered in the past and predicted to be present in the future, and how they can be overcome. This exercise is important or individuals will falter at the first setback.

Much time is also devoted to spotting opportunities in everyday work which they can exploit to learn from and to practise their newly acquired skills. Staged learning and development is recommended as is the gaining of positive reinforcement or reward at each step. The spotting of opportunities is helped by using learning styles questionnaires. Particularly useful is the questionnaire and supporting literature produced by Honey and Mumford (1983, 1986). It enables individuals to review their development needs in the light of how best they learn. Learning or development activities can then be chosen to produce results in the most satisfying manner possible. Examples of activities chosen are as numerous as the individuals choosing them, but they include the more expected formal training, interactive video, tuition, mentoring and suchlike, as well as chairing in-house meetings, writing précis of technical reports, co-working with a skilled colleague and presenting orally or in writing a review of a conference attended. The aim is to select activities which are available or easily requested within the normal course of work. There are self-managed development diskettes and checklists available which provide menus to help individuals consider a wide range of options. While most of these diskettes have been designed for a particular company, a general self-managed development diskette is currently in preparation (Craig, Gregg & Russell Ltd, 1991).

The development plan needs to be formalized, agreed and signed off as a contract between the individual and his/her manager. The contract should cover the following headings:

- Objectives: What needs to be developed?
- Activities: How will the development be actioned? What activities will be involved?
- Resources: What is needed to enable the activities to take place?
- Assessment: What is the criterion/measure to show development has been achieved?
- Duration: When will development begin, when should it be completed?

The final development plan or contract should have the following features:

- It needs to be owned by the individual and the line manager;
- It needs to be specific in terms of activities;
- It needs to be measurable, to have assessment points and criteria to be met;
- It needs to be attainable by the individual within a reasonable timescale;
- It needs to be timed; and, finally,
- It needs to be monitored and reviewed.

One of these features deserves further attention. Development plans should be attainable. This has obvious implications for choosing activities that are within the remit and time of the line manager or department to deliver.

A balance must be struck between delivery on development and ensuring the functioning of a department. All department members attending off-site training programmes may fatally disrupt operations or, if not, may raise questions on overmanning. The cost of the development activities must also be considered and kept realistic.

Another subtle implication is in the definition of development objectives. Some 'development needs' cannot or will not be developed by the person concerned. These need to be addressed by an alternative career path position and/or by managing the realism of aspiration during the feedback process.

Sponsoring development

Development can be blocked, sometimes by an unsupportive line manager. This block can occur out of ignorance or fear. Either way it can be very effective in shrivelling awakening motivation and drive for self-improvement. Two concurrent activities may help prevent the damaging effects of the block. The line manager needs to be involved in as many aspects of the assessment and development planning process as possible. For instance, before the career development workshop described above, line managers were fully briefed on what was going to happen to their subordinates, what the output would look like and their role in the actual and ongoing process. Without involvement, line managers can feel left out and alienated. Their best efforts in sponsoring development cannot then be expected.

The human resources department has a facilitation role to play in the ongoing process. Often information on development options is sought by both the individual and the line manager and sometimes there is a need for arbitration if the commitment to activities is not being delivered.

Monitoring and review

The organization has a business and professional need to monitor development progress and performance against objectives set at a development meeting. There will also be a need for a periodic review of the objectives as they are surpassed, achieved or neglected.

The monitoring and review process needs to be defined and set up before development plans are drawn up. In some cases, it is an information collecting and reporting activity with the review tied into an annual progress meeting. In other cases, the monitoring and periodic reviews take place in small groups of developers, usually facilitated by human resources managers.

The need to monitor and review progress against objectives is essential. The format should fit in with organizational procedures and practices so that planned development is seen by all to be part of the normal range of work systems.

Implementation

This section is intended to highlight some of the issues which, if not adequately addressed, can impede or slow down implementation in competency-based career development.

Promotion vs. development

Not only does the balance between assessment and development need to be fixed to meet programme aims but all parties need to be briefed on just what those aims are. It is vital to managing participant and line manager expectations that all are clear on whether fairly immediate promotion can be expected as positions are currently vacant or whether the purpose is to provide opportunities for progressive development towards a promotion position or alternative career path at some time in the future. The willingness to participate, motivation to action development, and the ultimate success of the programme will depend heavily on an accurate understanding of the goals. The objectives, once set and communicated, should not be changed by later actions.

Commitment to deliver

While installing a programme for career development begins the process of delivery, it is all too easy to allow operational contingency to postpone full delivery. Realism is needed and must be communicated in setting the menu of development options and in the design and agreement of individual development contracts.

Briefing Participants, line managers and their managers, plus human resource managers need to be briefed. All need to have a full understanding of the process, the possible outcomes and their roles in each part of the process. Briefing is especially important when promotion centres or career development workshops are being used. It is often useful to begin these briefings by eliciting expectations, hopes and fears as this provides the opportunity to remove myths, perceived hidden agendas and unrealistic expectations.

Nomination process A programme that is open to some now, some later, and some not at all requires an accurate and 'felt fair' nomination process. The competency-based approach lends itself to self and manager nomination, using rating forms of a similar but simpler format to the potential assessment form described in the career review technique. The final decision needs to be made by human resources managers, as independent arbitration, and the reason for inclusion now, later or not at all needs to be communicated.

Feedback Whichever assessment technique is used, feedback of the results in a constructive and meaningful manner is critical. Poor feedback, or lack of it, quickly produces a pass/fail mentality in the minds of both participants and line managers. This mentality makes managing expectations difficult. It can lead to over-confidence followed by disappointment when expectations are not immediately met or when others are not sufficiently appreciative of their abilities. Conversely, it can lead to a sense of hopelessness and an inability to strive for intermediate or alternative goals. Training in feedback skills should be given to all those who will be responsible for feedback. This includes assessors, observers and line managers.

An open sharing of information is preferable, including written confirmation of performance results, strengths and development needs. The information should where possible be devoid of ratings as these tend to create the pass/fail mentality. A mechanism to avoid this is often to provide a descriptive feedback sheet which acts as a structure for preparation and for the feedback meeting itself.

Addressing these implementation issues before and during the introduction of competency-based career development ensures that full advantage can be taken of the approach.

The impact of a well-designed competency-based approach leads to tremendous benefits for both the organization and the individual. Those benefits most worthy of mention are:

• The standards for promotion are made clear for line managers, human resources personnel and for the individuals. Identifying potential and managing expectations and aspirations is made easier.

- The assessment process is usually seen as fair and unbiased. Objectivity and feedback combine to produce a satisfying experience for both individuals and the organization.
- Planned development can be achieved to ensure that individuals have the capability and skills to handle the next-level position.

References

Craig, Gregg & Russell Ltd. (1991), 2 Churchill Court, 58 Station Road, North Harrow, Middlesex HA2 7SA

Honey and Mumford, (1983, 1986), published by Peter Honey, Ardingly House, 10 Linden Avenue, Maidenhead, Berkshire SL6 6HB.

A competency approach to role and career management restructuring

Michael Pearn

The company　Glaxo Manufacturing Services is the manufacturing arm of Glaxo Holdings, one of the largest pharmaceutical companies in the world. It operates two large factories in the UK and also provides engineering, technical and other services to the group's operating companies all over the world. The company had recently undergone significant reorganization, a new vision had been created, and a mission statement with associated values had been developed.

An important part of the structural change was the subdivision and restructuring of the large factories into a number of more commercially meaningful and customer-responsive manufacturing centres, each under the control of a single manager. Associated with this change was the introduction of advanced manufacturing technology and new working practices with great emphasis on team working. The company was also de-layering, replacing five levels of supervision with only three. A new culture was being created which emphasized total quality, customer service, world-class manufacturing, team working, openness, flexibility and the development of the potential of all employees.

The three levels of management being created for the manufacturing centres were:

1　the overall manufacturing centre manager who formed part of the factory site executive;
2　a team of functional operational managers responsible for the specialized activities necessary for running the manufacturing centre, including human resources, finance, logistics and customer service as well as production and packaging;

3 the team managers who would be directly responsible for the efficient working of groups of flexible operators; several would have specialist or technical skills.

Various attempts had been made to define the three new roles and to specify the personal qualities needed to be successful, but a systematic method had not been used. Consequently, the various attempts to define the roles appeared incomplete, overlapping and inconsistent. Previously, the company had not operated formal or systematic methods for assessing external candidates for selection or for assessing employees for promotion. There was also very little in the way of systematic training and development of managers. Consequently, different sites and different departments tended to do their own thing, resulting in inconsistency and an *ad hoc* approach to the development of people.

The company had grown dramatically from a medium-sized pharmaceuticals company, to one which in just a few years found itself to be a major player on the world stage. It lacked its own management ethos and also a strategy and the structures necessary to create and develop its own management. The combined effects of dramatic growth and the desire to restructure the factories into manufacturing centres had created a strong awareness of the need to become more systematic about the selection, training and development not just of managers but of all its employees.

The company then decided that it needed to have assessment centres, in part because there was a belief that assessment centres in themselves were a good thing but also because many other companies of their size and standing were making use of assessment centres and had been doing so for many years. It was realized at the outset that the essential building blocks of a management development programme had not been put in place, namely a set of management competencies that could communicate to the workforce what was expected of them as managers and also provide the basis for assessment and development.

The company was keen to become self-sufficient as soon as possible and entered into a contract with external consultants that they should work in such a way that the company would have no residual dependency on the consultants at the end of the contract period. The consultants saw their role as equipping the company with the knowledge and skills necessary to carry out competency analysis, to design and run assessment centres, and eventually to evaluate and continuously improve the process. At the same time, the company needed to develop a strategy on human resource development.

Objectives

The formal objectives were:

- to analyse the three new managerial roles;
- to create a structured and systematic role specification for the new roles;
- to create a competency model for the three new levels of management;

- to use the model as the basis for the design and construction of a series of assessment and development centres;
- to develop a core group of experts within the company who would be able to design and run assessment centres in the future.

A team of ten managers, who were already working in the new manufacturing centres, was formed as a task group. They were drawn from three factory sites as well as from head office and were, deliberately, a mixture of line and personnel managers. The first activity was a workshop lasting three days in which the whole concept of management competency and the assessment centre method was analysed and explored. The secondary objective of the workshop was to develop an appreciation of the importance of job analysis and in particular to acquire skill in running critical incident interviews, repertory grid interviews, structured job analysis interviews and also structured group discussions.

At the end of the workshop the task group decided on the 40 or so people who should be interviewed, and the type of interview that should be used. It was decided that there were two broad categories. The first included those people who were currently working at the three new levels of management, even though some of them did not as yet have the formal titles, and who were judged to be operating in the new management style required by the new culture. The second category of people to be interviewed consisted of a smaller number of employees who were labelled 'visionaries'. These were people who had a long-term view of where the company was going or who had been involved in the company project to formulate the structures and working methods of the new manufacturing centres. Some of them had been specifically brought into the company from other organizations which had already undergone similar changes.

Altogether about 40 interviews were carried out and another 30 people participated in structured group discussions. It was not felt necessary to obtain data and views from all these people but some of the interviews were conducted to ensure that no relevant group felt they had been left out of the study.

Competency model

Once all the interviews and group discussions had been carried out and the reports written up into large folders, a second workshop was run for the task group in which the fundamentals of data analysis and interpretation were explained and a working methodology was developed for identifying and describing appropriate competencies. The first output of the task group's analysis was the production of generic role definitions and structured person specifications. The task group concluded, on the evidence available, that the same core set of 12 competencies was equally applicable to the three managerial levels, though the focus and level of performance expected would vary. The overall structure of the competency model is presented in Figure C.3.

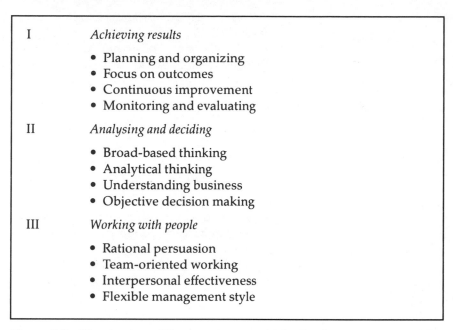

I   *Achieving results*

- Planning and organizing
- Focus on outcomes
- Continuous improvement
- Monitoring and evaluating

II   *Analysing and deciding*

- Broad-based thinking
- Analytical thinking
- Understanding business
- Objective decision making

III   *Working with people*

- Rational persuasion
- Team-oriented working
- Interpersonal effectiveness
- Flexible management style

Figure C.3   *The structure of the competency model for the three new managerial roles*

The competency model is divided into three broad categories: achieving results, analysing and deciding, and working with people. Technical and functional competence were also considered to be important but were not directly relevant to the generic model of managerial competence. Functional specialists operating as managers would still be expected to conform to the generic model.

The three broad clusters were defined as follows:

Achieving results

Effective job holders maintain a clear focus on what needs to be achieved and persist in the face of difficulties. They display enthusiasm and commitment, and communicate this to others. They have determination and confidence and achieve results through detailed planning and organization. This enables objectives to be met within agreed timescales and they also develop methods to check performance and monitor progress. The effective job holder is constantly seeking to bring about improved ways of working and is aware of both short- and longer-term objectives.

Analysing and deciding

Analytical thinking provides the basis for a clear understanding of the issues and helps the individual reach sound conclusions. However, broad-based thinking is also important. This enables the effective job holder to take into account a wide range of issues and to consider the overall implications of a particular course of action. Sound analysis also requires a good understanding of how the business operates, the factors affecting profitability and the commerical environment in which the company operates. The combination of these various elements helps the effective job holder to make timely and appropriate decisions and to establish clear priorities.

Working with people

An important characteristic of the effective job holder is the ability to develop and use structured arguments based on well-organized facts. However, this is also accompanied by strong interpersonal skills which encourages two-way communication and build commitment in sub-ordinates.

There is also an appreciation of the value and benefits of team working, and an emphasis on continually finding ways of improving the effective-ness of the team. Regular meetings are used to improve communication and to encourage ownership and accountability for performance. Effec-tive job holders, therefore, adopt a participative and consultative style of working which places high value on the contribution of all members of staff.

The true significance of the clusters, as defined, lay in the way in which they departed from past experience. Previously, the management style had tended to be authoritarian or paternalistic and was somewhat secre-tive. Consequently, lower levels of supervision in the company had tended to be rather passive and narrow in focus.

For each of these three clusters there were four specific competencies, making a total of 12 as shown in Figure C.3. For each of these competencies there was a specific behavioural definition. The definitions for the *Achieving results* cluster are shown in Figure C.4.

Achieving results

1 Planning and organizing

Achieves results through detailed planning and organization of people and resources to meet/identify goals, targets or objectives within agreed timescales.

2 Focus on outcomes

Maintains focus on results to be achieved, persists in face of difficulties and ensures others achieve successful outcomes.

3 Continuous improvement

Constantly seeks and brings about better/improved ways of working in both short and longer term.

4 Monitoring and evaluating

Finds ways of checking performance, both ongoing and at critical points, to assess progress towards specified targets/objectives.

Figure C.4   Definition of competencies within the 'Achieving results' cluster

Behavioural indicators

But even the behavioural definitions of the specific competencies are not precise enough for development and assessment purposes. They could easily be interpreted in different ways by different people with different functional perspectives. In order to complete the process a set of behavioural indicators (both positive and negative) was developed for each competency. Initially, a generic set of indicators was developed in order to provide a precise definition and anchoring of the competencies to actual behaviour. However, at a later stage, when assessment centres were being developed and exercises were designed, a specific set of behavioural indicators for each exercise was also developed enabling very precise assessment and development of candidates. An example of the performance indicators developed for use with a practical exercise and to assess continuous improvement is given in Figure C.5.

Continuous improvement

Positive indicators
- seeks advice from others, e.g. team, customers, suppliers, service departments
- proposals aimed at permanent solution not just quick-fix
- involves team at all stages
- sees potential for reaching and maintaining higher standards

Level 2 manager as above plus
- shows awareness of impact of proposals on customer service and quality
- considers use of off-the-job approaches, e.g. quality circles

Level 3 manager as above plus
- suggests reallocation of resources, reorganization of structure to ensure effective solution
- balances cost of improvement against customer and quality requirements

Contra-indicators
- proposes short-term solutions without considering long-term consequences
- fails to consult others or to build on their contributions
- focuses on only one or two opportunities for improvement
- does not recognize alternative ways of tackling problems, e.g. special project team, quality circles.

Figure C.5   Performance indicators for continuous improvement (practical exercise)

The immediate application of the competency model was the construction and design of assessment centres for the three new layers of management, to be used both for selection and for development-oriented assessment of current job holders.

One of the striking things to emerge from the study was the conclusion that the same set of twelve competencies could apply equally to the three levels of management. The difference in interpretation of the competencies would arise primarily by reference to the performance indicators which would reflect the differences in function and objectives

- **Purpose**
- **Structure**
  —responsible to
  —responsible for

- **Key dimensions**
  —timescale
  —internal/external focus
  —revenue budgets
  —direct/indirect staff
  —product range
  —standard value
  —capital employed
  —annual capital budget spending

- **Key accountabilities**
  —financial
  —quality
  —customer service
  —safety
  —people
  —organizational development
  —projects
  —internal contacts

Figure C.6   *Structure of the role specifications*

of the three levels of management, as defined in the three role specifications. The structure of the role specifications is shown in Figure C.6.

For example, the key dimensions would greatly influence the behaviour that was considered appropriate for the three levels under the same heading. One of the key dimensions was timescale in terms of each manager's forward thinking, and planning and organizing. For the centre manager the timescale was 1 to 5 years regularly, and 1 to 12 months occasionally; for the operations manager it was 1 to 12 months regularly, 1 to 5 years occasionally; and for the team manager it was from immediate to within 3 months regularly and 3 to 18 months occasionally. Internal/external focus was also a significant factor in interpreting the same competency for the three levels of management. For the centre manager the external focus (i.e. to the manufacturing centre) was 60 per cent; it was 30 per cent for the operations manager and 10 per cent for the team manager. These are obviously relatively crude guidelines but they were very effective in influencing the interpretation of the same competencies at three different levels of management.

Although the immediate application of the competency model was the design and development of assessment/development centres, it was quickly recognized by top management that the competencies succinctly and vividly captured, in behavioural terms, many important aspects of the new culture that they were trying to build in the organization. Consequently, it became a useful tool for communication (in terms of what is expected) as well as for assessment and development. The same competency model has also been used by the company as a basis for annual job performance appraisals and also to help structure the process by which performance-related pay grades are determined.

The company is beginning to develop a common vocabulary for assessing, training and developing its stock of managers. There has also been considerable feedback, by way of follow-up questionnaires, that the assessment/development process based on the competency model is seen as fair and effective, and is thus regarded as a popular move within the company. There is a growing pride in the professionalism of the overall process and a sense that, in terms of an evolving management ethos and an associated management development strategy, the company has begun to catch up with its dramatic and sophisticated growth in other aspects of its operations.

Consistent with its thinking about the restructuring of the organization and the development of a new culture, the company also decided to take the competency model and associated assessment procedures downwards through the organization right down to the entry level operator grade.

Career movements

While the company was removing the traditional multi-level hierarchical structure and replacing it with a more fluid, flexible and competency-based structure, a study was carried out to identify the competencies and levels of performance required at each of the three new operator grades and also within each of the five or six cells that made up each level. The outcome was highly task- and output-oriented. What the company lacked was a systematic basis for deciding how individuals should move between levels, moving either vertically, horizontally or diagonally across the matrix. A further study was carried out and the results indicated that a simplified competency model could be created for the new flexible operator structure by collapsing components of the managerial competency model. The resultant structure of the competency model for the three layers of the operator matrix is presented in Figure C.7.

Attached to each of these competencies was a set of behavioural indicators and an assessment process consisting of psychometric tests, a self-assessment questionnaire, and work-sample tests which are currently in use for assessing movement between as well as within the operator matrix.

The company has now achieved a consistent and compatible set of behavioural competencies that run all the way from entry level operator grades through technical operator grades to team manager and all the way up to manager of a manufacturing centre. This enables the company to achieve systematic and consistent assessment of the behaviours necessary for quality performance of the jobs from bottom to top of the manufacturing organization. This feature is a concrete manifestation of the company's commitment to the new culture it was trying to establish as an essential step in creating the necessary conditions for meeting its corporate objectives.

Operator Level 1	Operator Level 2	Operator Level 3/4	Management competency model
Work habits	Approach to work	Planning and organizing Continuous improvement Maintaining standards	'Achieving results' cluster (four competencies)
Job requirements	Company knowledge Solving problems	Business appreciation Judgement	'Analysing and deciding' cluster (four competencies)
Team participation	Team contributions People skills	Team working Interpersonal skills	'Working with people' cluster (four competencies)

Figure C.7   *Relationship between the operator competencies and the management competency model*

8 Competency, pay and performance management

Derek Torrington and Will Blandamer

The ideas of linking pay to performance and of performance management are inextricably linked with the idea of human resource management (HRM), which has the potential to transform the people management processes in and around organizations.

The largely academic debate about the qualitative differences between personnel management and HRM has produced at least some consensus as to the nature of HRM, if not a consensus on what it actually looks like in an organization. Human resource management represents a shift away from collective (industrial) relations towards individual (employee) relations, and is undoubtedly unitaristic in style, with a greater emphasis on initiatives taken by management rather than initiatives agreed with trade unions. Hence there has been renewed interest in the more direct forms of employee participation such as quality circles, team briefings and employee share ownership. In HRM thinking there is little scope for collective bargaining, and, although it has been suggested that HRM is not necessarily non-union, the role unions play is significantly diminished.

HRM values are essentially individualistic in that they emphasise the individual–organisation linkage in preference to operating through group and representative systems. (Guest, 1989)

This approach can be seen in the proliferation of the 'people' approach to management and the growth of customer care schemes, best exemplified by Peters and Waterman in *In Search of Excellence*. Employees are seen as a strategic variable: an asset in which the company seeks to invest, rather than a cost to be reduced. Assets are also, however, exploited and the logical way to exploit the benefit of the people asset in the business is to focus on performance.

As a product of this there has been a growth in individual responsibility initiatives, with the emphasis firmly on individual performance. Performance appraisal and performance-related pay and a renewed interest in training initiatives representing investment in the human resource are manifestations of this approach and are at the centre of any conceptualization of HRM (Keep, 1989).

Obviously, one of the main components of any human resource policy will be the management of the reward/compensation/pay/remuneration package. One of the intriguing by-products of the whole interest in payment has been the use of all sorts of different words to describe it, almost as if it must be different because we have thought up a new word for it. The potential motivating effect of pay is a subject of considerable debate, but it is clear that any shift towards a performance management culture will have implications for the size and type of the payment to employees.

Through the bulk of the post-war period arrangements for payment have had one or both of two underlying philosophies. The *service* philosophy emphasized the acquisition of experience, implying that people became more effective as they remained in a job and rewarding their service through incremental pay scales. These scales were typically of five to eight points, encouraging people to continue in the post for five years or more, as there was still some headroom for salary growth. The *fairness* philosophy emphasized getting the right structure of differentials. The progressive spread of job evaluation from the 1960s onwards was an attempt to cope with the problems of relative pay levels that were generated by increasing organization size and job complexity. Legislation on equal value gave further impetus to this approach.

Accompanying the growth of pay systems emphasizing service and fairness was a steady decline in incentive schemes. These had been developed, almost entirely for manual workers, from the early part of this century until the late 1960s, but had then begun to decline under the weight of union attack, employee ingenuity in outwitting the work study officer, and the changes in production technology. The 1980s was the decade in which the incentive idea was re-invented: the *performance* philosophy. Length of service is useful, fairness is necessary, but what really matters is the performance that the employee produces.

Performance-related pay

Performance-related pay (PRP) is one approach which in theory fulfils the requirements of a reward system in HRM. A survey in October 1990 reported that 93 per cent of personnel managers regarded pay for performance as a major or emerging priority.

Performance related pay is one of the most dynamic issues of human resources management and arguably the most topical component of reward management today. (Bading and Wright, 1990)

The aims of PRP are to reward those who are performing well, to motivate all employees, and to focus the effort of individuals on appropriate tasks through the use of appraisals and objectives. Another survey, by Kinnie and Lowe in 1990, identified the following perceived benefits of PRP:

- Improvements in staff commitment;
- Improved job satisfaction (because employees feel they are being listened to);
- A way of focusing attention on the individual employee;
- Better communication by improving dialogue between managers and their subordinates.

Another benefit of PRP is that it can act as an important cultural signifier, or mechanism of cultural change, in the organization. A well-structured and well-implemented performance-related pay strategy gives clear messages about the direction and values of an organization. As such it can be used to reinforce current types of behaviour or support change (Bading and Wright, 1990).

An example is the National Health Service, which at the time of writing is trying to move away from the predominant bureaucratic culture towards a culture emphasizing individual initiative, responsibility and autonomy. There is therefore much debate within the NHS about the use of performance-related pay, not so much for any great belief in its ability alone to increase performance, but more as part of an overall initiative to move towards a performance-based meritocracy.

Problems of PRP   There are however significant problems with the operation of performance-related pay schemes. The survey by Kinnie and Lowe (1990) suggested that only 20 per cent of personnel managers considered their appraisal systems effective and only 11 per cent believed that their system effectively linked pay to performance. This is very significant when one considers the cost of introducing PRP, which tends to be in the range of 10–30 per cent of the first year's salary bill.

Kinnie and Lowe also asked respondents what they considered to be the major barriers to the effective operation of the PRP system. The survey mentioned the following problems:

- Carrying out the appraisals, including the difficulty of setting meaningful individual objectives, and the apparent lack of ability or training of the appraiser to assess the subordinate;
- Translating appraisals into pay, including the opportunity for bias and favouritism to undermine the credibility of the scheme;
- Trade union attitudes and employee scepticism. The trade unions viewed PRP as implicitly threatening, not least because of the lack of an objective appraisal system.

As a conclusion to the study it was suggested that 'PRP, if not handled properly, may actually become divisive and inconsistent with team working' Kinnie and Lowe (1990).

If the scheme does not actually become divisive it may be subject to considerable manipulation. For example, if managers know they are being evaluated according to certain criteria, a disproportionate amount of time may be spent on activities contributing to those objectives, perhaps at the expense of other equally important but not appraised activities.

There are clearly problems with PRP schemes, and it is not turning out to be the 'cure-all' solution its advocates would have us believe. There is a growing conviction that PRP is merely the latest in a long line of 'flavours of the month', like quality circles and self-financing productivity deals.

A competency-based approach to performance management

This chapter seeks to explore whether a competency-based approach to rewards and performance management could alleviate some of the problems of PRP outlined above. If it could, it would perhaps not only be regarded as the salvation of many ailing PRP schemes, but would also allow a competency-based approach to take its place at the 'great table' of HRM.

There are several different definitions of competencies already in this book, but all have in common that the competent person is able to perform some task effectively, there is a described standard for that performance, and it can be measured or assessed. That carries with it the lowest common denominator problem: when you pass your driving test you are competent and the fact that some drive better than others is irrelevant. In contrast to that, PRP is seeking to stimulate and reward extra performance, but pressures in the social system of the workplace, to say nothing of the appraiser/appraisee relationship, make that difficult. The distinction therefore needs to be drawn between the competent performance of a job that implies merely satisfactory performance, and a competency required to perform a job to an excellent standard. This builds on the analysis by Woodruffe in Chapter 2 which made the distinction between areas of a competence and competencies which are associated with highly effective performance.

Those on PRP schemes who do not earn their reward seldom accept that their failure is their fault. It is either that the objectives were not properly set or they were not fairly assessed. This tension in the appraisal process can totally undermine the effectiveness of the scheme, if there is to be any impact on the levels of performance.

Three aspects of the appraisal process can be identified: the setting of the objectives of the appraisal system, the setting of the objectives against which the appraisee is to be judged, and the actual appraisal process. We consider these in turn.

Appraisal system objectives

Cameron (1982) quotes Singer (1974):

Many of the problems connected with performance appraisal stem from the lack of clarity in determining what it is intended to achieve.

Generally, people regard the objectives of appraisal as assessing future potential/promotability, assessing training and development needs, and assessing past and current performance with a view to improvement. It is our suggestion that a competency-based approach would help in fulfilling these objectives. A framework of competencies explicitly brings into the appraisal process a judgement on the future potential of the appraisee and relates this to a training needs analysis. It allows an identification of, and focus on, those aspects of an individual's potential that are crucial to the future success of the enterprise. Hence a competency-based approach provides a framework in which the objectives of the appraisal process can be drawn out with clarity, and related to the strategic role of the reward and performance management initiative. Furthermore, in a performance management setting a competency-based approach to appraisal would allow earlier identification of those people who should be retained, and included in the 'core' of the workforce.

Objectives for the appraisee

Another problem with appraisal schemes is the setting of objectives for the appraisee. Dissatisfaction with PRP schemes often arises if the objectives are seen to be remote from those that the individual can achieve. For example, the health of a patient in a hospital is not only dependent on the level and quality of care given by the nurse, but also the skill of the surgeon, the thoroughness of the cleaners and the nature of the patient's illness. There are, however, a number of activities of the nurse that are essential to the effective performance of the job.

A competency-based profile could set more appropriate objectives. It could set a performance standard representing a level of performance that would ensure the job was being performed effectively. It would be especially useful in those jobs that do not have readily available output criteria. In a bank there are only a few employees who can be set performance targets on a market basis—the manager and the people responsible for the marketing and operation of particular accounts would be examples. The majority of staff are required to perform their job competently and no more, even though a secretary who forgets to pass on a crucial message could lose an important client. A competency-based approach would allow performance targets to be set and would also fulfil the goal of the appraisal process of monitoring the potential of staff. Such an approach would perhaps allow PRP to move further away from its traditional managerial base.

Appraisal process

A key issue in the appraisal process is the ability of managers to carry out an appraisal interview, an essential element of most schemes. Long (1986) suggests:

Although most managers acquire a good deal of experience in interviewing techniques during the course of their everyday activities, the performance review discussion tends to be approached with as much circumspection by the reviewer as by the reviewed.

Not only is there the inability or reluctance of managers and supervisors to conduct appraisal, there is also a great reluctance to give poor ratings. When schemes are individualized, it is always difficult to keep pay rises down for poor performers. Few managers have the stomach for passing on the bad news and then hoping to get a satisfactory working performance out of the person who has not had a pay rise. It is argued that a competency-based approach would not only provide a framework for conducting the appraisal, it would also give managers the confidence to appraise honestly, and lead to a more frank and open exchange of views between appraiser and appraisee. Indeed, a competency-based approach allows discussion and feedback with appraisees on

sensitive and potentially emotive issues . . . [such as] . . . how they are perceived by others, the interpersonal aspects of their job performance or their failure to secure an appointment for which they applied (Glaze, 1989)

Clearly, appraisal schemes that appear overly dominated by paperwork are disliked by managers, but the potential advantages of a competency-based approach to appraisal—couched in 'scientific' terms and thus having a certain credibility—are great. Furthermore, although appraisal often represented an unwanted and unnecessary intrusion into working relationships between managers and the workforce, a competency-based approach allows the identification of training needs of individuals, and a potential interest in the appraisal by the employee.

Creating a common language

A further major problem of performance-related pay schemes cited in the study by Kinnie and Lowe (1990) was the attitude of trade unions and employees to its introduction. Trade unions feel threatened by PRP; it represents an increase in that part of the pay package that is not open to collective bargaining and negotiation. Furthermore, they feel that the system is too vulnerable to manipulation and subjective bias. The survey reports one personnel manager saying that if the system is not 'seen to be justifiably consistent, personal antagonism between employees and supervisors can cause potentially damaging confrontations'.

Bading and Wright (1990) suggest PRP systems 'can be potentially divisive, inappropriately focused or generally difficult to justify in terms of performance improvement'.

There are clearly messages here about the need to communicate the nature and content of the scheme to a largely sceptical workforce. A recent example we saw in a multinational company operating in the north-west of England sets out with great clarity the principles behind the scheme, its relationship to the business strategy, and the actual internal workings of the system. It does not, however, discuss in any detail the criteria upon which the employees are appraised. It is our contention that a competency-based approach could provide a common language of performance objectives that would help to overcome the fears of the employees and their representatives. Again, the ease with which a competency-based approach can lead to a training needs analysis is relevant, for the employee representatives are likely to be more willing to accept a scheme that will have beneficial consequences in terms of the identification of potential and the implementation of appropriate training.

Much of the dislike of PRP schemes is a product of the subjective nature of the appraisal, which is to a great extent the result of the seemingly arbitrarily determined criteria. One of the most thorough schemes we have studied is in a computer company that has the performance philosophy central to their business to such an extent that they will cut all sorts of other costs in order to sustain their PRP arrangements. Even in this well-developed scheme performance is assessed on the criteria of team working, decision making, initiative, creativity, safety and planning. The terms used in assessment are unacceptable/acceptable/good/very good/excellent/exceptional. It is inevitable that these appraisals will be prone to subjectivity.

A competency-based approach would provide a more reasoned and detailed analysis with greater scope for breaking down each of the identified factors into subsections directly relating to behaviour. Once again we can suggest that the apparently scientific roots of the competency approach lend the system a certain legitimacy. If competencies produce a common language through which effective and non-effective performers can be identified, there is a further benefit.

Pay/ performance link

Another difficulty with PRP schemes is the general rise in expectations that they create. People respond to PRP because there is the prospect of more money, and the prospect has to be of significantly more money if it is to be attractive. Therefore, the management 'grease in' the scheme by indicating how much one can expect. An enthusiastic, performance-enhancing response (which is the sole purpose of the exercise) will bring with it a widespread expectation of lots more money, and will not be delivered without the expectation.

In all the schemes we have examined the cost has exceeded management forecasts, despite some quite Draconian measures to contain it. It is quite common to structure the scheme to guarantee some losers by pre-setting the distribution, with set percentages required in each category, for example:

Outstanding	5 – 10%
Exceptional	15 – 25%
Above average	25 – 45%
Developmental	25 – 45%
Unsatisfactory	5 – 15%

Hence, by definition, a large minority of the workforce is going to be classed as below average. This would appear to be the major demotivational effect of PRP schemes. To brand an employee as below average at a time when that employee has a rising expectation of the level of reward because of the introduction of PRP is to create a divisive atmosphere. It is equally illogical, but less of a problem, that a significant minority are to be identified as exceptional or outstanding. A competency approach would at least lessen this effect by providing positive guidance and allowing the employee to identify those aspects of performance that are producing the below average rating.

We have so far considered some of the problems of performance-related pay schemes in practice and suggested how a competency-based approach could reduce the apparently large gap between theory and practice. There is, however, a further issue that we have mentioned only briefly. The term 'performance management' is a very seductive concept for managers, implying as it does notions of 'excellence' and 'striving to achieve'. A competency approach, however, sets standards for minimum performance: that which is required in order to do the job to a satisfactory standard. Now for many jobs this is all that is required, and indeed is all that can be encompassed in any objectives.

Competency defined as excellence

This begs the question: 'Are performance management and a competency-based approach incompatible for those occupations where a job holder has significant opportunity to surpass the immediate requirements of the job?' This is not to say that a competency approach is not relevant to performance-related pay, for the arguments above suggest that it may have a valuable contribution to make. It is to suggest that its application may be limited by the user's definition of competence, as there is a fundamental difference between a competent performance of a job, for which the job holder should nevertheless be rewarded, and an excellent, high level of performance in a job.

The National Westminster Bank uses a system of 11 competencies which they feel relate strongly to management performance in a turbulent business environment. Cockerill (1989) says:

I should make it clear that the 11 competencies are not concerned with mere 'competence'—with sufficiency or adequacy; rather they are forms of managerial behaviour which will raise performance beyond adequacy to excellence.

Jacobs (1989), however, suggests that:

Users of competency based assessment should be aware that it provides one relatively partial view of performance. Its strong emphasis on the need for scientific rigour tends to lead to a rather narrow perspective which, on its own, is barely capable of reflecting the rich and often paradoxical nature of human behaviour.

We take a position at some point between these two views. A competency-based approach may well provide a method of alleviating the difficulties encountered in establishing performance-related pay schemes, as has been suggested above, but for many jobs its application will be to provide a criterion of minimum standards. To this end it is perhaps more appropriately employed in merit pay systems which generally cover those jobs in an organization that are not sufficiently autonomous for performance standards to be set in business terms.

We studied a PRP scheme for management categories that had been operated in an organization over the preceding three years. Clear objectives were seen to be crucial to its success and managers could qualify for PRP ranging between 0 per cent and 20 per cent. For clerical grades, however, a merit bonus of 2 per cent, 3 per cent and 5 per cent was awarded and objectives were not set. Perhaps it is at this level that a competence approach based on the idea of minimum standards would be best employed.

Beer *et al.* (1985) say the following about payment schemes:

Of the four major policy areas of HRM, this is where we find the greatest contradiction between the promise of theory and the reality of implementation. Organisations sometimes go through cycles of great innovation and hope as reward systems are developed, followed by disillusionment as these systems fail to deliver.

Nowhere is this more problematic than with the development of performance-related pay. Competency-based thinking may well alleviate some of the barriers to an effective system, by providing clarity of objectives, a vehicle for a two-way communication process between the appraiser and appraisee, and a basis upon which training can be developed. It may also go some way to overcoming the distrust of such schemes by trade unions, through providing a common language for describing levels of performance.

Many of the problems of implementation of both performance-related pay schemes and competency approaches are that they are often imposed on an organization as an imported idea. The lack of organization-specific systems compatible with the dominant culture is perhaps at the root of failed schemes. Performance pay alone will have little impact and will not survive unless it is part of a fundamental shift of culture towards a performance basis. That requires much more than tinkering with the pay and appraisal systems. It requires commitment, action and follow-through in all aspects of the organization's management.

References

Bading, L. and V. Wright (1990) 'Performance related pay', *Personnel Management* Factsheet, 30 June 1990.

Beer, M., B. Spector, P. Lawrence, D. Mills and R. Walton (1985) *Human Resource Management: A General Manager's Perspective*, New York: Free Press.

Cockerill, A. (1989) 'The kind of competence for rapid change', *Personnel Management*, 21(9), September 1989, 52–6.

Glaze, A. (1989) 'Cadbury's dictionary of competence', *Personnel Management*, 21 (7), July 1989, 44–8.

Guest, D. (1989) 'Human Resource Management: Its Implications for Industrial Relations and Trade Unions', in J. Storey (ed.) *New Perspectives on Human Resource Management*, London: Routledge.

Jacobs, R. (1989) 'Getting the measure of management competence', *Personnel Management*, 21(6), June 1989, 32–7.

Keep, E. (1989) 'Corporate Training Strategies: The Vital Component?' in J. Storey (ed.) *New Perspectives on Human Resource Management*, London: Routledge.

Kinnie, N. and D. Lowe (1990) 'Performance related pay on the shopfloor', *Personnel Management*, 22(11).

Long, P. (1986) *Performance Appraisal Revisited*, London: Institute of Personnel Management.

Peters, T. and R. Waterman (1982) *In Search of Excellence*, New York: Harper and Row.

Singer, E.J. (1974) *Effective Management Coaching*, London: Institute of Personnel Management.

A competency approach to performance management

Clive Mosley and Jane Bryan

The BSS Group began trading in 1899 as British Steam Specialities, distributors of steam valves and fittings in the East Midlands. Since then BSS has grown both organically by extension of product range, and by acquisition, to become the major distributor of industrial heating, process, pipeline and mechanical services equipment in the UK and Eire. Its policy is to provide a local service through its network of more than 80 distribution branches nationwide, extending from Aberdeen to Plymouth and from Hull to Belfast, with the head office in Leicester.

The drive towards quality

The successful growth of the company was evident and in the early 1980s group performance had improved significantly. However, the market was becoming increasingly desensitized to price variations and increased market share was not available merely through careful pricing strategy. Internally, it was recognized that there was a need on the part of the management team to manage more effectively to stay competitive in the 1990s.

The buyers of BSS's services were contractors whose primary concern was the speedy acquisition of suitable products rather than price alone. It became clear then that BSS had a major opportunity to differentiate themselves and enhance their competitive position by improving the quality of the service they provided.

In 1987, the company embarked upon a total quality initiative. With the help of PA Consulting Group, a programme was designed to address company-wide quality improvement, ranging from products and customer service to communication, and commercial and administrative support.

With an emphasis on disciplined, ordered change going from top to bottom the programme involved a diagnosis of the company's current position. Structured interviews and workshops with senior managers helped to identify the company's views on quality and areas where an improvement in quality could have a major impact on the company's performance. Each quality improvement area was costed in terms of prevention, appraisal and failure, in order to quantify the business benefit of any initiatives. An assessment of employee attitudes and perceptions on how the company was run helped to assess the reality of work practice in contrast to what was desired or, indeed, required.

Finally, interviews with customers and a review of customer perceptions completed the data put forward to senior management to allow them to make decisions to move forward with an effective total quality management programme across the company.

People make quality

Throughout this whole process the influence of staff on quality became increasingly apparent. Satisfying the customer's needs efficiently and cost effectively was intrinsically linked to recruiting the right staff and ensuring appropriate training and staff development. Equally, motivating staff towards the desired behaviours meant that the HR strategy needed to be derived from, and supportive of, overall business philosophy and objectives. Through management workshops an HR strategy was generated under the banner of 'People make Quality'. The strategy was made up of four main areas:

- recruitment and selection
- competency profiling
- pay and grading
- objective setting and appraisal

Each component built on the others and all were driven by the BSS philosophy to be recognized as *the* quality company in its chosen field of operations (see Figure C.8). The dominant and critical values behind the strategy were that supporting HR systems and methods of managing human resources should be consistent across the group and should encourage individual contribution and development. That is, all systems and measures should be input- and process-driven rather than output-focused, so building the competencies critical to future success.

In order to build consistency, there was a need to identify the level and type of performance that was required and the competencies to be displayed in order to meet customer requirements. The concept of the 'Branch of the Future' was developed to articulate how the total quality mission would work in practice.

Two examples of how the organization failed to recognize customer needs as drivers of business strategy will illustrate how this concept was developed.

- Traditionally, branches were organized as independent trading units with their success measured by area sales. Practically, to meet customer needs, the computerized stock system and branch delivery service meant that the source of the product was irrelevant to the cus-

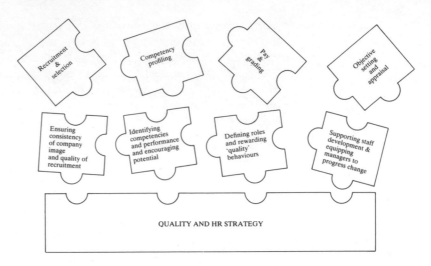

Figure C.8   Quality and HR strategy

tomer. Speedy and accurate service took priority. Flowing from the
TQM mission therefore was the need for the accelerated evolution of
the branch network from profit centre to service point.

• Branches were organized into two areas, sales and distribution. Sales
  staff were typically school leavers who gained both product and business knowledge within the internal sales function which equipped
  them to become external sales representatives in the future.

The distribution area was responsible for the distribution and delivery
of orders. However, these made up only 70 per cent of all sales. A
further 30 per cent came from the trade counter which was typically
attached to the back of the warehouse. BSS recognized the potential
benefit of developing this area as a point of sales. However, the trade
counter staff were typically from a warehousing background and
therefore possessed strong product knowledge skills but no selling
skills.

To meet customer needs it became clear that all staff in direct contact
with customers, either by phone or face-to-face, needed a practical
knowledge of how products were used and of product alternatives to
extend the sales process. The differentiation in career paths for the
sales and distribution areas therefore had to be eroded and each role,
with its required competencies, more clearly defined.

The aim is that staff within internal sales and trade counter sales will
be interchangeable with overlapping competency profiles. A trial is
currently under way to create an open sales office with a single point
of contact for customers.

The HR implications of these examples demonstrated a need for greater
consistency in role definition, recruitment procedures and selection
processes, and more explicit staff involvement in suggesting business
improvements through more direct manager/employee feedback.

Developing the HR strategy

Having identified the pieces, BSS was now able to start to piece together the HR strategy jigsaw. It began by visualizing its 'Branch of the Future', evaluating why some branches were more successful than others, and thus generating the competencies, roles and supporting systems to recreate and maintain this success throughout the branch network. The process followed the stages outlined below.

As a first step, a full organizational analysis was undertaken to identify competencies for all roles from director through to secretary. Critical incidents and repertory grid analysis were used to define those competencies in staff which distinguished success. A total of 21 key competencies were identified together with those behavioural indicators that reflected good versus poor performance. These were used as a basis to develop language ladders. The ladders gave both a general description of the attribute and a detailed definition of the level to which that attribute could be displayed. Each competency could therefore be defined on a 1 to 14 scale that could be applied consistently throughout the company. An example of the language ladder for the competency of 'motivating others' is shown in Figure C.9.

BSS LANGUAGE LADDERS

Motivating others

General description of attribute

Having the skill to gain interest, drive and commitment from others and sustain this over time. Involves viewing motivation in the widest sense, not just as a reward system. The skill comes to the fore in motivating others and managing their work performance even when career development opportunities are not apparent or available.

Level	Description
ONE	No previous experience of motivating others, does not have the opportunity to demonstrate this skill.
TWO	Minimum level of understanding of this skill, or no requirement to motivate others in his/her own work.
THREE	Tends to be uninvolved, distant and aloof when dealing with others. May not inspire or motivate others.
FOUR	Begins to demonstrate some attention to motivating others but may lack knowledge of individuals' aspirations. Tends to dominate and impose his/her own standards.
FIVE	Appreciates individuals' aspirations. May set unrealistic targets.

Figure C.9   BSS language ladders

Level	Description
SIX	Sets appropriate targets but does not always provide any positive feedback. May tend to criticize others.
SEVEN	Is able to, and frequently does, provide positive feedback. Sometimes fails to show or to explain development opportunities.
EIGHT	Seeks to understand individual aspirations. Demonstrates a sensitivity to morale and levels of individual satisfaction.
NINE	Takes an active interest in what subordinates are doing. Works hard at building a team spirit. Enjoys working with others and listens to their views.
TEN	Builds on team spirit by recognizing good ideas and effort. Is encouraging and able to gain staff commitment.
ELEVEN	Transfers his/her enthusiasm to others. Gets involved and devotes time to finding interesting things for them to do.
TWELVE	Uses the reward system effectively, providing motivating incentives and targets, keeps abreast of motivation techniques.
THIRTEEN	Is a natural motivator of staff. Finds ways of establishing career development opportunities.
FOURTEEN	Demonstrates the whole range of skills to motivate others at director level. Is a powerful motivator for all staff.

Figure C.9   cont'd

Building on this work, BSS was able to develop a competency profile for each role within the company. The profile has four main clusters of competencies:

- people skills
- commercial
- personal skills
- total quality

Again, this range of competencies can be applied to each role within the company. It is only the level at which it is applied in a particular role that will differ.

To these core competencies is added the profile of technical skills. This describes the procedural and technical knowledge required for a particular role, and will therefore vary between roles and functions.

The framework for defining individual roles across the company having been set, the competency profile of each role could be defined from a generic base. The approach had many benefits.

- It concentrated on inputs to a role rather than tasks to be completed and thus emphasized the benefits of process to achieve quality;
- It recognized the contribution of both technical skills and competencies to a role;
- It used customer needs as a focus for job design;
- It provided common elements by which jobs could be judged and ensured consistency of role definition across the company.

Competency and personal development

By defining what level and mix of competencies were necessary to perform effectively in each role it was possible to assess each job holder against the competency profile for their role. The profile therefore took on a second purpose, as a focus for personal development. This was planned according to the match of an individual's competencies against the profile for their role. It was therefore possible to plot the individual's level of competence in a particular area, identify where this fell below the level required in that role and thus assess development needs. In addition, the profile acted as a tool to help managers identify potential for progression into more senior roles or to areas in which currently underutilized competencies could be exploited.

Managers were required to engage in a dialogue with their staff, to confront issues of good and bad performance, and to address development needs. This represented a fundamental change in the managerial philosophy of the company. It underlined the importance of involving all staff in developing a quality approach and placed an onus on managers to highlight and address issues that constrained its development.

It was now possible for individual roles to be defined by three components:

- The *role definition* described the reporting relationships, main purpose and key elements of each role. This defines why the role exists within the company and the minimum expected returns.
- *Procedures* are contained within an operating manual and describe the standard forms and procedures for each role, thus ensuring consistent application of quality standards.
- *Core skills* are defined through the competency profile and are therefore consistent across all roles. For each role there is a level of competency which is required for the individual to perform effectively. The level of competency required will vary according to each role and falls within a range to allow for learning and progression.

As an example, the competency profile for a warehouse person is shown in Figure C.10. In this case, it is not necessary for all

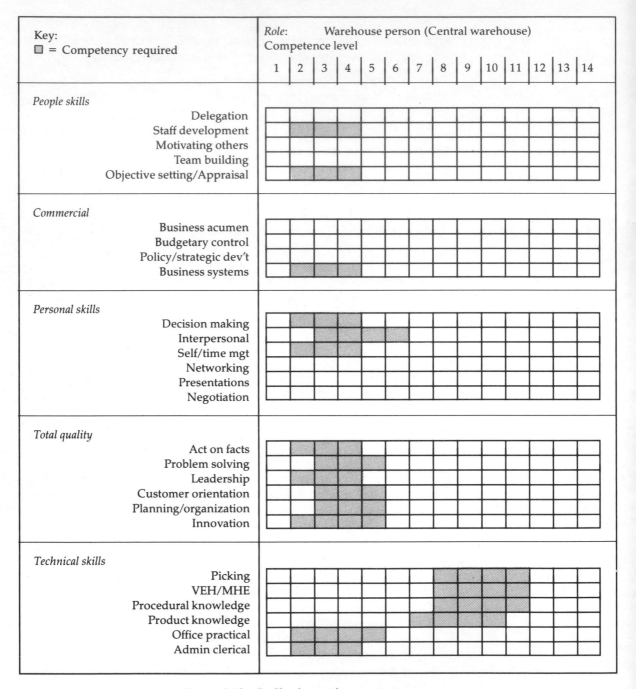

Figure C.10   *Profile of a warehouse person*

competencies to be displayed in order to perform effectively in that role; for example, the possession of competencies for delegation and business acumen are not viewed as a component of the job. However, as the profile shows, there is a requirement for interpersonal skills.

The pieces of the HR strategy were beginning to interlock. Having established competencies and a mechanism to identify variances, it was important to reinforce the new values by rewarding those staff who displayed quality behaviours.

Pay and grading

Another piece in the HR strategy jigsaw was pay and grading. One of the necessary building blocks in ensuring BSS had quality people was a fair, equitable and effective reward policy. Role evaluation provided the framework that enabled this to be put into practice.

A factor-based evaluation scheme was developed using factors consistent with the core competencies identified as determining success. As with the competency profile, definitions were attached to each of these together with a scoring system on a six-point scale, A to F. The factors identified were:

- people and leadership skills
- personal skills
- decision making
- change orientation
- role impact
- theoretical and technical knowledge
- skills acquisition and practice

A selection of framework roles was taken, which were seen to be representative of the majority of roles within the company. Each was assessed by a panel made up of staff from various levels and functions within BSS, to determine to what extent each displayed the factors listed above. From this assessment the panel was able to define the relative size of roles in the organization based on the particular values and competencies the company wished to promote. The careful definition of the factors ensured that the ranking of jobs reflected their contribution to the achievement of the BSS quality mission and thus gave a clear message to staff of changing values and culture.

However, the rewards policy had two further objectives:

- First, to reward people fairly and equitably, taking into account the different roles that people undertook and the different levels of performance they achieved in their role.
- Second, to ensure that total remuneration levels were at such a point compared with other employers that BSS was able to recruit and retain high-quality staff.

Linked to the role evaluation scheme was a market-facing pay and grading system. Following the application of consistent role evaluation criteria to ensure compliance with equal value legislation, jobs were clustered into job families. These families reflected the working patterns and location of staff and took into account desired progression routes. The three groups identified were head office, central warehouse and field staff. A grading structure was developed for each family and linked to market salary levels, taking into account BSS's desired market positioning. This approach had the advantage of allowing variable salary scales according to job family, so giving the company the ability to extend salary range maxima and maintain progression opportunities in volatile labour markets.

The individual's position within these salary scales depends upon:

- their position in the salary range and relationship to target salary
- their performance in their role judged against agreed objectives
- their progression in developing skills, discussed as part of a personal development plan and related to the level of competencies required in their role.

A scoring chart was developed to assist managers in this process. The chart was based on the competency and technical profiles, and provided a vehicle for the allocation of points according to performance and the achievement of objectives, and the development of competencies. The point system links into a recommended overall score which in turn feeds into pay levels. Points always fall into a range and the link to pay relates to a recommended salary range into which the individual is placed. Managers retain the discretion to award salary levels above this range in cases of exceptional performance.

The salary range is determined by the company's desired and actual positioning within the salary market and its ability to fund pay awards based on overall company performance. The pay and grading exercise therefore performed two main functions:

- It provided a mechanism to control structure costs;
- It was founded on the mix of competencies most likely to bring success and therefore provided a vehicle for cultural change by clearly rewarding the demonstration of quality values and behaviours.

Communicating the changes

For the first time in the history of BSS, the rewards system was being used as an open communicator of business objectives. The communication of the approach was therefore critical to the acceptance and application of the scheme.

A quality and HR director had been appointed at the beginning of the quality initiative to develop and implement the HR strategy. He was now to act as a missionary to ensure that the new approach was understood and accepted by managers and staff. He embarked upon a roadshow of all BSS offices to explain the new approach to quality, competency, performance and pay. This also underlined the company commitment to the quality philosophy and its determination to succeed. Visits and workshops were backed up by clear and user-friendly staff communications aimed at allaying fears of change and managing expectations. The content of the communications literature was generated through management workshops which attempted to pre-empt staff concerns and answer key questions on how salaries and performance were judged and managed.

Objective setting and appraisal

The final piece in the jigsaw was objective setting and appraisal. Objectives are set within the following categories, again to emphasize the link between individual behaviour and the achievement of corporate objectives:

- people
- commercial
- personal
- total quality

We have noted that the move from a closed to an open pay and grading structure was a fundamental change in the BSS management philosophy. Managers had to be prepared and able to take on the challenge of addressing staff pay, performance and development issues face to face. Significant time was invested in ensuring managers understood the logic and purpose of the new systems. The development needs of staff identified by the skills profile were also addressed.

The basis of the HR strategy was now in place. BSS had addressed:

- Recruitment and selection: ensuring consistency of company image and quality of recruitment procedures;
- People, development and performance: identifying the mix of competencies most likely to bring success and encouraging potential and self-development;
- Pay and grading: defining roles and rewarding quality behaviours;
- Training: supporting staff development and equipping managers to progress change.

Evaluating success

So how can we evaluate the strategy's success?

It should be said that managers did not immediately accept the value of the open, competency-based approach. Mark Parrish, quality and HR director at BSS, said: 'Going public with pay and grading closed off all the hiding places for managers and they were confronted with the enormity of the interpersonal skills required by the philosophy. The prospect of being questioned by their people generated a great deal of nervousness.' Of particular concern was matching the individual against the competency profile, together with measuring performance against agreed objectives. However, by building and selling the HR strategy piece by piece, managers were gradually able to see the value of the system as a support to their role. The systematic approach to pay and grading provided them with a rationale and a sound, logical defence for pay decisions.

From the employees' perspective, careful communication of the purpose of change and the new competency profile meant they had a clear understanding of the competency evaluation process and saw it as enhancing their career development prospects. There was an understanding of and a commitment to the quality philosophy which focused behaviour and performance towards customer satisfaction. With regard to the pay and grading system there was obvious concern among staff about how they would be affected by changes. Questions such as 'How did you decide my salary?' and 'If I work to develop my skills, will it be worthwhile?' were common. These concerns have been addressed by open and thorough communication and by training of managers. At this early stage in the scheme's development it is difficult to know whether this is sufficient. The reactions to results of salary reviews will provide a firmer basis on which to judge.

On the part of the managers, concerns were expressed over the results of the pay and grading review which upset traditional relativities through an emphasis on 'new' values. Problems were foreseen with the move to an open pay and grading system through the comparison of roles and the disturbance of internal relativities. Again, it is too early to gauge whether these fears are founded but every care is being taken to allay concern and present a fair and objective picture of new roles and relativities.

What is clear is that by using the total quality management approach to define the company's goals and philosophy, the HR strategy and systems are consistent with and support the business strategy. This has helped to ensure that the company's internal organization and management is aligned to and driven by the needs of the customer to enhance the company's position and the service it provides in a tight and competitive market.

The emphasis on competency development recognized the vast opportunity for organizational progress through focus on individual ability. BSS places value on each individual within the organization and emphasis on their development. As a result, the company and its employees are working towards a common goal and together are progressing to move that goal forward to achieve greater organizational and business success.

9 Using a competency approach in a business change setting

Viv Shackleton

The only thing that's certain is change.

In May 1989, Howard Hughes, the managing partner of Price Waterhouse UK, was quoted as saying:

Life is becoming very tough for firms in the middle ground. To stay in the big league requires tremendous investment in the future and the cost of that investment is enormous. Therefore, a certain size is essential. If you are caught trying to compete without the capacity to develop, you face real difficulties. A large number of national accounting firms are caught in that trap. (*Sunday Times*, 21 May)

He was responding to the mergers that had taken place, and would take place in subsequent years, in the accountancy profession. Just two days earlier, Ernst & Whinney and Arthur Young had announced that they were to combine to form Ernst & Young and become the world's largest accountancy firm at that time, with offices in more than 100 countries and billings of $4.3 billion.

At another level, what Hughes was referring to was change in the world of business. The last few years have seen enormous changes in many British industrial and commercial companies. Restructurings, redundancies, mergers, acquisitions, takeovers, bankruptcies are just a few of the words that hit the headlines and convey the notion of change to even the least business-aware person. Below this tip of the iceberg lies much more change, occurring every day and in every way, inside organizations themselves. The supposedly cosy world of the professions, and particularly the accountancy profession, has not escaped this onslaught of change.

Responding to the future is what continuing business success is all about. As Elwyn Eilledge, the proposed co-chairman of Ernst & Young International, said on that important day in May 1989: 'We are merging with an eye on the future, on the 1990s. I am sure other firms will be re-examining their strategies.'

They certainly will. But what Hughes, Eilledge and others may not have been aware of was that one of the 'middle ground' firms referred to by Hughes had been working hard for more than two years on just the problem he outlined. Their strategy was to invest, and invest heavily, in the development of their staff, using a competency-based approach.

This chapter sets out that firm's approach to the problem, the steps it went through and the eventual outcome. But before we describe the case of Finserv, we should examine the issues and options a manager faces when he or she wants to construct a forward-looking competency profile.

Future competencies

It is easy to think of competencies at the present time, as in, for example, the competencies required to do this present job of mine, or the essential competencies required in a candidate for a vacancy. But, as Charles Woodruffe states in Chapter 2, competencies should not be based solely in the past. Particularly in times of rapid changes in organizations and their environment, they should be forward-looking. They need to include those competencies which are becoming important or may become important over the coming few years. To do otherwise is to keep competencies and the organization rooted in the past.

However, arriving at future-oriented competencies is far from straightforward. There are a number of options or methods which can be employed, depending on the circumstances.

The main approach is to employ the usual methods of teasing out competencies, like repertory grid and critical incidents, but to push them constantly into a forward-looking frame of reference. So, elements in the repertory grid technique can be 'an ideal person for the newly created role' or 'someone who is most likely to be successful in the future' or 'someone who is good at seeing future requirements in the role'.

Similarly with critical incidents. Instead of just asking for examples of successful incidents and major failures ('dropped bricks'), respondents can be encouraged to think more about the future. They can be asked to imagine what incidents of critical success or failure are going to be increasingly seen in the future. And what successes and failures of the past or present the respondent thinks will become rarer or irrelevant.

Both the above techniques rely largely on hypothesizing. More pragmatic is looking at best practice from other companies in the same sector, or in other sectors undergoing similar strategic changes. In-depth interviews with those individuals in the company undergoing the change who have good knowledge of, and contacts with, the outside world can yield great insights into the competencies required for the future. So, more surprisingly, can inviting respondents to imagine how their best competitors do things. Or to imagine the best of all possible worlds. Given generous amounts on interview time, a skilled non-directive interviewer and an informed and communicative interviewee, much useful information of future competencies can be gained by in-depth interviews.

Other techniques sometimes employed are business scenarios and the

Delphi technique. Both involve speculating about the future, and so have much in common with forward-looking repertory grids, critical incidents or in-depth interviews. Business scenarios involve asking senior managers to imagine possible future events, good or bad, such as high growth, declining growth, turnaround situations, a merger, high profit, low profit, and so on. For each of these scenarios, the key managerial characteristics and competencies can be guessed at.

According to Greek mythology, people interested in seeing what fate had in store for them could seek the counsel of the Delphic oracle. Today, competency analysis similarly can be informed of the future by consulting experts. The Delphi technique is used mostly as a systematic way of collecting and organizing the opinions of several experts into a single decision. The process has many steps and starts by writing to experts who put forward ideas of the future. One person then collates all the individual responses and sends them to the experts, who comment on each of the collected ideas and propose future ideas. This process continues until there is a reasonable consensus of opinions. In the context of future-oriented competencies, these ideas might be concerned with the impact of new technologies, or working practices, or consumer demand, on job requirements. From this lengthy and extensive process, competencies which many people feel are the key ones for the future can emerge.

Background to Finserv

Now that we have explored the options to eliciting future competencies, let us return to the example of Finserv (short for Financial Services), a real but anonymous organization, well known to the author. They had a pressing need for a major business change, and based this firmly on a forward-looking competency profile.

For Finserv, the future looked bleak in 1987. It was caught in a trap. It wasn't big enough or small enough, and saw itself increasingly being squeezed.

Finserv is a medium-sized, British-based accountancy firm. It is one of the 'middle ground . . . national accounting firms' described by Hughes. So it is not one of the 'Big 8' that used to be, or the enormous five or six of the present time. But nor is it the small-scale, local accountancy partnership catering for a local clientele of shopkeepers, doctors, family firms or small limited companies. Both ends of this spectrum were doing well. The respectable, big, household name accountancy firms are attractive to major industrial and commercial companies for 'compliance work' (mostly auditing) and a host of other services from corporate finance to personal financial planning for directors, and not forgetting management consultancy, the growth business of the 1980s.

The smaller, local niche players were also not doing too badly. Because of their more personal nature, their lower fees and the convenience of having your accountant almost round the corner, they were surviving and in many cases prospering.

It is the middle market who had, and have, most to fear from the future.

They are not big enough to offer a complete range of services, nor do they have the credibility to appeal to the major blue-chip companies. But they are not small enough to win out over the three or four-partner firm.

Finserv has offices in many major towns and cities in Britain. It has links with continental European accountancy firms but no overseas offices solely its own. It has in the region of 150 partners with about half of them based in the City of London. London is not only the largest office, but by far the most profitable. It has also enjoyed the largest growth rate in fee income over the last five years.

Organization structure

The chief executive is called the managing partner. He is elected by fellow partners, and can be removed from this role and replaced at any time by a vote of partners. There is a management board, comprising eight partners, each responsible for a significant part of the business. These responsibilities are based mostly on geography (so there are the partners in charge of the London office, the Midlands, the South East, the North, etc.) but also by function (such as the partner in charge of management consultancy and the insolvency partner). The managing partner is, of course, also on the board and chairs the meetings. The management board is concerned with strategy, planning, rewards, senior appointments and promotions, and everything to do with important policy making and execution.

There are also business unit leaders. In London and the larger regional offices (Birmingham and Bristol, for example) these are the partners in charge of a functional unit such as auditing, insolvency, consultancy or corporate finance. Smaller offices have one business unit leader (BUL) in charge of all functions at the branch (so BUL Leicester or BUL Winchester, for example).

External environment

This has been changing rapidly recently. Since Big Bang in 1986, when there were major changes in the working of the London Stock Market, the environment has been much more competitive. There has also been major growth in the financial services market as a whole, particularly consultancy. The number of consultants in most of the Big 8 firms has increased at more than 20 per cent a year, year on year, for at least the last six years.

Along with this has gone a number of mergers and acquisitions. This has meant that medium-sized firms, like Finserv, have been squeezed and are prone to being taken over.

Issues

There were several issues that led to Finserv deciding on a competency-based approach to change.

Strategic perspective

If change is endemic in business, the place to start is the future. This in essence was the view of the managing partner of Finserv.

The issue was this. Like many small and medium-sized professional partnerships, Finserv had grown and prospered up to the time of this consultancy exercise without much conscious or formalized strategic planning. It was almost enough simply to 'be there' to attract custom. And the custom came neatly packaged. Clients' needs were for auditing, or for insolvency, or for help with an acquisition or a divestment, and so on. An expert would offer the client a specific service, whatever the nature of the client's business. If you wanted your books audited, it mattered little to the accountancy firm whether you were a ship builder or a manufacturer of toy trains, a high street retailer or a market gardener. And if you wanted additional services, say raising finance, you went either to another source, a merchant bank, or hopefully to another expert in the same accountancy partnership.

But clients were expecting more. Increasingly, they expected that an accountancy firm should offer a full range of services. More important still, the firm you chose would know about your business, be it cars, computers or kumquats.

The response of a number of firms has been to merge, as we have seen, in order to provide the necessary specialism. For others, it has been to become more niche players. A few middle-ranking firms, of similar size to Finserv, were beginning to make a name for themselves by specializing in just a few business sectors. One, for example, had established a reputation in travel, transport and tourism.

So Finserv had to change. No one saw this more clearly than the managing partner. And it had to change in a number of ways.

A managed business   First, it had to become a more 'managed' business. This meant greater emphasis on targets, fee generation, profitability, marketing and internal controls. Management had to become tighter and partners more accountable. Specifically, the managing partner was proposing that:

- The large number of small, fragmented clients should be rationalized;
- Non-profitable clients should be dropped;
- The marketing effort should be more targeted;
- A management information system should be introduced so that partners could see, on a day-to-day, week-by-week basis, how they and the firm were performing financially;
- Rewards for partners should be much more closely tied to performance;
- Partner fees should be increased to avoid them being lured away by attractive remuneration packages, as was happening;
- Non-performing partners should be sacked;
- Non-performing regional offices should be closed.

An entrepreneurial culture   By an entrepreneurial culture, the managing partner meant a lot of things, but they all centred around moving the firm's culture from a traditional accountancy one to a business success culture. Some of the ideas about a 'managed business' in the previous section relate to this, in the sense that they put in place reward and control mechanisms which encourage a concern for profitability and other indices of business success. But a managed business is mostly about managing the 'inside'. An entrepreneurial culture is more about managing the 'outside'.

By an entrepreneurial culture the managing partner meant:

- Identifying selling opportunities;
- Selling on from one service to another for the same client;
- Making presentations, liaising with bankers, attending conferences, networking, and so on, with the aim of meeting and selling to prospective clients;
- Improving partner skills in selling, presenting and understanding clients' needs;
- Offering services in new areas with new clients where an opportunity existed.

Both these two sets of changes, a managed business and an entrepreneurial culture, were summed up by the partner in charge of the London office. He said: 'One of the fundamental things we must try to do is to turn our accountants into business people.'

Why consider competencies?

Once the key business problem of Finserv had been articulated by the managing partner and his core team, and understood by the consultants, it was time to turn to practical action.

If Finserv was to develop in the way proposed by the managing partner and senior partners, it was important that each of the key players (mostly partners) understood the changes required and developed the competencies needed to carry the organization forward. An explicit, competency-based approach to cultural change has many advantages. First, couching change in competency language means that people more easily identify with the change. It becomes personal. It says 'these are the skills, qualities and attributes I and/or my colleagues must possess if we are to succeed'. Other, less personalized, culture change programmes have a poor record of success.

Second, the early stages of competency analysis, with interviews, repertory grids, and so on, often have the immediate effect of promoting thought and discussion about the future. The process of drawing up a list of the competencies required for successful performance in the future helps the organization articulate, often for the first time and in a public way, what it is asking of job holders and groups of individuals. Key job holders have a say in designing competencies for the future. Each person interviewed is forced to think strategically. And those not involved in formulating competencies will see in clearly stated terms how the organization views the future by learning through various feedback mechanisms what competencies are required for success.

Assessment development workshop

A major plank in the development of the organization was an assessment centre for development purposes. The terminology used was ADW (assessment for development workshops). Similar terms employed by others to describe the same or similar process are CDW (career development workshops), A4D (assessment for development) or just DC (development centres). But why was this 'technology' decided upon at all?

In any individual or business development, there are a number of steps:

1 First, the desired end point needs to be stated. This has already been described above.
2 This vision then needs to be couched in competency terms. So the skills, abilities, aptitudes and personal characteristics needed by the key players must be specified. The competencies must reflect the 'new organization' even more than the present one.
3 Then the competencies and aptitudes of the key players need to be assessed.
4 Gaps between 2 and 3 are then highlighted.
5 The key individuals themselves need to become aware of the competencies and any gaps in their portfolio of skills.
6 Training and development activities need to take place to close the gap.
7 Some individuals may choose not to make the changes needed by the new organization, or may not have the capacity for change. These people need to self-select themselves out of the system or be selected out by others. This may involve them leaving the organization altogether, or moving to less turbulent waters inside it.

The reader will see that the assessment centre technique with a developmental focus is ideally suited to this change in business culture and the demands it will place on key personnel.

The model   The model shown in Figure 9.1 outlines the thinking and stages behind the competency approach to business change at Finserv. In many ways the model appears little different from any model that one would expect

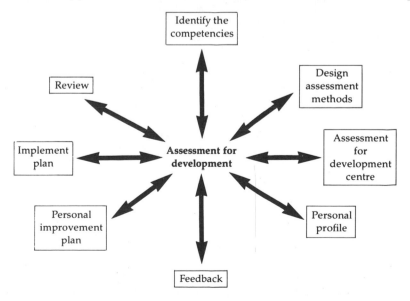

Figure 9.1 Competency-based business change: the model

to find describing any assessment for development exercise. However, there is a crucial difference. Within the box labelled 'Identify the competencies' lies the process of eliciting not only present competencies but also attempts to identify the competencies partners will need for the future. So the competency model is future-oriented. It reflects the strategic view of where the business should be going and what skills, abilities and personal qualities the key human resources will need to implement the strategy.

Job analysis methodology

The consultants who identified and made explicit the competencies had their job made easier by the clarity of the vision of the managing partner. He clearly expressed his view of the future direction of the business, and this has been outlined above.

However, it was important to check this strategic plan with other key decision makers within Finserv. To what extent did they all see the world in the same way? How much were they in agreement with the managing partner? Would they be prepared to pay the price of change? Most important of all, what competencies did they see as necessary for partners to possess in order for them to carry the organization forward?

So in-depth interviews were held with senior partners on a one-to-one basis. These interviews used repertory grid and critical incidents, focusing on key attributes and skills needed in the future. This allowed us to describe the vision in competency language. To this collective picture were added any major competencies which the consultants knew to be important in the management of a professional service business.

An example of a repertory grid will serve to convey the flavour of the interviews, which typically lasted around two hours. The repertory grid technique is developed from personal construct theory and personal constructs are personal and highly individual ways in which we view the world. The repertory grid is a way of obtaining these personal constructs. In competency analysis, the objective is usually to differentiate good performers from the poor in terms of competencies possessed. But it can be used to elicit competencies in a strategic change application, as explained at the beginning of this chapter. The constructs are elicited in the normal way by asking respondents to consider certain objects or concepts known as 'elements'. For future-oriented competencies, the elements should reflect the future.

In the Finserv study, elements varied, but the following serves as an example. There are a number of steps to elicit constructs. These are:

1 The interviewee is asked to think of three partner colleagues. Two of these should be close to the 'ideal' in terms of adopting the role expected of a partner in the next five years, while the third does not behave in this way. Let's call these two roles 'new role' and 'old role' respectively. There is no need for the respondent to name the people he or she is thinking of.
2 The interviewee is asked to describe how the two 'new role' individuals

are similar in the way they carry out their role as partner, and different from the 'old role' partner. For example, the respondent might say that the two 'new role' individuals are good presenters, unlike the third individual.

3 The next step involves the process of laddering. The partner is probed on the original construct, in this case presentation skills, in order to gather more detail. This can include what the respondent means by this construct, how they know the person is a good presenter, what behaviours indicate it, to whom they present, how, when, in what ways the 'old role' person doesn't present well, and so on.

4 When the laddering or probing is complete, the process is repeated. The respondent is asked to think of other ways in which the two individuals differ from the third, and this construct is probed to make it concrete. When the first three individuals chosen give rise to no new constructs, the respondent is asked to think of another trio of colleagues, and the process continues until the person interviewed runs out of constructs or is starting to repeat ones given earlier in the interview.

The point to note in this example is that the interviewee is being encouraged to think in terms of future role requirements for job incumbents, not only present requirements. The elements were 'new role' and 'old role'. Other elements that were employed were major aspects of the 'new organization' as seen by the managing partner. So respondents were asked to think about colleagues who took a 'strategic perspective' or were 'entrepreneurial' versus those who were less so. Successful competitors were also used as elements to elicit constructs which described how their ways of working were different from Finserv's current methods. The important issue is that repertory grids, in-depth interviews and critical incidents can each be used in parallel, as was the case with Finserv, to explore future scenarios so as to build a more complete picture of future-oriented competencies.

As a result of this process, a list of competencies was drawn up. These are given below, each with a brief definition.

List of competencies for partners

1 *Identifying selling opportunities*   Being alert to and acting on indications of opportunities for expansion of existing business into new areas of the client company and/or diversification into new categories of business.

2 *Understanding the client/colleague in their own terms*   Active listening, clarifying, reflecting back the content and feeling behind statements, avoiding jargon and misinterpretation.

3 *Commercial awareness*   Using questions and statements to indicate an understanding of the totality of the business, i.e. strategy, marketing, competition, etc., as well as its financial structure.

4 *Flexibility*   Modifying own approach or style in order to achieve set goals.

5　*Communicating persuasively and effectively*　Clear and fluent oral communication of ideas with persuasive impact on the listener; clear, concise written communication.

6　*Goal setting*　Setting realistic targets, quantifiable or behavioural, that are well-defined, specific and measurable.

7　*Encouraging and building on ideas*　Assessing ideas objectively and building on them; encouraging (verbally and non-verbally) others to contribute; avoiding irrational criticism.

8　*Giving feedback*　Commenting on both the negative and positive aspects of others' behaviour and performance in a clear, balanced and constructive way.

9　*Delegating*　Effective use of colleagues; knowing when, how and to whom to delegate responsibility.

10　*Leadership*　Ability to guide and direct individuals or groups towards the achievement of objectives; taking the initiative.

11　*Helping groups to achieve consensus*　Looking for common ground; mediating between opposing views; being prepared to compromise on own views (after full discussions) for sake of group.

For the workshop, longer, behavioural indicators for each competency were provided for delegates. An example for the fifth criterion, communicating persuasively and effectively, is shown in Figure 9.2. Providing

---

Behavioural indicators: Communicating persuasively and effectively

Oral communication

- Explains complex information in a clear and concise way
- Demonstrates enthusiasm, interest and conviction when presenting ideas
- Non-verbal behaviour to support the spoken word, e.g. eye contact, gestures, posture

Formal presentation

- Uses a clear logical structure for presentation; emphasizes main themes; clearly links themes together
- Uses language, free of jargon, which is meaningful and at an appropriate level for the needs of the audience
- Uses appropriate visual aids, examples to relate key messages
- Maximizes use of time to convey messages and actions
- Is a confident presenter

Written communication

- Uses simple, concise, grammatically correct English
- Structures written communication and includes key information, supporting data, conclusions and recommendations; clear links between analysis and conclusions where appropriate.

Figure 9.2　*Behavioural indicators for the competency 'Communicating persuasively and effectively'*

detailed descriptions of criteria in terms of behavioural indicators serves a number of purposes. It explains fully what the workshop was designed to assess and develop among participants. It provides detailed information for participants when they come to assess their ability to perform in relation to the criteria. Finally, and crucially, it is a clear way of signalling to partners the importance of the competency for their own success and for the success of the firm.

Design assessment methods

It is at this point that the more scientific, systematic methods used earlier in the process, such as repertory grid or key attribute interviews, have to give way to artistry or craftsmanship. For there is no easy way to turn competencies into exercises which measure and develop them.

The workshop at Finserv comprised talks, discussions, exercises, simulations and tests. Each 'hands-on' activity (exercise, test or simulation) was designed to measure a number of competencies. So, in typical assessment centre style, each activity measured more than one competency and each competency was measured by more than one activity. The resulting matrix is shown in Figure 9.3.

Development centre

The assessment for development workshop (ADW) comprised a number of activities. These included:

- group discussion
- client meeting exercise
- coaching role play
- strategy and leadership talk and discussion
- psychometrics
- personal profile and feedback
- personal improvement plan

Group discussion

Here six or seven participants (the typical number on a workshop) were each provided with information unique to them, consisting of data on a fictitious department within an organization, as well as general information on the whole issue (the problem faced by the organization as a whole). They met as a committee to discuss where economies could be made. In essence, the exercise was one of negotiation and cooperation. They were asked to persuade their fellow committee members of the soundness of their individual case, but also to come to a consensus regarding cuts for the organization as a whole. A summary of the brief for participants is shown below.

Brief for group discussion

Task 1   Individual

You are a member of the Finance Committee which will determine the basis on which cuts in budgets to a number of departments within your company will be made. Seven departments (the number corresponding to the number of participants) and budgets are under threat of cuts and have been singled out for further investigation.

Designing and achieving competency

Exercise/Activity

Competency	Group discussions	Client meeting	Coaching	Strategy/leadership talk & test	Psychometric			Whole workshop
					A	B	C	
Selling		✔	✔	✔				
Understanding client		✔		✔		✔		
Commercial awareness	✔	✔	✔					
Flexibility		✔			✔			✔
Communicating	✔	✔	✔				✔	✔
Goal setting	✔	✔	✔			✔		
Encouraging ideas	✔	✔	✔		✔		✔	
Giving feedback		✔	✔			✔		
Delegating	✔			✔		✔		
Leadership	✔			✔			✔	
Consensus seeking	✔	✔			✔			

Figure 9.3   Competency matrix

You are also a representative of one of the seven departments that are under threat. You will be required to present a case of why you believe your department should be saved from the cuts. It is essential for the future of your department that you should put forward the best case you can. The staff and the work of the department depend on how well you represent your case.

Your fellow committee members will also be presenting the case for each of the other departments.

To help you compose a case, some facts and figures are provided together with some qualitative data that will indicate the key strengths and weaknesses of your particular department. All other committee members will receive a copy of the facts and figures but not the qualitative data. It is up to you to sell your case to the committee.

Task 2   Group consensus

In addition to presenting your case to the committee as a committee member, you are responsible, together with the other committee members, for drawing up the criteria and reaching agreement on which departments will face the cuts next. The committee has been asked to draw up a priority listing of seven departments. Those departments at the top of the list will face the next round of cuts. The aim of the group is to achieve genuine consensus and not to use such methods as voting or averaging in order to reach a decision.

Limitations of the exercise

1 It is not intended that you should use the figures provided in a totally definitive way. They are there as a guide to relative strengths and weaknesses across all seven departments.
2 The exercise is not intended to measure your numerical analytical skills, but your ability to present a persuasive case and operate effectively within the group to arrive at a consensus decision.

Timing

You will have 3 minutes to present your case to the committee.

You will have 30 minutes for the group discussion, following the presentations.

Criteria for assessment

1 To what extent you demonstrate leadership of the discussion.
2 How effectively you help the group to achieve genuine consensus.
3 How effectively you encourage, develop and evaluate ideas from others.
4 To what extent you demonstrate a flexible approach.

This exercise has been described in some detail since it provides the reader with the format not just for this exercise, but for all exercises in the workshop. Points to note are:

• Participants are given adequate preparation time;
• They are fully briefed. They also know in principle the information that other delegates have received;
• Most importantly, they are told what competencies are being assessed by each activity, so they know the targets to aim for.

There was also a second group exercise, focusing around consensus seeking and cooperation among the team.

Client meeting exercise   Here participants were asked to sell the services offered by Finserv to a prospective client. It was a role play of an initial meeting with a finance director or similar person in a prospective client organization. Delegates were provided with information on the client company such as annual report and accounts, textline data and newspaper cuttings. The client company was real, though the client person was an actor. The role of client can be played by any knowledgeable, plausible individual, preferably not known to the participant.

Coaching role play

Similar in format to the client role play, this exercise was designed to assess and develop the skills of feedback to subordinates. It involved giving feedback, understanding a colleague's goals and encouraging and building on ideas.

Delegates were asked to meet with a colleague for 15 minutes during which time the participant aimed to find out what the colleague's main development needs were for the coming year, such as new areas of work and/or new skills to be acquired.

Strategy and leadership talk

Here the managing partner talked to the participants about the senior management's view of the future and its strategic importance for the health of the firm.

There was also guided discussion on questions of leadership, using a model of leadership, to raise the awareness of delegates to the issues of managing a team and leading the firm towards a new future.

Psychometrics

Three separate inventories were used to help delegates gain greater self-insight and to tap key competencies, as shown in the matrix in Figure 9.3.

Personal profile and feedback

The whole workshop lasted 48 hours. By the time the above activities had taken place, something like 40 hours had elapsed. Once this stage of the workshop had been reached, two key elements of the process could begin. These were to construct a personal profile and conduct a feedback session for the participants, as shown in the model in Figure 9.1.

Each partner on the workshop was offered an individual feedback and counselling session with the consultants. This served to pull together all the data on the individual so as to point to individuals' performance on the workshop, their strengths and weaknesses, training and development needs and other matters concerning the partner's career. Each partner had the chance to discuss these matters subsequently with his or her immediate superior after the workshop was complete. A written summary was also provided to the workshop participants but they were under no obligation to show it to anyone else, inside or outside Finserv. All this leads to the final key element, a personal improvement plan.

Personal improvement plan

Participants were able to focus immediately on their own development needs both for the present and, more importantly, for the future. This allowed them to know clearly where they could work to improve their competency. That in turn should have a direct and beneficial impact on their work performance and the performance of the firm as a whole.

Outcomes and evaluation

The exercise had a very stimulating effect on the participants. Some of the partners emerged as clearly able and willing to develop themselves and their roles in the partnership, and having the competencies to carry the firm forward to higher levels of service and performance. Others, while perhaps fully effective in their present roles, identified the changes taking place, and their ability or willingness to change too, as something they had doubts about. They had been forced by the ADW to consider their strengths, weaknesses and preferences and hence their future career aspirations.

Crucially, the exercise enabled the firm to communicate expectations to partners in terms of performance standards for the future. It allowed both senior management and the partners themselves to predict who had the capacity to take on the challenges of the future, and where their individual talents could be most usefully employed.

There were numerous ways in which implementation took place. These included training, counselling, mentoring, a job move, a reorganization of a department, greater emphasis on interdepartmental cooperation, a team-building workshop for a regional office, and many other small-scale initiatives. And, of course, the implementation and review process is still going on.

All participants on all the workshops agreed that the rewards were beneficial and immediate. The partner in charge of the London office was unequivocal. He said:

When these weekends started, you could sense the resistance. But meeting those who took part in the first one immediately afterwards, they were all positive about it. To have got them to think about themselves, to face up to their strengths and weaknesses, was really something.

The firm's personnel director, who was instrumental in commissioning the work and aiding in the design, was equally positive about the workshop:

It has raised the awareness that you have got to be more than just a technician. It has got everyone interested in what is going on. For the first time ever, we are now beginning to know what we have got in terms of human resources.

Application issues

Applying competency analysis to any organizational issue is not something that can be done simply, as previous chapters have made plain. There are some additional issues that have to be faced when applying a competency-based approach to strategic change situations. The main one is, how certain or confident can one be that one has identified the key competencies for the future? The answer is, of course, that one can never be certain. Much depends on whether the vision or mission is a correct one for the organization. And that may never be known. To the extent that an appropriate strategy has been formulated, then competencies derived from it will undoubtedly help the strategy to succeed. This is not just because key players have a chance to develop the competencies required by the organization. It is because competencies can give a language to the whole organization, a language that expresses in practical terms what has to be done to succeed 'around here'. Competencies help articulate strategies in terms people understand because it relates to what they do.

Another issue in competency analysis concerns identifying the gaps. Repertory grids, critical incidents, and other techniques help formulate what employees feel are the key competencies now and in the future. But often, it is what gets left out that is instructive. No one in a major retail chain where we recently conducted a competency analysis ever mentioned the issue of quality; a professional partnership never mentioned internal customer service, i.e. between departments, and a manufacturer never mentioned staff development. Skilled practitioners of competency analysis learn to help an organization to see that what gets left out of their list of competencies for the future can be as important for the successful implementation of the strategy as what is included.

Finally, this chapter has concentrated on a vision driving the competencies. The reverse can sometimes be true. The need to specify competencies can act as a spur towards creating a top management vision, where one doesn't exist. Encouraging respondents to think through what skills, aptitudes and abilities will be increasingly needed by their organization can move the organization towards a more complete picture of where it is headed.

Pointers for success

Finally, we need to look at why the assessment for development process was a success in helping the partnership adjust to business changes. Some of the keys to the success of the exercise are:

- The assessment for development process was clearly focused strategically right from the start.
- This was incalculably helped by a visionary chief executive, who saw clearly where the profession as a whole was headed.
- There was a sophisticated personnel director. He was able to develop a strategy for human resources management as an integral part of the corporate strategy.
- The personnel director was familiar with the language of competency and saw the potential of the ADW approach.
- There was also a good degree of consensus among the partners of what was needed for the future, even if to start with they were unsure who or what was needed to take them there.
- After initial hesitation, there was organizational commitment to the competency-based approach from the very top down.
- The firm and its partners had virtually no experience of management development. Yet they had a willingness to learn about themselves and to develop once the need had been highlighted.

PART THREE

An assessment of the strengths and weaknesses of competency-based approaches

10 Where do we go from here?

Paul Sparrow and Rosemary Boam

Existing competency work

In attempting to review the 'state of the art' within the competency field and identify 'where we do go from here' there are two fundamental issues that need to be addressed. These are:

- How do you extend the 'shelf life' of the competencies identified and ensure that they are forward-looking?
- How do you get competency-based approaches deeper into existing personnel systems?

Most managers would only wish to consider the second issue—getting competencies deeper into the personnel systems—once they felt they had built a sufficiently sound basis for doing so by resolving the first issue.

Previous chapters in this book have demonstrated how competency-based approaches can be used very effectively to tackle problems in recruitment, development, performance management and the management of change. In this sense they are capable of providing:

- the 'glue' to integrate recruitment, reward and development strategies;
- a focal point for cultural change.

But can competency-based approaches be used to address the pressing strategic change issues and triggers outlined in Chapter 1? The answer, we feel, is a qualified yes. The qualifications are concerned with the limited use of competencies in some application areas, and a number of methodological issues needed to strengthen the analysis and identification of competencies. Most applications of competency-based approaches to date have been in connection with the identification and assessment of individual potential focused on a target job as part of a recruitment or career development process. Less attention has been given to the analysis of competencies which encompass a broad perspective, such as for roles, career streams, the management of sector or business activities, or competencies that relate to the organizational strata. Where analysis has been undertaken on a broad basis, it tends to be directed towards areas of competence or minimum standards of performance (such as the MCI initiative).

In Chapter 2, Woodruffe defines competencies in relation to a 'position', but acknowledges that the position may encompass broader levels such as roles or career streams. However, in Chapter 7, Craig rightly pointed out that once competencies are derived at a level of analysis beyond a target 'job' position, there is a danger that the resultant behavioural indicators become too generalized, and therefore lose much of their power. This is indeed true, but we feel in many cases this merely reflects poorly constructed or thought-out analysis methods. As individuals we can still bring sets of behaviour patterns that are appropriate to, and can be analysed in relation to, broader roles, career streams or business issues.

Another criticism that can be levelled against competency-based approaches is that the proliferation of work aimed at considering individual-to-job fit has made it quite legitimate to rely heavily on analysis techniques that primarily provide evidence of existing or past perform- ance. However, in order for competency-based approaches to be used in this more strategic fashion we need to develop the methodology. Many of the data-gathering techniques are also limited by the 'imagination' of the individual being interviewed. Simply selecting the 'best performers' will not always address the problem. The best performers in a job that is designed in a way that produces low customer service might not be the people to interview about this competency. In many cases, the demand to understand a new competency comes at a time when the job holders' knowledge of the competency is at its lowest! Identifying the competencies required is an educational process in itself and the need to use techniques that help clarify this learning should not be ignored.

The potential of the approach to realize the significant business benefits gained by addressing future business issues has therefore been largely untapped. Morgan (1989) has pointed out that:

In developing managerial competencies we must do more than drive through the rear view mirror. It is not enough to look at what excellent organisations and managers are already doing. It is also necessary to be proactive in relation to the future: to anticipate some of the changes that are likely to occur and to position organisations and their members to address these challenges effectively.

This chapter therefore concentrates on the need to ensure that competency-based approaches are dynamic in nature, rather than becoming the 'dodo looking for a mate'. It introduces a number of methodologies, tools, techniques and practical examples that demon- strate ways in which traditional competency-based approaches can be enriched by a future focus. In so doing it attempts to answer the following questions:

- When is it appropriate to make a competency profile forward-looking?
- What does good performance mean when we talk about the future?
- Can we assign a 'life cycle' or 'shelf life' to competencies?
- How do we move from profiling competencies to forecasting future requirements?
- Can we push competency-based approaches deeper into existing per- sonnel systems?
- What have we got to do to link competencies to specific strategic busi- ness issues?

Forward-looking profiles

We have said that one of the strongest criticisms of competency-based approaches is that the profiles draw too strongly upon historical evidence. They also base profiles on the mindset of individuals to date. By design, therefore, it is extremely difficult for such techniques to gather information about the future. Frequently, job holders who are providing the information comment: 'But of course it is all going to be very different in the next few years, isn't it?' The answer is invariably yes. The need to capture as much forward-looking 'intelligence' and build it into the competency identification process cannot be overstated.

In deciding how to balance and draw the line between competencies that are grounded in, and supported by, current performance data, and those forward-looking competencies that are more intuitively derived, managers need to be clear about two issues: what is the competency information going to be used for and what do we really mean by 'effective performance'?

A range of reasons for taking a competency-based approach were highlighted in Chapter 1. More forward-looking techniques should be considered if it is likely that the competency profiles will be used to:

- identify the requirement for future managers;
- recruit people who will be able to cope with the present and the future;
- plan long-term personal development;
- address business or strategic issues.

As a basis for these issues we need to establish how the current requirements will change and what new competencies will be required. In view of this it is necessary to move away from one of the acknowledged strengths of competency-based approaches, i.e. their use of scientific and psychometrically sound techniques to derive hard and observable evidence of the behaviour patterns associated with effective performance. Once we consider the future we have to incorporate a more intuitive definition of 'effective performance' based on a process of deduction. This may give some academic purists a feeling of unease, but in most cases the business justification used to support the high investment of time and money to identify competencies in itself make the argument valid.

Good future performance

The most obvious criterion for effective performance is 'whatever is needed to achieve results'. When the environment is known it is sensible to base this definition around successful job performance. When the environment is not known we change our criterion of effective performance. Cockerill (1989) has described how National Westminster Bank based their future competencies around the need for high performance in a high change (unknown) environment, i.e. What is it that managers have to do to be able to react to and capitalize on high levels of change? Woodruffe has outlined these competencies in Chapter 2. He made the useful distinction between talking about competencies for change—and the need for changing competencies.

Performance criterion	*'. . Being effective in a turbulent world'*	*'. . Enabling organiz- ational change to happen'*	*'. . Creating strategic and sustainable advantage'*
Organization	SHELL CANADA/ YORK UNIVERSITY COMPETENCIES PROJECT	BRITISH PETROLEUM	CADBURY SCHWEPPES
Reference	Morgan (1989)	Bognanno (1990)	Dale (1990)
C	*Contextual* Building bridges and alliances Reframing problems to create new solutions Acting nationally and locally Social responsibility	*Open thinking*	*Adaptability*
	Reading the environment Scanning and intelligence functions Forecasting and futurism Scenario planning Identifying fracture lines	*Personal impact* Bias for action Knows what makes others tick Concern for impact Self-confidence	*Decisiveness* Innovation Integrity
O **M**	*Proactive management* Proactive mindset Managing from the outside in Positioning and repositioning skills	*Empowering* Coaching and developing Building team success Motivating	*Leadership* Risk taking
P	*Leadership and vision* Using vision to frame action Communicating an actionable vision	*Networking* Influencing others Reaching others Shared achievement	*Self-motivation* Vision
E **T** **E**	*Empowering people* Valuing people as key resources Developing abilities to relish change Blending specialist and generalist qualities		

N
Managing in an environment of equals

Remote management
Helicoptering
Managing through an umbilical cord
Promoting self-organization
Managing ambiguity
Making specialist staff user-driven

C

Creativity, learning and innovation
Developing an appropriate corporate culture
Encouraging learning and creativity
Striking a balance between chaos and control

I

Using information technology as a transformational force
Developing new products/services
New network concepts of organization
New work designs
Real time decision making
Planning with evolution in mind
Information management mindsets
Strategic role of software

E

S

Managing complexity
Managing multiple stakeholders
Managing many things at once
Managing transition

Figure 10.1 Future performance criteria and associated competencies

The approach taken by organizations like Shell Canada (Morgan, 1989), British Petroleum (Bognanno, 1990) and Cadbury Schweppes (Dale, 1990) has been to define and characterize effective performance in the future in terms of *those behaviours that enable organizational change to happen*. This equates to the idea of 'competencies for changeability' discussed by Woodruffe in Chapter 2. Figure 10.1 outlines the competencies these organizations derived.

In justifying the need to move towards more forward-looking competency profiles it is important to avoid extremes. In the examples given it can be seen that some of the indicators represent clear competencies, while others have reverted back to generic areas of competence, albeit relevant ones. To realize the power of such profiles the implications for competencies should be tested out against the most appropriate hypotheses about the future in a way that is still sensitive to the organization's context.

There is a very thin line between intuitive deduction and speculation. In throwing lots of relevant-sounding behaviours at the future it is easy to create 'laundry lists' of desirable characteristics and behaviours which may—but there again may not—bear any resemblance to what will actually be needed to achieve results. Forward-looking competency profiles should represent powerful distillations of effective behaviours linked to a number of defensible hypotheses about the organization's future. Woe betide the organization that bases its personnel systems around a trendy 'wish list' that picks up all the latest writings of the management gurus, but little else.

Competency life cycles

The one thing we can be certain about is that we will have to live with complexity in the future. Peters and Quinn (1988) point out that our view of what constitutes effective performance will inevitably be dynamic and changing. We need to develop a more flexible framework about the relevance of competencies to the present and future, and appreciate that the more forward-looking our 'intelligence' is, the lower the degree of specificity and therefore the less worthwhile it will be to invest in it. But it is clear that as an organization moves through different business environments, or itself matures, then the relevance that any one competency has is bound to alter.

Rather than creating generic lists of competencies that are associated with 'coping with change' or 'making change happen', we should develop a more sophisticated picture of competencies at the organizational level by thinking of any particular competency as having a life cycle. In Chapter 2 Woodruffe argued that a categorization of competencies in terms of time would have some merits. The relevance of any competency to an organization (or to a career stream, or individual job) will wax and wane. Standing in the present and looking out to the future, we would expect to see four different categories of competency (Figure 10.2).

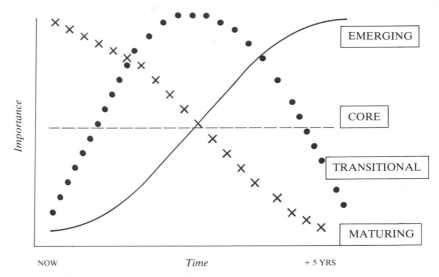

Figure 10.2 *Competency life cycles*

Emerging   Some competencies may be termed 'emerging'. These competencies may not be particularly relevant to the organization and its jobs at present, but the particular strategic path the organization is pursuing will undoubtedly place greater emphasis on them in the future. For example, a public sector organization that was in the process of privatizing in the late 1980s was able to identify that the demands of planned price control regimes, regulated standards of customer service, business diversification, shareholder expectations of increased profitability, and devolution of responsibility within the business would increase the need for its senior managers to demonstrate more outward-looking behaviour, commercial and competitive awareness, anticipation and planning of business change, better utilization of resources and a general shift away from the management of activities towards the leadership of people. In designing a career management system to identify and fast-track managers capable of performing successfully in this new environment, the organization had to be able to identify competencies that no amount of interrogation of existing managers would have evidenced.

Maturing   In other cases the opposite applies. Some competencies may be called 'maturing'. They may have played an important part in organizational life (and the jobs within it) in the past, but will become increasingly less relevant in the future.

Transitional   A third category of competency may be termed 'transitional'. Take an organization that wants to identify some senior managers to head up a new business area as it embarks on a major business expansion and acquisition programme. In the early stages of their new role these managers will probably be required to demonstrate a high capacity to live with uncertainty, to manage stress (in themselves and their new colleagues), to cope with pressure and manage conflict. Because these competencies are associated with negative aspects of the future—and may only be relevant for a short period of time—they may be over-looked when competencies are being identified. Yet the change can only be achieved or managed smoothly by placing greater emphasis on these competencies. They are transitional but represent an integral part of the change process and so are still highly relevant.

Core   Finally, there is a fourth category of competency which may be termed 'stable' or 'core'. These are enduring competencies that will remain as important tomorrow as they are today. In any organization environment there will be competencies that remain at the heart of effective perform-ance despite the current or forthcoming flavour of the business plan and its strategic direction. Evans (1991) observes that we are in danger of becoming obsessed with change, improvement and transformation at the expense of those competencies needed for continuity and imple-mentation. Reasoning or analytical ability are likely to be core competencies in most settings. Other core competencies may relate to the way business is carried out in the particular industrial sector the organization is in. The health service has received much attention in relation to the management of change, but examples can be found in which a fascination with the future led to serious difficulties. A depart-ment within a health authority was about to undergo a major change, converting to agency status. Competency profiles were established in order to recruit a group of external managers into senior positions. The profile included the expected new focus on communication skills, strategic planning, and so forth. However, subsequent comparison to competency work done elsewhere in the health authority showed that, in focusing on the future priorities, the profile had totally overlooked a number of core competencies that would be critical for the new managers. These included organizational and political sensitivity. The managers who were recruited were in fact very poor in these areas. The result was that they failed miserably in their task and the high investment was wasted. The need to build in core competencies that provide continuity should not be lost.

Updating competency profiles   In thinking about—and classifying—competencies as being stable, emerging, declining or transitional, it becomes easier to understand the need to attach a 'shelf life' to any competency profile. Clearly, the rela-tive focus or weighting that can be given to a competency will change in proportion to the speed of change within the business environment and nature of the job. However, through the process of classifying competencies in relation to their life cycle as described, it can be seen that the time and cost spent in an 'updating process' need not be as onerous as some critics might suggest. The more forward-looking the profile is, the longer its shelf life. The more it is possible to classify competencies, the easier it is to update only those competencies that have a changing emphasis. The questions to be asked are:

• Have the 'emerging' competencies become so relevant that they become a central part of the profile from now on?
• Have the 'maturing' competencies now become of such reduced

importance that it is no longer worth investing in them?
- Do we still need to consider the transitional competencies?

The first exercise in updating such a competency profile is likely to be one of shifting the weighting given to various competencies, rather than having to re-establish their existence all over again. It is of course impossible to put a finite figure in years, months and days on any profile. However, it would be reasonable to assume that when the life cycle of the competencies that make up a profile is considered, an organization would only need to re-identify the competencies once every three years or so.

Competency requirement forecasting

What we have been describing in this chapter is a new approach in the competency area. Rather than talking about 'competency profiling'—which implies examining existing and/or historical competencies, or considering generic areas of competency to cope with change—a pressing requirement is for organizations to undertake 'competency requirement forecasting'. In order to reap all the benefits of a competency approach, it becomes essential to extend the shelf life of the profiles. Unless this can be done, few organizations will feel that they are getting sufficient return on their investment. It is, we believe, possible to maintain a sound basis for identifying competencies while incorporating an element of forecasting. The main elements of such a methodology are outlined in Figure 10.3 and developed throughout the rest of this chapter.

Top-down clarification

The most important reason for starting a competency requirement forecasting process—with top-down clarification of the strategy, the organizational drivers and job demands—is to ensure that the competencies that are identified are set in context. There is a time and a place for any behaviour within an organization, and it is only by setting the scene that we will know if it remains an appropriate behaviour that will produce the desired outcomes.

This scene setting, as previous authors have commented, is best done by a group of senior managers and strategists. In some cases, as for example in the case described by Shackleton in Chapter 9, the organization may have already gone through a period of thinking about its future and the general strategy, mission and values may be neatly laid out. However, in many cases, the managers responsible for implementing a competency-based approach do not have the benefit of such clear thinking. The senior managers themselves may still see the future as being as clear as mud—or even worse may each be working on their own (different) assumptions about what will constitute effective performance.

How can you forecast competencies in the absence of a ready formulated business strategy? In our experience, organizations can draw upon the following approaches:

- 'Visioning' workshops designed to help managers articulate and clarify their underlying thoughts about a particular aspect of the organization, its structure, or job roles;

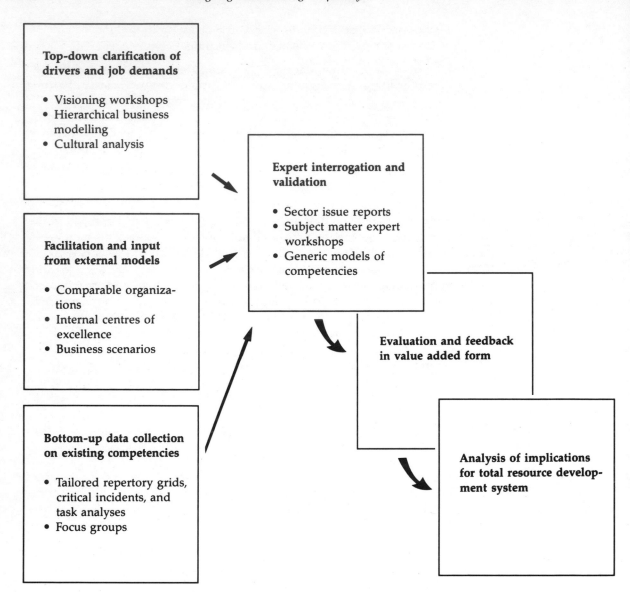

Figure 10.3   Stages in competency requirement forecasting

- Hierarchical business modelling to establish the key functions and tasks necessary to achieve effective performance in new business areas or services;
- Analysis of the desired versus the existing culture of the organization.

Visioning workshops   It is not the purpose of job analysts constructing a competency requirement forecast to create a strategy or mission for an organization that does not have one. However, the analyst does need to have a clear—and agreed—picture of the resulting vision. In Chapter 3, Kandola and Pearn pointed out the need to undertake values-driven analysis of jobs in order to identify competencies in situations where the changes are not entirely understood by current job holders. It is necessary to know:

- What are the success criteria that will be associated with a particular role, job or career stream in the future?
- What will this mean for performance?

A workshop run for a financial services organization helps to illustrate the stages involved in a visioning workshop. The organization was in the process of introducing a new organization structure within its IT department. As a result the job holders had taken on new responsibilities and accountabilities. They experienced new reporting relationships within their own department, were talking to different customers and were facing very different (and higher) expectations about their performance. The key problem facing the organization was how to create new career streams within the organization and how to identify the most appropriate staff for progression. Launching into a traditional competency analysis would either pick up old ways of working, or very variable (and as yet poorly understood) work practices. The vision of what the future roles were supposed to be about had not been articulated, and this had to be done before any analysis of the competencies involved could progress.

The workshop participants were senior managers, and the process was used to help clarify and express their thoughts about the future and then convert this into performance expectations about the role(s) in question. Such a workshop usually takes managers through a number of logical stages. Typical questions to be tackled by group or individual work include:

- What are the problem areas with the existing roles?
- What sort of changes in the roles has the reorganization brought about?
- What aspects of people's work have changed?
- How are these changes intended to be achieved?
- What further changes in the outside world and within the organization will impact the roles?

As a result of this thought process the participants grouped the resulting statements into a series of dimensions. In the example of systems development project management roles, the vision was expressed under the four main headings of organization, culture, management control and people.

The next stage was to build on this clarified vision of the future roles by pursuing a new line of questioning. Under each dimension and against each main factor agreed upon by the managers, the line of questioning was:

- What will you see in the organization or the performance of the job holders to evidence the desired criterion?
- What are the most appropriate outputs or achievements?
- Why are these important?
- How might these be measured?

The result was a precisely defined set of success criteria—expressed in terms of desired events or outputs. Running the workshop made it much easier to consider subsequently the underlying competencies associated with the new role demands.

Hierarchical business modelling

Visioning workshops can be used to clarify and articulate a poorly understood picture of the future. In some situations, a more detailed understanding of the future may already exist. All that is needed is a technique to convert this understanding into a picture of future competency demands. In this situation hierarchical business modelling techniques—in which business experts are taken through an analysis process that identifies all the business functions required for a service and activity and then breaks these functions down into their components—can be used to build up the understanding. The approach is very similar to hierarchical task analysis which is used to analyse the tasks carried out in a job. The only difference is that functions are analysed at the business service or activity level. These models can be used to break down a planned business function into the requisite tasks and activities. Comparison between existing functions and planned functions identifies the new and deleted tasks. Traditional job analysis techniques such as those described in Chapters 3 and 5 can then be adapted to analyse the competency demands that the new business functions will create.

Cultural analysis

In some cases, the detailed business functions may as yet be unclear, but the culture that will be necessary—the values, attitudes and behaviours that staff will need in order to be successful—may be clear. A number of questionnaires have been designed by academics or consultancies to represent dimensions of culture (PA Consulting Group, 1990; Trompenaars, 1991). These—or any tailored set of questions—can be used to establish data on the existing culture and the desired (or implied) culture that results from the business strategy). Again, traditional techniques can then be used to explore the competency implications of the major shifts in the culture.

The example shown in Figure 10.4 resulted from an analysis of existing styles and values in a financial services organization compared with

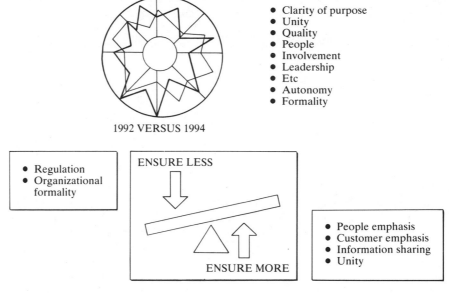

Figure 10.4 *Cultural analysis*
Source: PA Consulting Group (1990)

those defined by the top team as part of their business strategy planning. The implication (and future reality) was that over the next five years the organization needed to reduce its formality and structure and increase its people emphasis. This cultural shift was in the process of being designed into the organization's policies, systems, procedures and technology. The same principles would inevitably apply to management behaviour. The definition of what constituted good management performance had been changed. Adapting job analysis techniques to explore the implications of each cultural shift can reveal powerful behavioural indicators of what is a culturally sensitive view of good performance.

As organizations undertake cultural changes such as total quality management, customer service programmes and decentralization, and as these changes increasingly work themselves into the organization's policies and procedures, we can expect to see calls to identify the generic competencies associated with specific cultural changes so that they might be adapted and explored within the context of each organization.

Facilitation and input from external models

Business scenarios

Another common approach is to develop a scenario of competency changes alongside the business plan. The sorts of scenarios investigated—such as business turnaround, start-up, exploiting profit, managing decline—tend to characterize the current phase of the organization

Senarios	Start up	Turnaround	Dynamic growth	Extracting profit	Redeploying efforts
Scenario demands	• High financial risk • Limited management team cohesiveness • Few organization systems or procedures in place • Little operational experience • Endless workload: multiple priorities • Generally insufficient resources to satisfy all demands • Limited relationship with suppliers, customers and environment	• Time pressure for • Need for rapid situational assessment and decision making • Limited resource; skills shortages; some incompetent personnel • Re-evaluation of business position • Inappropriate reporting channels • Re-orientation of organization mission: cost/profit	• High financial risk • New markets, products technology • Multiple demands and conflicting priorities • Rapidly expanding organization in certain sectors • Inadequate managerial/technical/financial resources • Unequal growth across sectors of the organization • Likely shifting power bases • Constant dilemma between doing current work and building support systems for the future	• 'Controlled' financial risk • Unattractive industry long-term • Need to invest selectively • Internal organizational stability • Moderate to high managerial/technical competence • Adequate systems and administrative infra-structure • Acceptable to excellent relationships with suppliers, customers and environment	• Moderate short-term risk • Unknown long-term risk • Resistance to change • Bureaucracy in some sections • High mismatch between some organization skill sets • Highly operational orientation in executive team

Scenarios	Start up	Turnaround	Dynamic growth	Extracting profit	Redeploying efforts
Management characteristics	• Vision of finished business • Hands-on orientation • In-depth knowledge in critical technical areas • Organizing ability • Staffing skills • Team-building capabilities • High energy level/ stamina • Personal magnetism/ charisma • Broad knowledge of all key functions • Creating vision of business • Establishing core technical and marketing expertise • Building management team	• 'Take charge' orientation • Strong leader • Strong analytical and diagnostic skills, especially financial • Excellent business strategist • High energy level • Risk taker • Handles pressure well • Good crisis management skills • Good negotiator • Rapid accurate problem diagnosis • Fixing short-term and ultimately long-term problems	• Excellent strategic and financial planning skills • Clear vision of the future • Ability to balance priorities • Organizational and team-building skills • Good crisis-management skills • Moderately high risk taker • Excellent staffing skills • Increasing market share in key sectors • Managing rapid change • Ability to build towards clear vision of the future	• Technically knowledgeable • Knows the business • Sensitive to changes • Ear to the ground • Anticipates problems • Strong administrative skills • Orientated to systems • Strong relationship orientation • Recognizes need for management succession • Stresses efficiency • Works towards stability • Senses signs of change	• Good politician/ master of change • Highly persuasive— high interpersonal influence • Moderate risk taker • Highly supportive, sensitive to people • Excellent 'system thinker' • Good organizing and executive staffing skills • Established effectiveness in managing change • Supporting the dispossessed

Figure 10.5 Business scenarios and associated management characteristics *(after Child, 1984, and Whetton and Cameron, 1984)*

within the business life cycle. McBeath (1990) has described how BAT Industries held interviews and group sessions with their top 200 managers to build a visionary view of the relevant business scenarios and associated competency profiles. Shackleton also refers to this approach in Chapter 9. It is important to tailor any generic demands that particular business scenarios may place on competencies. However, based on the research of Child (1984) and Whetton and Cameron (1984), it is possible to outline a number of generic competencies that should be considered in so doing.

Comparable organizations

There is a truism that 'there is nothing new under the sun' and it can often be applied to thinking about future competencies. Someone, somewhere, has probably experienced many of the features of the environment that you are so unsure about. There are a number of existing models or sources of information that can form the basis of 'intelligence' in establishing forward-looking competencies. The most commonly used intelligence, above and beyond the research on generic change competencies or business scenarios already discussed, is to:

- examine the demands and competencies seen as important by organizations that are going through a similar business change;
- identify the internal 'centres of excellence' or parts of the organization that are already experiencing many of the aspects of the environment now seen as having a wider impact.

The manager has some choice over how the intelligence from these sources is incorporated. The external models may be organizations in the same sector who are further down the same track as your organization or, more commonly, they may be firms in a different industrial sector that has previously undergone a similar strategic change. In the turbulent late 1980s many state utilities undergoing privatization found, for example, that they could learn much from the financial service organizations that had already experienced deregulation.

Internal centres of excellence

The internal models are also easy to identify in many organizations. Somewhere there has probably been a department or division that has served as a pilot. The choice that has to be made is whether to include people from these areas in the initial interview sample during the data collection phase or whether to draw upon their views and experience as part of a 'validation check' after you have collected your own data.

Sharpening analysis of existing competencies

At this stage in a competency requirement forecast it is possible to incorporate the data gleaned from the more traditional sources described in Chapters 3 and 5. The bottom-up data collection process, involving interviews with job holders, provides the base line information to establish the competency requirements. Clearly, the main focus needs to remain one of establishing the competencies that have underpinned current and previous performance. However, it is possible to use the information from the top-down processes of clarification and the external models to create a more focused—and sharper—set of questions for existing job holders.

Repertory grid questions may be designed to tap particular features of work or new definitions of performance and critical incidents may be sought in the areas that are felt to reflect more likely events in the future.

Task analyses may also be used to explore areas that job holders—on the basis of their current activities—may ignore. An example may be drawn from a building society. In analysing the competencies required by branch staff a series of task analyses were carried out. Very quickly it became apparent that the job holders only thought of their tasks once the customer had reached the desk and once they began to process the various transactions. The analysis was therefore only revealing the competencies needed in relation to historical work practices. Had the approach been continued it would have produced a very truncated picture of the branch staff's work. The job analysts were, however, aware that the building society was in the process of launching a major customer service initiative and was also modifying its branch computer systems in a way that would free up considerable 'transaction time' and change the shape of the jobs.

A significant implication of this was that the branch staff needed to think of their jobs—and the interactions they had with customers—as starting before the customer walked through the door and ending once the customer had walked out of the door. The job analysts therefore had to 'shape' their techniques by ensuring that the job holders were in the right mindset as the jobs were analysed. This included:

- describing a number of customer service performance standards that could be achieved by effective branch staff, and then getting the job holders to identify the key tasks they could do in their job to achieve these standards;
- arranging a number of 'mystery visits' into competitive building society branches so that the job holders could observe and analyse at first hand alternative practices of carrying out the same customer transactions but using the new technology.

The second set of task analyses that were completed revealed a very different balance of competencies required for the jobs and one that more closely matched the imminent future.

Expert interrogation and validation

At the beginning of this chapter we argued that it is possible to draw upon apparently subjective information about the future and convert it into hard evidence of competency demands. It is appropriate to build in a period of expert interrogation or validation into any competency requirement forecasting approach.

At the simplest level, this can involve a project team collecting evidence from business sector reports and publications, or the various lists of competencies that have been produced by other organizations and institutions. The information can be used to assess, question and challenge the data-collection process and resultant competency profile. The sorts of questions used to interrogate the data include:

- Have we taken account of the relevant trends and factors?
- What was the evidence that backed up this competency?
- How likely is it that this change will happen?
- What levels of the organization will be affected by this change in our timeframe?

When competency requirements are being established for particular jobs or functions, Schneider and Konz (1989) have advocated the use of subject matter expert workshops to analyse and validate the future requirements.

Another issue to consider is the way in which competencies have been derived and to classify them in terms of their relevance. Many organizations are not able to focus their resources or attention on the selection, assessment and development of every competency that has been identified. It is often asked if it is possible to 'weight' or prioritize the competencies. While in theory managers need to attend to the whole range of competencies, since they are all by definition associated with excellent performance, in practice different priorities may be allocated to competencies. We have suggested this is done by considering their current stage in their life cycle. Classifying competencies in this way has to be a subjective process. However, by comparing the analysis of future competency demands based on the top-down process of clarification with that of existing performance based on the bottom-up data-collection process, it is possible to identify those competencies seen as having more, less or similar importance to the future. The more structured the analysis techniques, the more reasoned the judgement is.

Pushing competencies deeper into existing personnel systems

In order to design and integrate complete personnel systems around competencies, organizations will want to see more work done that links competencies to organizational-level issues as opposed to individual-level issues. A major focus of work in the 1990s will therefore be finding ways to push competencies deeper into existing personnel systems. The scope of competency work will expand to address the management of specific strategic issues. This is likely to involve a shift from analysing competencies for individuals within target jobs to analysing competencies for teams (strategic project teams, top teams, functional teams, and so forth) with specific roles.

There will also be developments of competency work within some of the existing areas of application covered in this book. The most pressing areas of development are concerned with career and performance management.

Structuring career systems around competencies

There will be a need increasingly to structure careers around competencies. Organizations will be able to use competency-based approaches to help them understand the shape and balance of competencies across its management levels. This understanding will make it easier to make decisions about:

- the pace and extent of decentralization or centralization, by examining the depth of management talent and skill against specific competencies (such as decision making, entrepreneurialism);
- the scope for 'de-layering' within the organization by examining the real 'vertical bridge points' at which competency demands shift significantly;
- the creation of new resourcing paths and the freeing up and planning of lateral career moves within the organization by examining the 'horizontal bridge points' at which organizational, business sector, functional, departmental or technical specialisms truly create new competency demands;
- the most appropriate resourcing option, for example whether to make, buy, temporarily lease, or recast specific competency needs.

More attention will be given to the design of career systems that are tailored to, and more sensibly reflect, the actual possession of competencies across the organization's labour force. Organizations will also be faced with decisions to invest in the development of competencies that are not immediately relevant, but that are forecast to have a key role in the future.

The business benefits to be gained by addressing these issues within organizations are significant indeed. However, our knowledge and ability to use competency-based approaches to these ends needs to be developed. From a methodological point of view we need to develop tools and techniques to help identify and quantify the discontinuities or 'break points' between competency profiles for different roles. We need to be able to answer the following questions in a less intuitive way:

- When does a competency profile really contain a new competency demand?
- In competencies that are present in several roles, when do the behavioural indicators that constitute the competency begin to demonstrate a different 'flavour' or focus?

From a philosophical or scientific point of view, we need to have a much clearer view about which competencies—or the skills, abilities and characteristics that underlie the observed set of behaviours—are capable of being developed in people and which competencies are not, and are therefore best selected for.

Using competencies to manage performance

As Chapter 8 by Torrington and Blandamer shows, there has been more limited application of competency-based approaches in the area of performance management, despite the fact that it offers much potential. Much of the work that has been done is based on the concept of competence, i.e. minimum standards of performance. Therefore, the potential to design reward systems around those competencies associated with excellent performance has been largely underexploited. The limited amount of work done in this area in part reflects the sensitivity of individuals and organizations to changing the way they think about pay. It also reflects the fact that—unlike in the fields of selection and development—there are alternative ways and competing theories about thinking about rewards. To recruit and develop people in relation to their underlying competency is hard to argue against. However, there are many jobs in which appraising people and paying them against performance expressed in terms of their skills and abilities would not be appropriate.

In some jobs it would be better to focus on the outputs from the job—what the performers achieve against measurable targets and objectives. In some cases, what is done—in terms of the tasks and process carried out—is more important. In yet others, meeting the expectations of customers or stakeholders represents the best measure. The focus in the 1990s will therefore be to find ways of determining when a competency-based reward and performance management system is appropriate and, having done this, finding ways of accommodating and improving the tools and techniques used to assess competencies in relation to reward. The case study by Mosley and Bryan does much to address these issues. There is, however, a significant gap in the application of competency techniques in this area.

Linking competencies to strategic issues

Strategic skill pools The building up of competencies around specific strategic issues represents an extremely attractive extension of competency work. Based on their work in Shell Chemical Company, Naugle and Davies (1987) argued that many organizations focus at senior levels on strategic issues by creating separate strategic business units. In so doing, they 'disaggregate' the organization into smaller units, finding that many of the common or underlying skills that provide competitive advantage to more than one of the business areas are overlooked, underdeveloped, or even lost to the organization. Organizations, it is argued, should look to identify and develop their underlying 'strategic skill pools' to exploit the new ideas, new business developments and new relationships that place demands upon the competency of organizations.

This means that instead of just concentrating on the competencies managers need in relation to their particular job or role—albeit in the context of what is needed for business success—we should also consider the strategic skills (from a competency perspective) that are necessary to manage specific business issues. The work on business scenarios covered earlier has made a move in this direction, but there is a need to consider the competencies managers need for more specific business issues, such as:

- coping with large-scale decentralization or de-layering within an organization;
- becoming, and working as, an international manager;
- managing a joint venture;
- integrating contrasting cultures.

In order to address these sorts of issues most organizations will be prepared to invest the necessary time and money in management development. There will undoubtedly be a call in the 1990s to define organizationally specific competency profiles that will both create the language for, and express the resultant behaviours associated with, the 'excellent' management of such business issues. Another extension of competency work in the 1990s will be to help manage less formalized groups of staff who direct many of the strategic issues. Competency work will move away from its current focus on the selection, development and performance implications of individuals (in relation to specific jobs). The new focus will be on the management of the performance of teams in relation to particular tasks or objectives.

Moving into team building

Nobody is perfect at everything. In creating an understanding of the competencies associated with the management of strategic issues (see Figure 10.1) it would be easy to imagine that organizations will be looking for some sort of 'superperson' who matches the template. In practice, any one individual is likely to display strengths in three or four competencies. Moreover, as the work of Belbin (1981) and Margerison and McCann (1990) has shown, individuals need to take on different roles within teams. We cannot and should not all be the readers of the environment, the visionary leaders, the innovators, the shapers or the chairmen.

We have to manage the mix of competencies across teams. Competency-based approaches can bring three main benefits to team building. They can be used to:

- express the success criteria for the team by describing the specific behaviours that reflect 'the way we do things in this team'. Most team-building exercises require the team to agree on how effective teams perform;
- identify and assess individual team members' strengths and weaknesses against this set of competencies in order to make a better selection of team members and build in project-related development during the life of the team;
- provide a common language for that team, aid communication and improve the identification process.

We could therefore see a shift from creating competency profiles, tailored to relatively stable jobs, towards the creation and exploitation of competency work in the area of more temporary teams. The most obvious candidates for competency-related team building include top management teams, temporary task forces or project teams managing high-cost projects (for example, large technological investments) and teams handling significant business changes. In other words, the current use of competencies to explore whole job roles will be superseded by more detailed work on the most important and specific business tasks that they carry out within their job.

Conclusion

In Chapter 1 we argued that competency-based approaches hold the promise of integrating a large number of initiatives in the human resources management field. The various contributions in preceding chapters demonstrate a deep understanding of the approach in a wide range of areas, notably recruitment and career development, improving the approaches taken by organizations in these areas. To date, however, organizations have made only limited use of the potential offered by competency-based approaches. Few organizations have used the approach across all their human resource policy areas. Our current level of understanding, we believe, already allows us to do this. Moreover, as we become more experienced at building in competency requirement forecasts, we can expect to see an extension of competency-based approaches into matters that affect the very success of the organization.

References

Belbin, R.M. (1981) *Management Teams: why they succeed or fail*, Oxford: Heinemann Professional Publishing Ltd.

Bognanno, M. (1990) 'Facilitating cultural change by identifying the new competencies required and formulating a strategy to develop such competencies', *Conference on Identifying and Applying Competencies within your Organisation*, 6 November 1990, London: Resource Ltd.

Child, J. (1984) *Organisations: A Guide to Problems and Practice*, London: Harper & Row.

Cockerill, A. (1989) 'The kind of competence for rapid change', *Personnel Management*, September 1989.

Dale, G. (1990) 'Management proven in the marketplace', *Conference on Identifying and Applying Competencies within your Organisation*, 6 November 1990, London: Resource Ltd.

Evans, P. (1991) 'Motivation revisited: striking a dynamic balance in the dualistic organisation', *23rd International Human Resource Management Conference*, 3–5 April 1991, Barcelona: Management Centre Europe.

McBeath, G. (1990) 'A competency-based approach to improve individual and corporate performance: a business strategy', *Conference on Identifying and Applying Competencies within your Organisation*, 6 November 1990, London: Resource Ltd.

Margerison, C. and D. McCann (1990) *Team Management: Practical New Approaches*, London: Mercury Books.

Morgan, G. (1989) *Riding the Waves of Change: Developing Managerial Competencies for a Turbulent World*, Oxford: Jossey Bass.

Naugle, D. and G. Davies (1987) 'Strategic skill pools and competitive advantage', *Business Horizons*, 30 (6), 35–42.

PA Consulting Group (1990) *Organisational Styles and Values Questionnaire Handbook*, London: PA Consulting Group.

Peters, T. and R. Quinn (1988) *Beyond Rational Management: Mastering the Paradoxes and Competing Demands of High Performance*, New York: Jossey Bass.

Schneider, B. and A. Konz (1989) 'Strategic job analysis', *Human Resource Management*, 28, 51–62.

Trompenaars, F. (1991) 'The effect of culture on international human resource management', *23rd International Human Resource Management Conference*, 3–5 April 1991, Barcelona: Management Centre Europe.

Whetton, D. and K. Cameron (1984) *Developing Management Skills*, Glenview, Illinois: Scott, Foresman.

Glossary

Assessment centres (ACs)   A process by which an individual, or a group of individuals, is assessed by a team of judges using a comprehensive and integrated series of techniques. Used most frequently for selection purposes.

Behaviorally anchored rating (BAR) scales   Scales which allow the rater to make a more reliable judgement based on the behaviours that can be observed. Developed by Smith and Kendall.

British Psychological Society (BPS)   Professional body that provides chartered status for psychologists in the UK.

Career development workshops (CDWs)   Similar to an assessment centre, but used to identify long-term potential in relation to developmental career goals. Assessors act as facilitators as opposed to judges. Also known as development centres (DCs) and assessment for development workshops (ADWs).

Competence (areas of)   A set of deliverables, outputs and roles that people must be able to perform in a position.

Competency   A set of behaviour patterns that the incumbent needs to bring to a position in order to perform its tasks and functions with competence.

Council for Management Education and Development (CMED)   Formed in response to the call to improve management development in the UK. Initially sponsored by the Foundation for Management Education, the Confederation of British Industry and the British Institute of Management. CMED published a consultation document on 'A new pattern of management education awards' and is involved in the 'Management competences project'.

Critical incident technique (CIT)   Job analysis technique that systematically identifies the characteristics or psychological factors which contribute to effective job performance. Developed initially in the 1950s by J.C. Flanagan.

Competency requirement forecasting (CRF)   A structured process aimed at profiling existing and future competencies associated with a particular position, career stream or organization.

Delphi technique   A long-range forecasting technique in which qualitative value judgements are made about information. Judgements are made independently and anonymously, are pooled, summarized and then fed back to judges for another round of opinion.

Hierarchical business modelling (HBM)   A structured analysis technique used to break down any business activity (current or planned) into a series of constituent functions and subfunctions.

Human resource management (HRM)   A phrase used to include a range of personnel policies and practices covering the recruitment, selection, placement, career development, exiting, performance management, reward, employee relations, and work design for staff within the organization.

Institute of Personnel Management (IPM)   Professional organization responsible for setting codes of practice and examinations for personnel professionals in the UK.

Job Components Inventory (JCI)   Job analysis inventory developed by the Social and Applied Psychology Unit at Sheffield University.

Leaderless group discussions (LGDs)   Exercises used for assessment purposes in which a group of participants discuss and resolve a business problem without the aid of a pre-appointed chairperson.

Learning styles questionnaire (LSQ)   A self-administered inventory developed by Honey and Mumford, aimed at identifying the way in which an individual learns most effectively.

Management Charter Initiative (MCI)   An initiative launched by CMED in 1988 with the intention of mobilizing a group of 'management charter' organizations to commit themselves to a ten-point code of practice on management development. Developed an inventory of the main competences needed by the well-rounded middle manager and first level manager.

Occupational personality questionnaire (OPQ)   A personality inventory based on an interlinked series of questionnaires and designed specifically for industrial settings by Saville and Holdsworth Ltd.

Performance-related pay (PRP)   A pay system that links salary progression to an assessment of the merit of an individual and/or their performance.

Position Analysis Questionnaire (PAQ)   A structured job analysis technique based on a taxonomy of job behaviours. Developed initially in the 1960s in the US by McCormick.

Realistic job preview (RJP)   An approach that provides candidates with an accurate picture of a job for which they are applying through the use of first-hand experience, films or demonstrations.

Repertory grid (Repgrid)   Analysis and data gathering technique that elicits and identifies the personal constructs that individuals use to view the world. Used to reveal the conscious and subconscious interpretations that individuals use to describe and articulate events.

Subject matter experts (SMEs)   A small group of experienced individuals who can bring to bear their expert knowledge to assess and provide guidance on the validity of uncorroborated information.

Work Profiling System (WPS)   Integrated job analysis system developed by Saville and Holdsworth Ltd, used to profile jobs, tasks and human attributes.

Index

Ability tests:
  competencies measured, 63–64
  guidelines for use, 64
  psychometric properties, 65
  recruitment, 97–98, 109
Accomplishment records, 71, 120
Advanced Occupational Inventory, 67
Advanced Progressive Matrices, 64
Advanced Test Battery, 64
Advertisements, 93–95
AH Series tests, 64
Applicants:
  attracting, 93–95
  targeting, 92–93
Application form design, 96
Appraisal systems, 135, 139–142, 155
ASE, 64, 110
Assessment:
  analogous approaches, 50, 51–62
  analytical approaches, 50, 62–68
  miscellaneous approaches, 50, 70–71
  reputational approaches, 50, 68–70
  recruitment, 96–100
Assessment centres:
  benefits, 72
  design principles, 71–72
  guidelines for use, 72
  psychometric properties, 73
  recruitment, 104–110
  role review, 134–135
Assessment for development work-
      shop (see Development centres)
Assessor training, 102, 110

BAT Industries, 190
Behavioural event interviewing, 43
Behavioural indicators, 18, 39, 44–45,
      87–88, 99–100, 109, 133–134,
      166
Behaviourally anchored rating scale
      (BARS), 62, 69, 119
Benchmarking, 158, 190
Biodata, 70–71

Body Shop, 92
British Petroleum, 23, 178
British Psychological Society, 35
BSS Group, 146–156
Business, change, 4, 7, 157–160, 175
Business strategy, 89–90, 160–161

Cadbury Schweppes, 23, 178
Career bridges, 112, 192–193
Career development, 111–127
Career development workshops (see
      Development centres)
Career plans, 124–125, 170
Career review meetings, 119–120
Cattell's 16PF test, 66
Change competencies, 177–181
Change programmes, 9–10, 12, 157–
      172
Checklists and inventories, 46–48
Combination Job Analysis Method, 34
Competencies, area of, 17
Competencies:
  benefits of approach, 12
  classification, 25, 105, 116, 144, 178–
      182
  definition of, 16–17
  determinants, 26–27
  generic, 18, 21–22
  identification, 31–49, 79–88, 113–116
  level of analysis, 176
  number of, 20–21
  organizationally specific, 23
  technical skills, 19
Competency analysis:
  choice of method, 32–35
  range of methods, 37–48
Competency life cycles, 180–183
Competency requirement forecasting,
      183–192
Competitive arrangements, 7
Computer-assistance, 34, 67, 100
Core competencies, 182
Cost benefit analysis, 102–103

Cost reduction strategies, 8
Courtaulds, 91
Critical Incidents Technique:
  contribution, 37
  future orientation, 158, 164, 190–191
  use in competency identification,
    41–43
Culture:
  change programmes, 8, 9
  competency identification, 161–162,
    186–187
  competency language, 115, 135,
    142–143, 162, 172
  rewards, 139

Delphi technique, 159
Demographic pressures, 7, 92–93
Development centres:
  business change, 163–172
  design principles, 72
  feedback process, 126
  logistics, 121–123
  sponsorship, 124
Diary methods, 39
Differential Aptitude Test Battery
    (DATB), 64

Emerging competencies, 179
Ernst & Young, 157
Equal opportunities, 101
Eysenck Personality Questionnaire, 66

Fleishman's Ability Requirement
    Scales, 34
Flexible organization, 7
Flexigrid, 79
Future autobiographies, 71
Future orientation, 27–28, 36–37, 71,
    111–112, 114, 158–159, 176–183

General intelligence, 63, 64
Glaxo Manufacturing Services, 128–
    136
GMA abstract tests, 109
Group exercises:
  competencies measured, 53–54
  competitive, 53
  co-operative, 52–53
  recruitment, 97–98
  leaderless group discussions, 41, 51,
    167–169
  production, 54
  psychometric properties, 54
  recruitment, 109

Hierarchical business modelling, 186
Human resource management:
  definition, 5
  range of solutions, 6–9, 137–138
Human resource planning, 8, 14
Human resource strategies, 6–9, 147,
    149–150

IBM, 91
ICL, 32
Industrial Society, 92
Information technology, 7
Initial screening, 96
Interest tests, 66
Internationalization, 7
Interview techniques, 39–41
In-tray exercises:
  competencies measured, 57
  production, 51, 56–57
  psychometric properties, 57
  recruitment, 97–98, 109

Job Components Inventory, 47–48
Job design, 91

Kuder Personal Preference Inventory,
    67

Language ladders, 149–150

Macquarrie test, 64
Management Charter Initiative (MCI),
    24–25, 32, 104, 107, 175
Management Interest Inventory, 67
Manchester Airport, 23
Maturing competencies, 179
Mechanical reasoning, 64
Mill Hill Vocabulary Scale, 64
Minnesota Form Board, 64
Motivation, 3
Motivation tests, 66

National Health Service (NHS), 139
National Westminster Bank, 23, 144,
    177
NEO Five Factor Inventory, 66
New technology, 7, 90–91
NFER-Nelson, 110
Numerical ability, 64
Numerical Reasoning Scale, 64

Observation techniques, 38
Office of Strategic Services, 52
OPQ Concept 5, 66

PA Consulting Group, 146, 186–187
Pay and grading, 153–154
Peer assessment, 68
Performance management, 137–145,
    146–156, 193–194
Performance related pay, 138–140, 143
Personal Construct Theory, 43, 44, 164
Personality tests, 65, 97–98, 120–121,
    170
Point-to-point correspondence, 51, 52,
    62, 121
Position Analysis Questionnaire
    (PAQ), 33, 34, 37, 40, 46–47, 48
Presentation exercises:
    applications, 51, 58, 170
    competencies measured, 59
Price Waterhouse UK, 157
Promotion centres, 121
Psychological Corporation, 64
Psychomotor tests:
    competencies measured, 60
    production, 51, 60–61

Quality pressures, 7, 146–148

Raven's Progressive Matrices, 64
Realistic job preview, 95, 108
Recruitment, 89–103
References, 68
Reliability:
    ability tests, 65
    group exercises, 54
    in-tray exercises, 57
    temperament tests, 66
Repertory Grid:
    administration, 80–83
    analysis, 84–88
    benefits, 37, 79
    future orientation, 158, 164–165,
        190–191
    use in competency identification,
        43–45
Reputational approaches:
    applications, 67–69
    competencies measured, 69
    validity, 70
Resource development, 8, 192–193
Role analysis, 113, 130–132, 149–151
Role play exercises:
    applications, 51, 58, 169–170
    competencies measured, 58
Roles, 19
Royal Insurance, 20

Safeway plc, 104–110
Saville and Holdsworth, 64, 66–67
Scenario creation, 115, 159, 187–190
Self-assessment, 68, 135
Self-managed development, 123
Selection, 89–103
Shell Canada, 178
Shell Chemical Company, 194
Situational interviews, 97, 99–100, 108
Skills supply, 10–11
Spatial reasoning, 64
Strategic skill pools, 194–195
Structural change, 8, 13–14, 128–129,
    135
Structured interviews, 108
Strong Campbell Interest Inventory,
    67
Subject matter experts:
    assessment centres, 72
    competency validation, 192
    reputational assessment, 69
    scoring methods, 62–63
Succession planning, 117–118
Supervisor assessments, 68

Team-building, 195–196
Temperament tests:
    career applications, 120–121
    competencies measured, 66
    guidelines for use, 66
    psychometric properties, 66
    range of tests, 65–66
Thematic Apperception Test (TAT), 67
Trainability tests:
    competencies measured, 61
    production, 51, 60–61
Transitional competencies, 179–180

Validity:
    ability tests, 63, 65
    assessment centres, 73, 104
    group exercises, 54
    in-tray exercises, 57
    recruitment, 101–102
    reputational methods, 70
    temperament tests, 66
    work samples, 63
Values-driven data gathering, 31, 36–
    37, 160–166, 172, 183–187
Verbal ability, 64
Versatile Job Analysis System, 35
Vincent Mechanical Reasoning Test,
    64

Visioning, 171, 183–186

War Office Selection Board, 52
Weschler Adult Intelligence Scale, 64
WH Smith, 23
Work Performance Survey System, 34

Work profiling system, 33, 34, 37, 46, 48
Written report exercises:
  competencies measured, 59
  production, 51, 59